D1474818

INFLATION OF SYMBOLS

Other Books by Orrin E. Klapp

Overload and Boredom, 1986
Opening and Closing, 1978
Models of Social Order, 1973
Currents of Unrest, an Introduction to Collective Behavior, 1972
Social Types: Process, Structure and Ethos, 1972
Collective Search for Identity, 1969
Symbolic Leaders, Public Dramas and Public Men, 1965
Heroes, Villains and Fools, 1962
Ritual and Cult, 1956

INFLATION OF SYMBOLS

Loss of Values in American Culture

Orrin E. Klapp

HM
101
. KL33
1991
West

Transaction Publishers
New Brunswick (U.S.A.) and London (U.K.)

Copyright© 1991 by Transaction Publishers,
New Brunswick, New Jersey 08903

All rights reserved under International and Pan-American
Copyright Conventions. No part of this book may be
reproduced or transmitted in any form or by any means,
electronic or mechanical, including photocopy, recording, or
any information storage and retrieval system, without prior
permission in writing from the publisher. All inquiries
should be addressed to Transaction Publishers, Rutgers-The
State University, New Brunswick, New Jersey 08903.

Library of Congress Catalog Number: 90-20349
ISBN: 0-88738-385-8
Printed in the United States of America

Library of Congress Cataloging-in-Publication Data

Klapp, Orrin Edgar, 1915-
     Inflation of symbols: loss of values in American culture/Orrin
E. Klapp.
        p.   cm.
     Includes bibliographical references and index.
     ISBN 0-88738-385-8
     1. Culture.   2. Social values.   3. United States—
Civilization—20th century.   4. Symbolism.   I. Title.
HM101.K633   1991
303.3'72'0973—dc20

90–20349
CIP

To Evelyn, Merrie,
and Curtis

Contents

1

What Is Symbolic Inflation?

There is a sense of loss in the world that comes with more of virtually everything. "Bigger and better" does not quite describe our progress today. Too many things are happening that are bigger and worse.

Paradoxically, this sense of loss is connected with *growth*, which has become a decidedly ambivalent term in modern countries (the negative side of which is implied by terms like *noise, pollution, clutter, overload of information, overpopulation, congestion, urban sprawl, redundancy, satiation, boredom*)[1] though developing countries don't mind having more of it.

This book does not address all of these formidable problems, but only one that enters into many of them and is bigger than at first it looks and deserves extension, being a name for many things in our modern life that are like balloons and bubbles that enlarge and then go flat suddenly or slowly—namely, inflation. Such images of the leaky balloon or bursting bubble apply to many things that, taken together, help to comprise what we call (with less and less conviction) "the American dream."

Today Americans are used to keeping tab on inflation by price indexes and interest rates, and restraining it by Federal Reserve monetary policy. But no tab is kept on other kinds of inflation—of symbols other than money. This book is a conceptual exploration of the latter neglected area, looking into what inflation might mean and how it happens in social relations, popular culture, mass contagions, fads and fashions, even smiles and kisses. The general effect of all kinds of inflation is to "cheapen," that is to weaken the "purchasing power" of symbols to get what they mean and what is expected from them in the social marketplace.

1

By social inflation I mean processes that act as magnifiers for a time to turn nothing into something, or at least little into much. Fads will do for an immediate example—a popular craze one day, gone the next—no institutional product that could be called progress. Which is not to say that bubbles cannot add a little excitement to more sustained social movements. In any case—whether we are talking of a fad, a crowd mood, a mass hysteria, or a prolonged inflation such as monetary—the center of a symbolic bubble is hollow and gives a sense of emptiness even before it bursts—one clue, perhaps, to what has been called the malaise of affluence, the inability of mounting consumer goods to give a true sense of fulfillment.

But to understand inflation in its broad connections we must take it beyond a specific (narrow) economic role in monetary inflation— even beyond consumerism—to processes that occur widely in culture. My view is that any symbol in culture—a medal, a certificate, a hat, a robe, a tradition, a fad, an idea, a promise, an entire output of symbols—which betokens (signifies, represents) a value can be inflated when certain processes occur.

Metaphors of the bubble and balloon seem appropriate for some inflationary social processes, especially when enlargement is followed by bursting, leaking, or other loss of value. We see in everyday life that expectations are often disappointed. Dreams of future uptopias collapse when as they are realized. Crowd and mass mentality often exaggerate and push people to extremes which are later regretted. Rhetoric has a gaseous quality. We see a prima facie case that much social behavior is bubble-like, or balloon-like, taking people up, then down. The loss of value may be a slow leak or sudden blowout—as in "The One-Horse Shay," "all at once, nothing first, just like bubbles when they burst."

What is inflation? A dictionary helps us begin with the common meaning:

Inflate
1. To swell with air or gas; expand; distend.
2. To puffup; elate.
3. To expand or increase abnormally, improperly; to extend imprudently; as, to inflate currency or credit.

Inflated
1. Distended, as with air.
2. Turgid, bombastic.
3. Expanded abnormally or unjustifiably, as prices . . .

Inflation   1. An inflating; state of being inflated.
              2. Disproportionate and relatively sharp and sudden increase in the quantity of money or credit, or both, relative to the amount of exchange business. Inflation always produces a rise in the price level.

(*Webster's Collegiate Dictionary*, 5th ed. Springfield, Mass.: G. and C. Merriam, 1942.)

A few examples from daily life may also recall ways in which the idea of inflation is commonly used: a general rise of prices, putting out rumors to falsely drive up the price of a stock, in South Africa, the National party calling demands of black militants "inflated," a conceited person's opinion of himself, calling a college instructor "professor."

We see from common use that inflation is not mere enlargement but excessive enlargement—abnormal, improper, disproportionate, false,—which leads to some loss of value. The simplest possible definition might be: a process that makes something seem bigger or more important that it actually is, where such enlargement, being excessive or exaggerated, causes "more to become less." Thus, hype and rhetoric make something seem better or more important than it actually is—when so perceived causing it to lose value. In the case of symbols (especially money) it seems often to be market oversupply which causes them to lose value.

Normally the loss of value is experienced in exchange (conspicuous consumption, display, presentation) of a symbol when it loses "purchasing power" in human response in terms like applause, admiration, respect, homage, credit, deference, authority, veneration, glamour. Such favorable responses are the meaning or value of the symbol. Inflation occurs when too many symbols have too little meaning.

As I see it, social inflation applies to all social processes where enlargement, expansion, or oversupply leads to loss of value of a symbol, which is, of course, disappointing to many people. Inflation of some sort has played a part in many sorts of picturesque follies, fiascoes, crusades, fanaticisms, polarizations, vilifications, confrontations, escalations, extravagant enterprises, stampedes, grandiose expectations, ill-founded hopes, disappointments, popular enthusiasms, hero worship, fads and vanities.

A contemporary literary critic holds that inflation pervades post-modern fiction, art, and culture. He describes a century-long inflation, of which this era is a climax—a "climax inflation,"

> not only of wealth but of people, ideas, methods, and expectations—the increasing power and pervasiveness of the communications industry, the reckless growth of the academy, the incessant changing of hand and devaluation of all received ideas. The Post-Modern era represents only the last phase in a century of inflation. (Newman 1985, p.6)

This is interesting and all to the good, but regrettably it does not analyze the mechanisms by which inflation occurs in a way that would please sociologists (which probably does not keep Professor Newman awake nights). Yet we do wish for some account of processes—psychological and sociological—that do regularly occur with predictable results, if we know what they are.

By what processes then does inflation occur? It occurs by what I call social magnifiers, which make things look bigger or more important than they actually are. Let us distinguish five types of social magnifiers, ranging from the simplest to market-like processes that resemble monetary inflation.

1. The simplest is mere overstatement, the exaggeration of claims, promises, boasts, noble intentions, expectations, fears, which sooner or later exceed the ability to deliver and lose credibility as reality is seen to fall short.
2. The second is crusading, the rhetorical inflation of a conflict into a war of good versus evil, with opponents as enemies and oneself as hero, and of victory into a grail-like goal.
3. The third type of magnification is contagious communication, often called hysterias or emotional contagions: going with the herd with uncritical suggestibility, which inflates by drawing larger numbers of people into excited actions that exaggerate the value of something and call for extreme actions. These contagions are in two main categories: crowd and mass.
4. A fourth type of social magnification is self-expansion by identification with others, and vicarious experience of the triumphs and careers of heroes and celebrities in media dramas and contests, which I call emotional hitchhiking.
5. After treating these forms of social inflation, we turn to the market-like type more familiar as monetary, in which oversupply of a symbol leads to its cheapening or loss of value conceived as "purchasing power" for desired responses in exchange. We try to see how this market concept might apply to such symbols as credentials, medals, smiles, kisses, greeting cards, religious tokens, fashions, and finally to information itself—John Stuart Mill's broad concept of the free market of ideas.

In view of such magnifiers, we may be able to see in the malaise of affluence an erosion of values, many kinds of which carry no price in a money market. It is an ailment of symbols which, for want of a better word, I call symbolic or cultural inflation. Such inflation may go on even when the monetary kind is checked. It has features that economists have less to do with than have anthropologists, sociologists, psychologists, linguists, in the way of claiming special jurisdiction. I propose as a sociologist to do what I can to bring into focus this vast, pervasive, largely unwitting sort of inflation that eats at the value of symbols.

The upshot is that we see inflation in a much broader perspective than the merely monetary kind and conclude by considering various conditions, such as massness, egalitarianism, and loss of scarcity that favor social inflation and thereby help us to understand (even to control?) social inflation as a source of disappointment in modern society.

Note

1. A substantial literature from 1960 on has questioned economic growth, expressed disenchantment with affluence, or detailed shortcomings of the American dream. There seems no need to detail these works, since most of them have not treated the connection between inflation, broadly conceived, and the phenomena indicated by the chapter titles of this book. The citations are as follows: Bethel (1969), Csikszentmihalyi (1975), Daly (1980), Ehrlich (1968, 1974), Galbraith (1958), Georgescu-Roegen (1971), Gorz (1967), *Global 2000*, Hardin (1972), Henderson (1978), Hirsch (1976), Hirschman (1982), Klapp (1986), Kohr (1977), Lapham (1987), Linder (1970), Menninger (1973), Miles (1976), Marcuse (1964), Maslow (1964), Meadows (1972), Mishan (1967, 1977), Rifkin (1980), Sahlins (1972), Scitovsky (1976), Schumacher (1973), Seabrook (1978), Shames (1989), Wachtel (1983, 1988). Fiction sustains the time-weathered theme of disappointments in affluence—of *The Great Gatsby, An American Tragedy, Death of a Salesman, Babbitt*, David Mamet's Pulitzer Prize-winning play, *Glengarry Glen Ross*, portraying conniving real estate salesmen in pursuit of the American dream. In such works, at least, Gatsby's green light seems to have turned yellow. These works attest to trouble with affluence, but none looks into the possible contribution of cultural inflation to that trouble.

2

Overstatement

There are people who think that if a little is good, more is better. This book is devoted to denying the universality of that proposition. If you expand something far enough, there always comes a point where more is not better.

We begin by considering the advantages of self-inflation. Some fishes—the balloon fish (among the Diodontidae) and the puffer (Tetradontidae)—have the capacity to swell themselves up, the latter with spines sticking out in all directions, to make themselves less attractive and perhaps more daunting to animals who might want to eat them.

They show that self-enlargement has tactical value for survival. Among other classic adaptations (fight, flight, camouflage, mimicry, feigning) there is the tactic of self-enlargement: to stand one's ground and pretend to be stronger than one is (bluff); or to claim to be better than one is, for self-gratification, self-confidence, or to impress others (boasting). It often pays to enlarge oneself.

Is it not relevant to the balloon fish's bluff that in 1988 came the news that, after a flirtation with compactness, Cadillac was stretching the Sedan de Ville's wheelbase by nine inches (making it seventeen feet long) while Buick was adding eleven inches to the Riviera?

But self-enlargement is not without its risks, illustrated by the well-known fable of the frog who, proud of his ability to enlarge himself by taking in air, was so tickled by flattery that he swelled up and burst. We recognize people who enlarge themselves as did the frog of fable. When unsuccessful, they are called showoff, blowhard, windbag, swelled head, big head, stuffed shirt, bull-shooter. The disaster of the self-inflationary frog is that he went beyond his limit. The fable would have little wisdom if it did not also apply to people who overextended themselves—bit off more than they could chew. Is

7

history not full of such mistakes? Did General Custer not overextend himself by recklessly going into battle outnumbered by Sioux Indians? Did Napoleon and Hitler not overextend themselves in invading Russia?

Let us look at a few more cases of the gains and risks of self-inflationary people. The apex of self-inflation is fame, having a public image, getting talked about (so providing material by which people can inflate their own self-images—see ch. 5). The boxer Muhammed Ali I should say was a successful puffer. He repeated audaciously and interminably, "I am the Greatest." By this, presumably, he psyched himself by building up self-confidence (in his undeniable ability) and dramatized his matches, bringing larger audiences either to see him win or fall. He never did oblige his enemies. Youthful blacks doted on him as a hero, and raised their own self-images. Another successful puffer was Babe Ruth, said to be the greatest baseball hero of all time. He was a flamboyant hitter, breaking all records for home runs to become "the Sultan of Swat." He had the instinct for the grandiose gesture, as in his unforgettable boast to the crowd, "I'll knock it out there."

But so easy would it have been for Ruth to have suffered the fate of the vain frog. This outcome is immortalized in the comic poem, "Casey at the Bat," in which, after letting two pitches go by, the great Casey struck out.

Dickens gives us another portrait of the puffer. It is of one who lives by big talk, bluffs, and promises, portrayed by Dickens' character of Wilkins Micawber, perpetually eluding a disaster that is enlarged by his own grandiose promises. No less is there overstatement of another type, as a way of getting attention, in Dickens' character of Mrs. Gummidge, who continually enlarges her troubles as a "poor lorn creature."

But, on the whole, self-enlargers are not complainers but persons of flamboyant temperament—showoffs, romantics, crusaders (see the next chapter), high riskers as psychologists define the type—prone to dramatizing themselves by bravado. We may think of General Custer's "last stand," or of General Patton with his pearl handled pistols and challenge to General Rommel to duel in tanks.

Among contemporary celebrities enlarging themselves by puffery, we might mention Colonel "Ollie" North, who is reported to have been a temperamental overstater. Co-workers described him as a "romanticist," behaving "bombastically." One said, "I never took anything he said at face value, because I knew that he was bombastic and embellished the record. . . . He had a touch of fantasy in his makeup that made him overdo, overestimate, and overstate." (Theodore Draper, "Iran-Contra Autopsy," *The New York Review of Books,* 17 December 1987, pp. 68–9.)

We have here glanced at a few personality types whose style is to inflate themselves by overstatement (boasting, putting best foot forward, grandiloquence, grandiosity, panache, bravura, foolhardiness). Over-statement may be a high road to heroism but it is also a slippery path to fiasco and total devaluation. To use a metaphor from poker, increasing bets raises the ante on both winnings and losses. If unable to make good on overstated expectations, one risks being hoist on his own petard.

For all this risk, self-enlargement by overstatement is the stuff that heroes are made of—the big gesture, the colorful deed, the stroke that slays the dragon.

On the other hand, understatement is a kind of insurance against risks of overstatement, expressed in the Buddhist proverb, "He who sleeps on the floor will never fall out of bed." Lowering claims makes one invulnerable to devaluation, as in Groucho Marx's one-liner, "I have worked myself up from nothing to a state of extreme poverty." He also quipped that he wouldn't join a club whose requirements were so low that they would accept him. The English preference for under-statement is well known. Understatement is also favored in sports which approve making little of injuries—as when a player being carried off a football field might say, "It's nothing." (But the wish to draw larger audiences has so corrupted this rule that now many performers are extravagantly obnoxious, egotistical, vain, effeminate, villainous, etc., in order to draw a crowd eager to see them defeated.)

Some cultures favor and even require understatement, as do the Zuni Indians described by Ruth Benedict. Their tribal collectivism suppresses individualism. They do not allow a soon-to-be leader even to speak on his own behalf, but he must put on self-effacing modesty until chosen by the tribe.

On the other hand, some cultures require overstatement, for all its personal hazards. The ruinous potlatching of the Kwakiutl Indians was a result of the cultural obligation to boast and make extravagant gifts and challenges to one's rivals. Traditional warrior ethics encourage boasting. It is told in Norse sagas that ancient champions would recite a list of ancestors as well as their own valiant deeds before doing battle (similarly the Japanese samurai).

Doubtless a reason for encouraging overstatement is that it favors comedy, prepares for the pratfall, and teaches a salutary lesson of humility, so is an element of folk humor (one thinks of Texas tall tales about Davy Crockett, and Paul Bunyan and his blue ox; or the makeup of the clown, his oversize feet and red bulbous nose).

Perhaps a deeper reason for the popularity of overstatement is its contribution to group pride and morale. Cultural permission is given to the hero to enlarge himself, to boast as much as he wants to, so long as it is complimentary to group (tribe, team, family, nation) achievement. Then what would be egotism in an individual is transformed into loyalty, team spirit, patriotism. In sports contests, one might say that a cheerleader is a designated group braggart. Even the clown's pratfall can be interpreted in terms of group pride, if it says, "we are not like him." When egotism is transformed into loyalty, a further strange and even dangerous effect can occur. Thinkers such as Reinhold Niebuhr, William Graham Sumner, and Gustave LeBon, have pointed out that there is almost no limit to what may be done or accepted in the name, or according to the mores, of one's group—not excluding lying, killing, bragging, strutting, gloating, self-righteousness, arrogance, intolerance, vengefulness, hatred of foreigners, ethnocentrism, the tyranny of the majority. Thus group egotism can be a blindness which keeps people from seeing how dangerously they are overextending themselves and overstating their case, in Sicilian expeditions, crusades, and the like.

From one pole to another—from the personal to the cultural—we turn to inflation in language, not as a tactical choice but as habits deeply ingrained in the speech and thought of almost everyone. We expect that language will reflect whatever faults of overstatement are habitual with people and common in culture. Words like the following tell that people are aware of shoddy values spread by equally shoddy words, inflation of which threatens our minds rather than our pocketbooks: hype, glitz, glamor, ballyhoo, hokum, B.S., flimflam, schmaltz, soft soap, puffery, boosterism, build-up, image-making, prestige, rhetoric (in a pejorative sense), hot air, hullabaloo, hoopla, much ado about . . . . It is reasonable to expect that a frequency count of such words could provide an index of cultural inflation.

We can distinguish six common types of verbal inflation: 1) hyperbole, 2) hype, 3) redundancy, 4) euphemism, 5) jargon, and 6) abuse.

1. Hyperbole consists of using words that are too grand, too strong, or too many for the matter at hand. Too grand language is said to be bombastic, pompous, grandiose, grandiloquent, boastful, fulsome, extravagant, exaggerated, purple. Too many words for the matter at hand are described as prolix, effusive, turgid, loquacious, verbose, wordy. Prolixity must have been what Voltaire had in mind when he said, "The secret of being a bore is to tell everything." George Meredith described the verbal inflation of one of his characters: The more he said the less he felt his words, and, feeling them less, he inflated them more."

Hyperbole is deeply ingrained in advertising. A man went into a drugstore for some toothpaste and asks the druggist for a small tube. He was handed one clearly marked large. The customer said, "I wanted small." The druggist said, "Mister, I've got family-size or economy-size, or large. But large is the smallest I got." And hyperbole is no less ingrained in politics. Will Rogers said, "The next time a politician talks about something big and important, notice that he isn't saying anything." Politics is much to blame, said George Orwell, for flooding English with stale and imprecise writing and speaking, because it calculatingly avoids clarity and chooses the "inflated style"; the "great enemy of clear language is insincerity." The National Council of Teachers of English now give annual Doublespeak Awards to those in public life who misuse language calculatingly. It is "strange," says the authority on the English language, H. W. Fowler (1974, p. 618) that the British "with such a fondness for understatement" should make excessive use of adverbs like *horribly, frightfully, dreadfully, fearfully, infinitely, fabulously.* "The downward path began with *awfully.*" Fowler (p. 282) adds: "There are naughty people who will say infinite(ly) when they only mean great or much or far."

However, masters of hyperbole like Rabelais and H. L. Mencken get away with flouting rules that apply to "purple" writers.

2. Hype is defined by a dictionary as "deceptively inflated advertising and promotion." It differs from idiomatic, habitual overstate-

ment in that it is not spontaneous but deliberately contrived for propaganda or promotional purposes. It is, one might say, a veneer over rhetoric, painted by professionals who study how to dress up a commonplace event or person by some theme that, added, will fascinate the public. It is overstatement that makes something look more glamourous and romantic than it actually is, the added element also often called glitz, schmaltz, hokum, or B.S.

Take the hype of Elvis Presley, who in his sequined, spangled costumes was called "The King of Glitz." Before him, Liberace in a white satin dress suit, playing the piano between two lighted candelabra, hands sparkling with jewels, deserved that title. Before that, we may recall Aimee Semple MacPherson giving her sermons in a long white gown with full-size wings resembling an angel's as the queen of evangelical glitz.

Now it seems almost impossible for a boxer or wrestler to have a professional career without a layer of hype and taking to himself names like "Rambo" and "The Macho Man." Musical hype is also called schmaltz or hearts-and-flowers. It is institutionalized in the cult of "corny" sentimental songs and dimpled dollies dancing and singing that generate romantic sentiment week after week and year after year. Surely it was a triumph of hype that a ruddy-faced cowboy twirling a lariat in "the spirit of Marlboro" should epitomize the health value of a "low-tar cigarette." In beverage sales we find hype making something out of nothing. The "Cola Wars" (1986–87) were supposed to be a merchandising duel to the finish between Coca Cola and Pepsi-Cola—both of which made greater sales. Behind that hype was the supposed mysterious formula of Coke in a vault guarded twenty-four hours a day.

The noise of publicity surrounding the annual football Superbowl ritual is an example of colossal hype in a sports event (with 24,000 sports writers covering it in New Orleans in 1986, to an audience confirmed at over 116 million viewers in America and abroad to thirty other nations), a spectacle surpassing the grandeur of the Nazi Party rallies in Nuremberg. When you get down to it, what would a superbowl game be without hype but just 22 men struggling over a ball?

The hyping of faddish merchandise adds enormously to consumer costs. In marketing basketball shoes to teenagers, for instance, the excessive price of the shoe is part of the hype. A shoe costing $20.00 to make in Korea is sold for $160.00 in New York—the difference between cost and price tag in the United States is largely promotional hype. A shoe retailer observes, "high price is part of the aura." (*Christian Science Monitor*, 8 May 1989.)

Astrology is cosmic hype. All the folderol about Scorpio, Aquarius, etc., signifying that cosmic forces are steering one, adds a dimension of celestrial meaning to an otherwise mundane life.

The media have their own glamor. The mere fact of being on camera or in the newspaper is enough to mysteriously exalt one above the common level.

With so many media pouring out hype (which can hardly be avoided where there is exposure of seven hours per day to television), we live in a bubblebath of overstatement, in which rival rhetorics claim our feelings, images are spread worldwide, voices clamor to be heard, any voice can be amplified, PR substitutes images for real people, media make events, people adore celebrities, fame lasts for fifteen minutes, showmen replace leaders, reality is what we verify by TV. Everybody seems to be trying to stand a little taller than he really is, and the first liar is lost in the shuffle.

In modern life, hype covers everything, like one of those ice storms that make trees, leaves, sidewalks—everything—glisten.

The chief faults of hype and hyperbole are shared with other forms of overstatement: their tendency to deny reality, and to raise expectations that sooner or later will be disappointed. Pervasive and prolonged overstatement contributes to a contempt for media, for leaders, for institutions purveying it—a sense of alienation that makes its contribution to the malaise of affluence.

However, I would not wish to give the impression that hype is all bad and no good. After all, the epics of Homer, Sir Thomas Malory, and Sir Walter Scott were puffery with full approval of their countrymen. How the Trojan War got blown up from a squabble over a woman to a great international cause in which the gods took sides would be difficult to explain without puffery—in this case called poetry. It can hardly be denied that, in such cases, hype and hyperbole, for all their falsity, in a Munchhausen-like way raise life above the humdrum level.

3. Another sort of overstatement lacks the extravagance of hype; and is often monotonous and boring, because it repeats beyond what is needed to convey a message. Communication theorists call it redundancy.

Most people think of redundancy as something one doesn't need, like a fifth wheel. Tell a man on the job that he is redundant and he will expect to be fired. A redundant message repeats what we know or have already heard and may not wish to hear again. In the latter case, it is boring, a waste of time, a kind of clutter in communication. Modern life is permeated with redundancy if only because of technical efficiency in transmitting, storing, repeating, and duplicating information.

But there is another kind of redundancy that is repetitious but not so boring. It is the kind we like to have repeated, at least on suitable occasions (anniversaries, family gatherings, etc.)—even to the extent of boring some. We might call it good redundancy because it carries good feeling, makes people feel warm and joyful. Everybody knows the good feeling that comes from contact with an important part of one's past—photo albums, school yearbooks, remembering good times together, reunions, candles on a cake, a letter to a teacher from a student who remembers her. Such redundancy brings warm memories and sentiments that restore identity—a sense of who one is, or was.

Plainly such "good" redundancy helps communication and social life generally (Klapp 1978, pp. 108–117). On the other hand, the "bad" sort, is stale, mechanical and boring, and so robs life of much of its liveliness and resonance. Unfortunately, modern media, if only by their technical power of communication and duplication, as already observed, favor "bad" redundancy, spreading boring sameness everywhere. So it is no surprise that, with all its redundancy, much of modern culture is boring (Klapp 1986). Boredom expresses the impoverishment of meaning from saying and hearing the same things too much. When news media have to generate a quota of words, day after day—story or no story— inflation is inevitable. We have yet to hear of the newspaper that has the nerve to print, "Nothing today, folks."

4. Euphemism substitutes polite and pleasant language for plain talk (e.g., unwell for sick). Obviously it plays a part in speeches, banquets, anniversaries, funerals, honorary ceremonies, and is the heart of politeness and tact in circumstances where blunt statement could offend and is not absolutely necessary. Useful though it is, euphemism tends to longer statement (prolixity, circumlocution) than does plain talk, and so is an inflation of language that can not only

waste words but make it harder to get at meaning. Necessary as it is, euphemism has also a sinister side when, by Orwellian transformation, it starts to call war peace, looting liberation, tyranny freedom, demagoguery democracy.

5. In jargon we have a proliferation of words that, by its ugliness, is the opposite of euphemism while getting no nearer to plain statement. To cite Fowler (1974, p. 315) again, the very word jargon connotes a strange, barbaric tongue: "talk that is both ugly-sounding and hard to understand." Our world is ever more filled with jargons that tax understanding (computerese, bureaucratese, legalese, officialese, sociologese, gobbledygook, bafflegab, eco-babble, psycho-babble, acronyms, and so on). Such jargons creep into language like a sort of verbal crabgrass. While grammarians unite in deploring them, no one seems able to prevent them from displacing plain speech by a sort of Gresham's law. According to Follett (pp. 286–87, 424, 684) the prevalence of jargon (as well as of vogue words and noun plague) is due to "the ease with which they can be substituted" for more precise words, "saving the trouble of choosing the right." Jargon "lengthens the expression of every idea." Analyzing a sample of verbiage, Follett found that 119 words could be reduced to 46, therefore that 73 (60 percent) were superfluous. The proportion by which verbiage can be reduced without loss of message would seem to be a measure of verbal inflation.

Even though jargon is so poor for thought and communication, we presume it is not without other functions—one of these being that it is some sort of status reward, entailing professional prestige. We note that while it baffles and puts off (and down) the public by its seeming profundity, it calls on an expert to tell what it means. So it puts a distance between the expert who knows the lofty language and the ignorant who know only plain talk.

Also, jargon and vogue words establish a bond among people who use them, a satisfaction of being "in the know," the right school of thought or social set. With such functions we could hardly expect bafflegab to die.

6. Lastly we come to inflation not from overuse of words but abuse so bad that it breaks down serviceable distinctions, loses the meaning of those words, and injures the language by what Fowler (p. 562) called the "crime of verbicide." The fault is amusingly illustrated by Sheridan's character Mrs. Malaprop in "The Rivals." She is

grandiloquent (as was Micawber) but blunderingly and consistently wrong (as Micawber was not). The audience laughs at her abuse of words, but it wouldn't be all that funny if writers got in such a habit and found that words no longer carried reliable meaning. The death of good words is not something for wordsmiths to celebrate, any more than a plumber would losing his best wrench. The question is, if one had thousands of Mrs. Malaprops pounding typewriters, writing news, advertisements, and fiction, and teaching school (to say nothing of editing dictionaries), how long would it take to bring about a sort of verbal bankruptcy? It might be the point at which the average person was so corrupted that he could not correct Mrs. Malaprop's mistakes even with a jury of his peers.

Advertising has long been blamed for abuse of words, especially about qualities (super, deluxe), sizes (jumbo, giant, economy, family), and the mislabeling of foods (such as natural and organic), which add to the blurring of standards and difficulty in telling (by words) which thing is better or cheaper than another.

Outside the domain of commercial puffery we find an interesting example of death by abuse of a good word in the sports field—for example, the remarkable changes in the meaning of *awesome* over the past decade. Beginning with the somewhat cryptic original use by a sportscaster to describe the performance of a football team, the word caught on until it seemed to apply to virtually anything which impressed or pleased somebody. For example, it might be applied to sports performance (a basketball throw, pitcher's fastball, a golf stroke, a quarterback's passing, a tennis serve). And outside the sports field, all sorts of things were said to be "awesome" (the profits of a firm, glaciers, the design of a hummingbird's wing, Tommy Dorsey's breath control on trombone, a Simon and Garfunkle song). I am waiting for an ice cream store to advertise its hot fudge sundae as "awesome." It seemed plain that by being inappropriately applied to so many things, "awesome" had lost its awe. It was not long before the entire field of athletics seemed permeated with "awesomeness." And not far behind were show business and politics. The only field that seemed no longer able to make much use of it was religion.

Other grossly abused words have lost some of their meaning, such as: fabulous (for remarkable), tragic (for accidentally fatal), catastrophic (for unfortunate), weird (for odd or strange), obscene (for undesirable), ghastly (for ugly), charisma (for attractive personality), super (for something a little better than average), liberal (for any political opinion on the left of right wing).

The destruction of the word *liberal* in the United States for years up to the 1988 presidential election was little short of verbal assassination. Its enemies so loaded it with negative meaning that it sank under its excess cargo. By deliberate misuse, it turned into a synonym for bureaucracy, welfare state, and even socialism. We note sadly its drift from the noble doctrine espoused by thinkers such as John Milton, J. S. Mill, and Voltaire, of the open society, intolerant to nobody, and learning from all points of view including the left. The question remained, could this pitiable wreck be raised and salvaged? Could conscientious correct use remedy the abuse?

Another example shows that even the strongest words—the most pungent expletives and "four letter" words—can be worn out by overuse and abuse. Applied habitually and indiscriminately in ordinary situations, they soon lose their shock value and are not much use to those who wish to swear. The question is left, then, what can one say when one really wants a strong effect? The jejune old naughties don't work any more, indeed they add to boredom and help make life flat emotionally. Aware of this weakening by abuse, one sees the rise of what might be called foul-mouthed theater and literature. An illustration is David Mamet's Pulitzer Prize-winning play, *Glengarry Glen Ross*. A good play, but why did those middle class businessmen have to swear so much? Perhaps it was to depict life as it is. But does that not speak to how boring life as well as theatre must be when even the strongest words have no effect?

We have looked at inflation of words by hyperbole, hype, redundancy, euphemism, jargon, and verbicide. All are forms of overstatement in which more words are used than the situation warrants or things are made to seem bigger or more important than they really are. They fit our minimum definition of inflation as a loss of value of symbols following increase in their supply. The more words are used in such ways, the less they mean. The loss of value, however, is not in monetary purchasing power but in their ability to convey meaning in social exchange.

Awareness of inflation of words, or overstatement of any kind, leads to a loss of what might be called their "purchasing power" to influence and convince people. Symbols are discounted (just as inflated money is) to make allowance for the tall tale, big talk, rhetoric, hype, hyperbole, and redundancy that they convey. Suspicion of communication and feeling the need to discount it are expressed in words like Babel, babble, ballyhoo, blab, bubble, bull, b.s., chatter, chitchat, idle talk, gossip, verbiage, rhetoric, propaganda, puffery, a line, hype, glitz, weasel words, purple, flimflam, softsoap, blarney—a vocabulary of disenchantment.

Such an idea, that words lose value as does money in oversupply, has been current for a long time, in one form or another. It is implicit in William Graham Sumner's likening of cliches and catchwords to "coins of thought" circulating in popular speech. Emerson deplored the degradation of old words, "perverted to stand for things that are not; a paper currency is employed, when there is no bullion in the vaults."

A market model of inflation implies operation of the supply and demand law on words, in which increase of supply tends to lower price.

Once the market model is applied to words, it also makes attractive the idea that Gresham's Law operates, in which "bad" symbols (crowd ideas, stereotypes, cliches, slogans, kitsch) drive out good from circulation. Such is the case with political discourse, according to a writer on public affairs, Geofrey Taylor, who holds that Gresham's Law, "which states that bad currency drives out good," has taken hold over large swathes of political discourse. Such an idea is especially applicable to popular culture, according to Dwight MacDonald (Rosenberg and White 1957, pp. 59–73) who wrote that "there seems to be a Gresham's Law in culture," in which kitsch, competing with good art, "drives out the good, since it is more easily understood and enjoyed," hence sold.

Even so, I would not wish to imply that a market model, even if applicable, is all that is needed to understand verbal inflation. Apart from the market aspect, we note that psychological processes called habituation (growing tolerance and loss of awareness of repeated stimuli), satiation, and boredom can cause overused words to lose some, even all, of their meaning. Boredom is an important sign and mechanism of inflation in words, a sign that too much talk is coming to nothing, meaning is being lost in verbiage, words are misapplied, overstatements are not coming up to expectations, a symbolic bubble is about to burst. These fundamental phychological processes seem able to deal with some inflation without invoking the more complicated, less parsimonious, idea of Gresham's Law.

But there is no need to view all overstatement negatively. It has its uses, as we have noted. Even among dreams we have a choice of a bubble that will burst or a balloon that will take us where we want to go.

We have so far only begun to look at types of overstatement, of personal tactics and words, as a cause of inflation. We need to get other types of social magnification into the picture. Let us now turn to crusading as moral rhetorical overstatement that glorifies conflict by ennobling one side.

3

Crusades

A crusade is a holy war of someone who thinks he is right against someone he is sure is wrong. We know crusades earliest as holy wars undertaken by Christians at the behest of the Pope from the eleventh to the thirteenth centuries to recover the Holy Land from the Moslems. Now the term crusade has come to refer to almost any vigorous, concerted action for some cause or idea or against some abuse. It might be a cause like women's rights, anti-slavery, birth control, civil rights, anti-abortion, humane treatment of animals, environmental protection (which, even though institutionalized by laws still has to be fought for)—anything that people care deeply enough about to make sacrifices for. Is it possible to have a crusade by oneself? (One thinks of whistle-blowers, or of fanatical reformers like Anthony Comstock.) The answer is no, for that could be merely an individual grudge or obsession. A crusade is a collective movement, in which heroes who lead the fight are backed up by comrades sharing the moral perspective of righteous fight against opponents who are not only mistaken or wrong but evil. This sense of moral militancy and righteous cause is well-expressed by one of the original crusaders: "I am marching with a goodly band, and we have placed ourselves entirely in the hands of God, for we go forth as His servants to accomplish His will." The early crusaders were firmly convinced that God was on their side; their battle cry was *Deus vult* God wills it). Faith in one's own righteousness is a chief mark of the crusader. To ascribe one's own goals to God's will seems gross arrogance, a self-righteousness that verges upon authoritarianism when one thinks only his own view is right and does not hesitate to impose it upon others. It is this spirit of righteousness, often on both sides, which distinguishes a crusade form a practical enterprise or a plain old war. Because of its moral militancy, a crusade is aptly symbolized by a cross that is also a sword.

Our concern is with how crusading acts as an inflationary factor—how it makes more out of what at first seemed little (take the Sacco and Vanzetti case, which grew into a *cause célèbre* in the 1920s). A crusade inflates by moral rhetoric, ennobling fighters into heroes battling against evil, and capable of drawing huge numbers of previously unaffected people into common cause. It recruits by mental contagion from crowds and the examples of heroes and martyrs, into a mass movement with a do-or-die spirit (morale, esprit de corps), which makes them ready to sacrifice for the noble cause (as one saw in the early Christians, or the soldiers of the Ayatollah Khomeini against those of Iraq). Crusades also enlarge action by reciprocal escalation: counter-crusades of people equally zealous for an opposite purpose (one thinks of "Right to Life" anti-abortion versus "Right to Choice).

It takes symbolic embellishment to make a crusade out of a practical enterprise or a plain old war—magnification by epic poets, news writers, photographers, propagandists, ballad-singers, and so on, to increase the scale of events and stature of heroes. One thinks of what writers like Malraux, Orwell, Hemingway, Dos Passos, and artists like Picasso, did for the Spanish Civil War, helping the world to see it as a crusade against the evil of fascism, which drew thousands of idealistic volunteers from many countries. As it happened, Homer, for all his eloquence, did not make a crusade of the Greek expedition to Troy, because the rhetorical elements were lacking—or if present were not seized upon. But Harriet Beecher Stowe (with apologies for comparing so minor an artist with Homer) did seize upon those elements, did supply in Simon Legree a villain bad enough to justify a crusade. And that book is much credited with having stirred up Northerners to the crusade against slavery.

Golden Age of Crusading in America

Americans rather like crusades. Perhaps that is why we have had so many of them. The historian Richard Hofstadter wrote of the reformist zeal that is at the heart of our penchant for crusading:

> Americans do not abide very quietly the evils of life. We are forever restlessly pitting ourselves against them, demanding changes, improvements, remedies. . . . There is a wide and pervasive tendency to believe . . . that there is some

great but essentially very simple struggle going on, at the heart of which there lies some single conspiratorial force, whether it be the force represented by the "gold bugs," the Catholic Church, big business, corrupt politicians, the liquor interests and the saloons, or the Communist Party, and that this evil is something that must be not merely limited, checked and controlled but rather extirpated root and branch. . . .

So we go off on periodic psychic sprees that purport to be moral crusades: liberate the people once and for all from the gold bugs, restore absolute popular democracy or completely honest competition in business, wipe out the saloon and liquor forever from the nation's life, destroy the political machines and put an end to corruption, or achieve absolute, total, and final security against war, espionage, and the affairs of the external world.

This history presumably provides rich opportunities to learn how crusades form and what results from them. If there ever was a golden age for crusading in the United States, it was probably the century before World War II, in which there were several peaks of reform and moralistic public action. Carl Bode describes the temper of 1840–1861 as:

one of the great reform periods in the United States. In sharp contrast to the cynical post-war era . . . . (it was) the heyday of crusades . . . for the insane, the poor, the disabled, for women's rights, for the 10 hour day for workmen, and above all for the abolition of Negro slavery. If we had to pick out any single example . . . of this crusading zeal, it would be Harriet Beecher Stowe's . . . *Uncle Tom's Cabin.*

In the struggle for abolition of slavery, let it be noted that, compared with Garrison, Lincoln was not a crusader but a gradualist calling for abolition within one hundred years. Following the post-Civil War cynicism came the period referred to by Hofstadter as the age of reform, form the Populism of the 1890s, the Bryan campaign of 1896, the Progressive movements and muckraking of 1900–1914, to the New Deal. These upsurges of reform were connected with trends and strains such as the chaotic growth of cities; infloodings of immigrants; rampant industrialism, investment, and economic exploitation; women and children in the labor force; the rise of the urban boss (the muckrakers' "devil"); increasing conflict between rural, native, white Protestants and immigrant Catholics; These all made possible penny journalism—or what was later coined "yellow journalism".

Filler (1939) describes well the crusading zeal of the muckrakers of these times—how, for example, Theodore Roosevelt arose as "a shining young knight in the habiliments of chivalry" from the ranks of the machine politicians—and the many muckraking campaigns, such as exposes of meatpacking (Upton Sinclair), the "shame of the cities" (Lincoln Steffens), the Standard Oil trust (Ida Tarbell), the "poison trust" and impure food (Dr. H. W. Wiley), the "white slave" traffic, and so on. A guiding faith of the liberal crusaders was that the cure for the evils of democracy was more democracy. This was our heyday of do-goodism and stop-badism. There was a keen sense of injustice and a desire to do something about it. And the moral conscience was still strong in the face of strains defined as evil, not merely "problems". There was conflict between cultures—not only immigrant but Protestant versus Catholic and rural versus urban. The intelligentsia were aroused and disturbed by status problems. And the awareness of issues was helped by the growth of a reading public and mass journalism.

World War I put an end to the golden age of crusading in the United States. Moralism in politics went out of style from that time on. Anyone who has studied documentary films or popular songs of the World War I era can hardly fail to be struck by the naiveté and chauvinism of the popular spirit—how different from the spirit, say, of 1939! World War I ended the muckraking era, says Filler, because it brought the liberals into "strange alliances" with people such as munitions makers and paid propagandists: "An age set in which held reform lightly." After Wilson, moral idealism suffered a kind of bankruptcy. The Prohibition Amendment was not the zenith but the last gasp of the puritan spirit in national politics. During its early history the American labor movement had the earmarks of a crusade from the left, with bitter strikes and anti-capitalist ideology, until under the New Deal it softened into a pragmatic effort for better wages and working conditions, institutionalized by the AFL-CIO merger and passage of the Wagner Act legally permitting collective bargaining. Gone was the crusading spirit of the Wobblies and the Knights of Labor. Let it also be noted that the New Deal, in spite of its vast reforms, was not a crusade but a pragmatic and opportunistic program with an anti-moralistic temper. The repeal of the 18th Amendment was a symbolic defeat for moralism in politics. The antimoralistic temper of the New Deal was expressed by Thurman Arnold's view of "trustbusting" as ritual, not practical, politics. Various intellectual trends were weakening the absolutism on which crusading spirit depends—for example, secularization, decline of belief in hell and sin, the waning power of religious fundamentalism, popularity of psychoanalysis, relativism in morality, environmental determinism, and the rise of humanism, hedonism, and the live-for-now outlook. World War II, though a desperate conflict (calling itself "crusade in Europe"), had little of the "make-the-world-safe-for-democracy" fervor of World War I.

During the 1950s came a quiescent, silent period, so well described by sociologists as an exhaustion of ideology, a drying up of radicalism, and a turning of concern toward culture and status rather than politics. This was a poor scene for a crusader. Other-directedness and bland conformity seemed to dominate, though disturbed by status anxieties and outbursts of moralism in politics such as McCarthyism. During this bland period, Senator Joseph McCarthy tried to launch what might be called a one-man crusade to search out and destroy "communists" in the United States government, but it did not catch fire; lacking enough consensus, he failed—but not before scaring a good many people and injuring not a few. On the whole, Eisenhower seemed a more representative symbol of the time. "Alienation" began to be a favorite term to describe the temper of both the vociferously discontented and the "silent" members of the American mass public.

It was not surprising, then, that entering the sixties "old fighters" remembering the "good old days" should find cause to lament that things were not the same—there were no causes to lance for anymore. Kenneth Rexroth, a "grand old man" of bohemianism, remarked that the socialist faith had run out on him.

> The moral content of the old radical movement has vanished . . . the classics of socialist and anarchistic literature seem at mid-century to speak a foolish and naive language.

Ben Hecht, a great fighter against censorship and puritanism, complained that there was nothing to crusade for anymore.

> When I first launched myself . . . as a writer, there was one great enemy. He was called morality, Victorianism, hypocrisy. Censors were strangling literature, strangling theater, ripping "September Morn" out of the window because she was nude. We all fought against Victorianism, morality and hypocrisy as if this was the greatest enemy of mankind. Well, I've lived to see that enemy laid by the

heels. . . . I was arrested . . . a long time ago, for writing a book that was supposed to be lewd, obscene, lascivious. The book could be printed in a ladies' magazine today. In fact, it might not be accepted because it's so gentle and sweet. The disappearance of the censor has really rattled me—I no longer know which side I'm on. . . . I hear things in the theater in New York that literally shock me, and I'm not easy to shock. They're the same words I heard in brothels. . . . The new playwrights are so busy with dirty words you'd think they'd discovered a new plot. But, as I say, I don't know which side I'm on—we fought for this freedom and we got it.

J. Allen Smith is quoted by Eric Goldman as having said: "The real trouble with us reformers is that we made reform a crusade against standards. Well, we smashed them all and now neither we nor anybody else have anything left."

"Nothing left" refers not so much to an absence of rules (we still have plenty) but to a lack of those categorical imperatives that put fire in the eye of a crusader. This is what I would call a "wet tinder" situation—a shortage of ignitable materials such as moral idealism, absolutism, ideology or utopia, and patriotic zeal. Crusading elements remain relatively small minority groups labeled "cornball" or "extremist" by the majority. This does not hurt their spirit, but it does their prospects. They are unable to "sell". Their wave does not spread to the majority because beneath apathy is a pervasive alienation which keeps many people from joining things or counting on each other, from hoping that "right" will prevail, or from focusing on one symbol of supreme good versus evil, and which fosters escapism in not a few. With distrust of ideology so widespread, even crusaders become tainted with Machiavellianism or manipulated by it: Galahad gets rust on his shield. In such an adverse climate of opinion, a crusade, if it starts at all, is like a wave that is breaking against an outgoing tide.

Then, about the time Americans had concluded they were a "silent generation," new bursts of crusading spirit exploded: the civil rights movement in the South; "free speech" demonstrations on college campuses; peace and anti-Vietnam war protests; and the beard (stimulated by beatnikism and Castroism) coming to symbolize protest against the Establishment. The crusading spirit of much of this was unmistakable.

INTERNATIONAL DAYS OF PROTEST . . . TEACH-IN . . . PROTEST WALK. We will meet in front of the Draft Board Office . . . the walk will proceed to the Army Recruiting Office and thence to the offices of our Congressmen. Next we will walk to the Copley Press, and finally to the Eleventh Naval Headquarters, where the walk will end. . . . YOUR PARTICIPATION IS

ESSENTIAL. . . . WE CANNOT BE SILENT ACCOMPLICES TO THE
UNNECESSARY KILLING OF AMERICANS AND VIETNAMESE. WE
MUST NOT ACQUIESCE IN THE FACE OF PENTAGON-DIRECTED
GENOCIDE. WE DARE NOT QUIETLY ACCEPT THE CONTINUING
ESCALATION, WHICH CAN ONLY LEAD TO NUCLEAR WAR. . . .
JOIN US.

Along with such protest came a surge of more practical idealism
in Peace Corps and Vista volunteering on college campuses. Sparking
all of this was probably the bus boycott led by Martin Luther King
in Montgomery, Alabama, leading to a Supreme Court decision of
October 1956 that segregated seating in municipal buses was illegal;
this gave rise to major new forms of militant nonviolent action, such
as the CORE sit-ins which began in February 1960 and the "freedom
rides" initiated by James Farmer. Likewise, from the radical right
came crusades against communism, viewed by many liberals as a re-
surgence of McCarthyism, and countercrusades against civil rights
fighters by white racist extremists, who were willing to attack crowds
of women and children with clubs, hoses, and dogs. When tried for
violent acts in Southern courts, they carried Confederate flags and received standing ovations when acquitted. It became clear that, on
both sides of the civil rights question, a real crusade was on, for
which people were willing to die.

A counter-crusader for white supremacy said:

They ask me—do you believe in violence? If it takes violence to defend our Constitution, the answer is yes!!! I love this Republic and I love this country and I
love the very principles down to the Constitution, but this bunch of gangsters in
Washington has violated it, has committed every act, from the top level of
treason right on down, against the white people, against God, against this nation.
Remember the words of Jesus Christ, who said, "You can't love two masters! You
love the one and HATE the other."

By an understandable dialectic, Negro revolt became more extreme
and sectarian. Extremist groups such as CORE, SNCC, the Black
Muslims, and the New York Black Panther Party threatened the
leadership of NAACP and the Urban League, urging "black power"
and rejecting moderation as "Uncle Tomism":

Allah will help us get . . . freedom, justice . . . we must have some of this earth
that we can call our own. . . . HURRY AND JOIN UNTO YOUR OWN
KIND! THE TIME OF THIS WORLD IS NOW AT HAND.

So the silent fifties seemed to have been followed by the erupting sixties.

But, as it developed, the new radicalism, for all its vehemence and alarming promise, did not become politically more than a "police problem". The activists on college campuses remained a small minority. No ideology emanated from it to reach a larger public—either radical left or radical right. (The "radicalism" of the right was based on the doctrine of laissez-faire, two centuries old; and that of the civil rights movement was collecting the last installment on the Emancipation Proclamation, over a hundred years old.) Esoteric doctrines like objectivism proclaimed by followers of Ayn Rand had little appeal to the man in the street. Indeed, the new radicalism was more mystique than ideology, a faith in action and involvement combined with mistrust of theory that made it ambiguous about goals. As one member of the "indignant generation" put it:

> The student movement is based on very general principles for rights, justice and so on. Many of us are for things that no political party has come out for—most of us are for banning the bomb. We just work on a broad set of principles, and as issues come up, we decide how to act. We approach all the problems without the strict theory that older people are so fond of.

Forced to find a label, one might say that whatever ideology or idealism there was in the new left could best be described as a kind of humanism that went beyond loyalty to particular mores, tradition, faith, or nation. "People to people", "people everywhere" were the slogans—which, rather than sympathy for communism, perhaps explains why so much crusading took unpatriotic forms such as burning draft cards, interfering with munitions shipments, or sending humanitarian aid to the "enemy." A statement by a teen teenager is typical: "I would give blood to the Viet Cong anytime. The important thing is people, not political systems." This humanism, though it was compassionate, lacked the sentimental self-righteousness of crusaders like Carry Nation or Harriet Beecher Stowe. It had no illusions about revising society by political methods to make everything right. One of the principal spokesmen of the new left, Edward M. Keating, said:

> The "New Left" does not fit within the political spectrum. If anything, it belongs to the social spectrum. The end sought is not a new system, since systems—whether the current one in this country, those in communist countries, or,

for that matter, any system of the past—are irrelevant. What is relevant is justice. Whereas the "Old Left" sought economic justice, the "New Left" has a far broader concern that encompasses social, economic, and political justice. Its ultimate goal is peace—domestic and international—and peace is impossible without justice. . . . We will have to let go of traditional rhetoric, stereotyped thought, preconceptions, and everything else that inhibits man from fulfilling himself.

However, while the New Left wanted change, it felt no great inspiration to crusade for economic and welfare legislation—Medicare, public housing, civil rights laws, minimum wage laws, revision of the Taft-Hartley Law, anti-poverty programs, extension of Social Security benefits, and federal aid to schools—of kinds already being achieved by the middle class; nor on the other hand, could it see in them the menace of "creeping socialism," as did the right. Thus a polarization grew between two factions in the United States which saw things in differently—not in terms of old issues, but from different world views: the humanism of man-is-one versus the melodrama of some-men-are-good-and-some-are-bad. To the New Left, mankind was one, even if it did not look that way; human rights were more important than property rights or even national interest; war was bankrupt as a method of international relations so some other means must be found. To the political right, the world was divided between communism and the free enterprise system; private property and the nation must be defended at all costs and to fail to do so is treason; communism as a world conspiracy is the single greatest enemy; war is justified to defend the nation and property.

Such an opposition, however, was not the kind one could readily settle by political methods. Indeed, the new radicalism, though it believed in "activism"—especially in protest—was, as Christopher Lasch said, more concerned with morals and culture than politics in the practical sense. Thus it was no surprise to see *Newsweek* observe in 1966 that student participation in the civil rights movement was waning; the "big exodus to the South" seemed to be over, one reason being diversion of interest to the Vietnam war, another that civil rights were becoming law, so that the movement lost some of its dramatic appeal. A student said: "It's still dangerous, but it's not a political act anymore. It's a wholesome, goody-goody thing because papa LBJ is behind you." And, by the end of that year, *Time* observed:

The old fire to hit the streets has largely faded. A new desire to work pragmati-
cally to tutor Negro kids and help out in slums is rising. . . . (At Berkeley) the
students once aflame with political causes are drifting toward the introspective
life of psychedelic drugs and the beat life. It is what Chancellor Assistant John
Searle calls "a move from the political culture to the hipster world."

For the vast majority, even among university students, crusading for
the left did not generate a wave; activists probably did not number
more than 2 percent.

Though the 1960s faded from their original promise of widespread
crusading activism, the fact remains that there was in this decade a
greater upsurge of crusading spirit than the silence of the fifties
would have led one to expect. Notable expressions were the effort of
students to take over Columbia University in April 1968 and the Poor
People's March on Washington, D.C. in the summer of that year.
Such events seem to indicate that crusading cannot be permanently
dried up, but that it is a spring which runs ever fresh even when conditions are unfavorable. Like hero worship, it is a generic tendency
whose sources are in human nature. Yet a social milieu which lacks
adequate moral base and belief in ideology is like wet tinder and cannot sustain enough crusading spirit for a long time to make much of
a difference in the course of history—except perhaps to symbolize
minority group feeling. Which is a good thing, pragmatists would
say, since they do not like crusading.

For all the fears that the crusading spirit had been dampened and
its fire gone out, the succeeding seventies and eighties gave ample
evidence that it had not faded. Not its thrust but only its direction
had changed. Major crusades with a sense of moral crisis were
mounted against: communism and its "evil empire" (to use President
Reagan's phrase); drug abusers at home and suppliers abroad (for
which war the military was drafted); polluters of the environment and
destroyers of wildlife species (epitomized by the protests of Green-
peace interfering with whaling). There was the widespread condem-
nation of the oil spill of the tanker Exxon Valdez and protest against
abortion, enough, one would suppose, to satisfy the most sanguine
crusader longing to put on his spurs and ride again.

All the same, it could not be denied that liberalism, once the
champion of causes, had become strangely languid and silent, unwilling or unable to respond to attacks from the right wing charging
that it was soft on communism and favored socialistic or centralized

government. By the end of the eighties (as noted in connection with verbicide), the very name—the "L-word"—had become anathema to the right wing.

Crusader as a Social Type

Having looked over a variety of crusading movements in the United States in over a century, we are in a position to define it more generically, and then perhaps to evaluate it in terms of these features. What symbolic elements make a conflict a crusade and a fighter a crusader? We propose here to look, first, at the social type of the crusader, then at what makes him different from other doers and movers on the stage of history, and finally at the crusade as a social movement, especially the rhetorical elements that enlarge it beyond an ordinary enterprise, and the absence of which causes a crusade to decline into an ordinary movement (as for example the American labor movement did).

What kind of person is a crusader and what is his role? If we are to go beyond a dictionary definition (such as one who undertakes a "remedial enterprise with zeal and enthusiasm"), it might be by considering people such as Harriet Beecher Stowe, William Lloyd Garrison, Margaret Sanger, William Booth, Billy Graham, Martin Luther King, Carry Nation, Susan B. Anthony, Gandhi, Richard the Lion-Hearted, Martin Luther, Mario Savio, and Ralph Nader. It is plain that Americans do not automatically consider crusading good or bad, but feel that various people of whom one approves or disapproves can play the role. The commonest things associated with crusaders were works or fights for a cause in which they believe, effectiveness in rallying people, and rebelliousness and the breaking of new ground. The range of personal traits—from Carry Nation to Mario Savio, from Martin Luther King to George Lincoln Rockwell—is great; we seek, therefore, something that might be shared by diverse persons, such as a stereotypical image, a role, and perhaps a mentality or outlook which different kinds of people could share. This is what I mean by saying that a crusader is a social type rather than a personality type.

The most stereotypical example of the crusading mentality and role is probably Carry Nation and her hatchet, symbolizing good versus evil, clearing the way for a new order, or defending the threatened values of an old order. This hatchet probably goes back in an unbroken line of symbolism to Don Quixote's lance and Richard the Lion-hearted's two-handed sword—indeed, to Excalibur, for all I know the first mythical hero in the distant past who came in time of need to strike a blow for the good. This is the militant spirit of someone who knows he is right and intends to do something about it—stir people up, even brave society's wrath if necessary. It is expressed in a speech by the slavery abolitionist William Lloyd Garrison:

> I determined, at every hazard, to lift up the standard of emancipation in the eyes of the nation, *within sight of Bunker Hill and the birthplace of liberty*. That standard is now unfurled; and long may it float . . . till every chain be broken, and every bondsman set free. Let Southern oppressors tremble—let their secret abettors tremble—let their Northern apologists tremble—let all the enemies of the persecuted blacks tremble. . . . Assenting to the "self-evident truth" maintained in the American Declaration of Independence, "that all men are created equal, and endowed by their Creator with certain inalienable rights—among which are life, liberty and the pursuit of happiness," I shall strenuously contend for the immediate enfranchisement of our slave population. . . . I am aware, that many object to the severity of my language; but is there not cause for severity? I *will* be as harsh as truth, and as uncompromising as justice. On this subject, I do not wish to think, or speak, or write, with moderation. No! No! Tell a man whose house is on fire, to give a moderate alarm; tell him to moderately rescue his wife from the hands of the ravisher; tell the mother to gradually extricate her babe from the fire into which it has fallen;—but urge me not to use moderation in a cause like the present. I am in earnest—I will not equivocate—I will not excuse—I will not retreat a single inch—*and I will be heard*. The apathy of the people is enough to make every statue leap from its pedestal, and to hasten the resurrection of the dead. . . . Posterity will bear testimony that I was right. I desire to thank God, that he enables me to disregard "the fear of man which bringeth a snare," and to speak his truth in its simplicity and power.

Another abolitionist, Benjamin Lundy, expresses the crusader's spirit:

> My humble exertions shall be directed to the one great end—my whole self shall be devoted to the holy work—my march shall be *steadily onward*—and neither sectarian pride, party zeal, nor even persecution itself, from the "Powers that be" or that may be, shall turn me to the right hand or the left.

And the modern crusader speaks in the sermons of Billy Graham: "The world is waiting tonight for a young man riding a white charger to say to the world: 'Follow me! Let's clean up the world.' "

Teddy Roosevelt was not an ideal crusader in his work, yet he stated the viewpoint—especially the sense of moral conflict—as well as many who played the role better:

> There are, in the body politic, economic, and social, many and grave evils, and there is urgent necessity for the sternest war upon them. There should be relentless exposure of an attack upon every evil man, whether politician or businessman, every evil practice, whether in politics, in business, or in social life. I hail as a benefactor every writer or speaker, every man who, on the platform, or in book, magazine, or newspaper, with merciless severity makes such attack, provided always that . . . the attack is of use only if it is absolutely truthful. . . .

The crusader's sense of wrong-to-be-righted requires him to picture the evil in terms which seem vivid and overheated, if not paranoid, to others who do not share his viewpoint. So the interviewer asks the Jehovah's Witness, "How do you know you are doing the right thing, do you ever doubt your faith?" And she answers:

> Oh I know but if I ever doubt or do something wrong it is because of the devil. Satan is still on the loose you see, he is always working against the Lord and trying to win people to his side. We Witnesses have to always guard against him. Still he gets some of us.

Seeing such evil, the crusader regards his role as an alarm to wake up the world from complacency before it is too late. It is the spirit of Paul Revere. Says the Liberty Bell Press:

> Help awaken others! Give *None Dare Call It Treason* to friends, relatives, neighbors, clergymen, school teachers, libraries. . . . Do we face a hopeless battle? Has time run out for America? The answer is up to *you*. . . . What can you do? . . . Enlist others. . . . Take action. . . . Get into politics. . . . J. Edgar Hoover said, "The basic answer to communism is moral. The fight is economic, social, psychological, diplomatic, strategic—but above all it is spiritual."

In any case, the moral militance and sense of alarm and need for action is a rebuke to those who sit around and will not join the fight; it is the rebuke of Quixote to Sancho Panza.

Whether we like a crusader or approve of his program or not, it is possible to agree, I think, that he shares certain basic characteristics with other crusaders. One of these is vigorous, militant activism with a sense of mission. Margaret Sanger remarked, "I would not contain my ideas, I wanted to get on with what I had to do in the world."

Second is determination to go ahead in spite of lack of public support, even with public opposition. Anthony Comstock said,

> I am resolved that I will not in God's strength yield to other people's opinion, but will, if I feel and believe I am right, stand firm. Jesus was never moved from the path of duty, however hard, by public opinion, why should I?

Susan Anthony on her deathbed, at the age of 86, said:

> Just think of it, I have been striving for over sixty years for a little bit of justice no bigger than that, and yet I must die without obtaining it. Oh it seems so cruel.

Third is an alarum-like effort to wake up the world, a sense of duty to fight an evil which others do not perceive or are complacent about. Fourth is taking oneself seriously: a lack of humor or ironic detachment toward one's role; a sense of noble purpose versus a complacent or ignoble world; a kind of high-mindedness or moralism which easily seems arrogant or foolish. This is the basic split between the crusader and most of us—between Quixote and Sancho Panza, between Galahad and Lancelot. In taking himself so seriously, the crusader is utterly committed or, to use a sociologist's term, lacks role distance. The rest of us, not so high-minded, may look askance at him, possibly may fear him.

Such traits of the crusader can be seen in Woodrow Wilson, whose seriousness and high-mindedness caused him to endure ordeals that others would have avoided. He insisted on seeing the role of the United States as fighting without a single selfish interest, without rancor,

> for democracy, for the right of those who submit to authority to have a voice in their own governments, for the rights and liberties of small nations, for a universal dominion of right by such a concert of free peoples as shall bring peace and safety to all nations and make the world itself at last free.

Herbert Hoover said of him:

> He was a man of staunch morals. He was more than just an idealist, he was the personification of the heritage of idealism of the American people. He brought spiritual concepts to the peace table. He was a born crusader. . . . His mind ran to "moral principles," "justice," and "right." In them he had deep convictions. In some phases of character he partook of the original Presbyterians, what they concluded was right, was therefore right against all comers.

Though not strictly a martyr, in a real sense he did die for his cause. Shortly before his death he said, "I am ready to fight from now until all the fight has been taken out of me by death to redeem the faith and promises of the United States." He carried on like a true crusader, even when warned that he might not survive his campaign to win popular support. He said, "Even though . . . it might mean the giving up of my life, I shall gladly make the sacrifice to save the Treaty."

Who, by contrast, is *not* a crusader? Among good men and important leaders in America, there are many who do not fit the role. Abraham Lincoln, for example, who, as historians describe him, when he signed the Emancipation Proclamation, did so rather late in a manner that might be described as footdragging and opportunistic. Nor was Lincoln Steffens a very good crusader, for all his muckraking. Unlike most reformers, Steffens mistrusted "righteous" people. He thought the world could be saved by intelligence—even intelligent dishonesty—whereas self-righteous men suffered from a blindness to the dishonesty built into middle-class culture—for example, the patronage system. (When Steffens pointed out to Theodore Roosevelt that patronage was "legitimate" bribery, Roosevelt became furious.) It was essential to Steffens to distinguish between man and system: to admit that a good man might have to do bad things; to see that the system needed reform even while one was playing by its crooked rules. He liked technocracy because of its scientific promise, but mistrusted the Russian revolutionaries (even while he approved of the Revolution) because they were "righteous". Nor does Franklin Delano Roosevelt qualify as a crusader, despite his historic achievements. Historians, such as Arthur Schlesinger, Jr., call him a pragmatist—a supreme one—and contrast him with the idealist Henry Wallace, and with Wilson. Roosevelt was, says Rexford G. Tugwell, "a supreme practitioner of the art of compromise." He lacked fixed direction and sense of righteous purpose, followed public opinion intuitively, and experimented freely, even recklessly, by "month-to-month improvisation." "Flexibility," said Tugwell, "was both his strength and his weakness." If one had to arrange the American presidents here mentioned in order of crusading spirit, Wilson would probably lead, with Theodore Roosevelt, for all his vigor, a poor second. Franklin Roosevelt and Lincoln—great reformers though they were—would fight for a very poor third. All this, despite the fact that

Wilson's major crusades—to end war and to establish a world court—
were both practical failures.

It may be generally said that politicians do not make good crusaders; they reject the crusading role almost instinctively. If they must
speak high-mindedly to satisfy public opinion, they nevertheless try
to act practically. They see the crusader by his high-mindedness
going out on a limb and burning his bridges behind him. They see
that although the crusader may occasionally win startling successes
when he appeals to the masses, the price of his role is high; the risk
and sacrifice make it a game with a high ante and large bets. The
pragmatist asks, in contrast, how can I get some of what I want with
least expenditure? Politics is the "art of the possible"—or asks
"where are the centers of power?" Politicians prefer influence and
manipulation to an all-out attack from which there is no retreat. Even
when they employ the "crusade" theme in propaganda, it is unlikely
that they act this way themselves. So we do not usually find the
crusader as a prominent leader in power structures, but mainly as
agitator, outsider, troublemaker to others who feel less strongly about
the morality of a cause, or act for it more practically.

In justice to pragmatists, let us admit the unsuitability of the
crusading spirit in day-to-day work. One would not use it to rally sec-
retaries, bureaucrats, or mechanics to action. Nor is it applicable to
judges or legislators—except, perhaps, in an emergency such as a declaration of war. Crusading appeals are called for only when the job
is so difficult and extraordinary that *heroic* energies must be
mobilized, and when there is a *moral* issue. Military men sometimes
like to think of themselves as "professionals" doing a job, but since
their calling is inherently self-sacrificial, based on moral duty rather
than excellent pay, it is natural for them to use the crusading theme
to rally others and explain what they are doing.

I have tried here to define the crusader as a distinct social type—
not in terms of personality but in terms of a "man-of-action" role
with a moralistic mentality and a militant program of action symbolized by the cross and the sword. The crusader is neither a
businessman nor a politician nor a philosopher (for all his ideals),
nor a social worker (for all his good deeds). Yet Gandhi shows the
practical mixture—a crusader with a peculiar blend of political pragmatism and sacrificial saintliness. The closer we get to a real
crusader, the closer we get to Don Quixote or Sir Galahad. The basic

quality that makes his role possible is that he takes himself and his own view of the world more seriously than others do—so seriously, in fact, that he is likely to be a big bore to those more playfully inclined because he cannnot laugh at himself. He will not compromise and may even put those who disagree with him in jail. His seriousness essentially comes from the fact that he sees a mortal struggle of good against evil—no laughing matter. This struggle is so serious that he wants all effort, even art and play, to serve his mission. He tends to be rather a puritan. As a man of action, his measures are militant, though not necessarily military. He believes in the sword, figuratively, because of his sense of war for good against evil; evil, he feels, requires stern measures.

But the man of the world looks askance at this serious, determined crusader. He regards him as a fool, or as a dangerous bigot or persecutor. So Samuel Butler describes "Sir Hudibras". And, in doing so, Butler speaks for all the anticrusaders—who probably outnumber crusaders—including those whose outlook is so rationalistic that they have no mystique of higher good or good versus evil, hence see no need for heroic action; those so satisfied with the status quo that they can find nothing to fight for; and those so alienated that they find it difficult to rally to righteous struggle and do not care for causes of any kind. These make up the audience to whom the crusader preaches, or the majority against whom he acts.

Crusade as a Social Movement

Then going from the crusader as a person, we take a broader view of the crusade as a movement. By what features does it develop *esprit de corps*, high commitment, and an opportunity to escape from ordinary life into heroism—even a new identity?

You cannot have a crusade by yourself. Like any collective process—a social party, a game, a conversation, a fight, a crowd, a culture—the whole is prior to the part. A crusade comes into being, then forms its members—their disposition, mentalities, and roles—according to its requirements. We have described the crusader as a type; individuals such as William Booth or Harriet Beecher Stowe are perfect—even stereotypic—examples. Still, it is fairly obvious that many more people enter a crusade and *acquire* its mentality and role than have it to begin with. Even those who lead become transformed from mere idealists, intellectuals, and reformers into eloquent speakers and battle-hardened veterans. Those who enter later become transformed not only by the struggle itself but by the models of the leaders and martyrs who went before. All acquire a certain aura of heroism. So, from the point of view of the recruit, the crusade is a role opportunity: to form oneself according to a pattern not ordinarily available, to rise to a higher level of input (commitment) and output (heroism), to test oneself by mortal encounter and engagement; above all, then, to find a new conception of oneself.

For this reason, then, we wish to examine the crusade as a collective process: the kind of self-finding opportunity it affords. We are especially interested in features which seem to mark the crusade off from ordinary movements—such as militancy, righteousness, sense of uphill struggle, and image of evil. While all activities called crusades do not equally have such features, one might say that those that do approach the ideal type of the perfect crusade thereby gain power to transform their members and generate esprit de corps. Take, for example, three crusades announced in the newspapers in the same town at the same time: (1) a "United Crusade" to raise funds for community welfare, which started its drive with these words: "Let's roll up our sleeves and get to work," (2) a "Stamp Out Crime" crusade inaugurated by the Independent Insurance Agents Association to honor individuals who come to the aid of the police, and (3) a "Christian Anti-Communism Crusade," which began its meetings with the national anthem, a flag salute, and a prayer that we may be "stirred" tonight for the "cause of freedom," and concluding its program of anticommunist songs and a speech with the statement "We have tried to survey the evil forces loose in the world."

There is little doubt which of these is really most crusade-like in spirit. So one might arrange activities called crusades on a scale of moral elevation and intensity, with the "United Crusade" at one end and Garrison fighting slavery at the other. The point is that people *do* not really care about many worthy social programs, but they do care about a real crusade. Moral intensity and elevation seem to describe two of these dimensions of caring: the feeling of rightness and the sense of being called upon to work for a higher purpose, performance beyond the requirements of ordinary duty. In general, bureaucracy has no crusading spirit. Military operations may or may not have it. Zeal, or caring beyond matter-of-fact job requirements, is the beginning of a crusading spirit. Fanaticism is its end point.

Let us, therefore, look at features of an ideal crusade, trying to understand how it develops esprit de corps, high commitment, and an opportunity to escape from ordinary life into heroism. The main features, which make a movement crusade-like are: (1) militancy, (2) righteousness, (3) sense of uphill struggle, (4) image of evil, (5) unwillingness to compromise, and (6) implied evangelism (catharsis and identity transformation).

1. Militancy. Emmeline Pankhurst, British suffragette, symbolizes the militancy of the crusade—by no means necessarily violent but extreme actions that shock or provoke people, such as hunger strikes, chaining oneself to gates, lying down in front of munitions trains, birth control demonstrations. Crusading militancy is not a matter of physical combat or male macho, but a matter of courage and moral commitment to fight and suffer, if need be, for a worthy cause. The crusader may be physically weak; loyalty is his strength. While crusades may operate within the context of education or social welfare work, they are nonetheless conflict groups with a sense of drive, of taking up the sword for and against something; they have rallying slogans such as "Save _____ _____", "Capture _____ _____", "V for Victory", "We shall overcome." Even a Cancer Fund crusade uses the symbol of a sword. Crusades draw fighters and encourage a spirit like that of this socialist:

> I fought on the kerbside, at the factory gate, in strike committees, in a militant march from Stepney to Trafalgar Square. I have walked with an ashplant in my hand confident, even hopeful, that the police would be forced to break up our demonstration and give the Party its martyrs. But if this sounds a little cynical to you, be assured that much of what I fought for as a Communist I fight for still as a Socialist. It has taken me eighteen years to realize that I have been carrying the wrong banner in the right fight.

As vigorous, concerted actions of fighters, crusades have thrust—a spear-like or spearhead quality. It may be a peaceful thrust, as in the Peace Corps as a "peace army," a "moral equivalent of war"; but all true crusades have an agonistic, striving motivation at the opposite pole from Buddhism, Taoism, and other quietistic philosophies—though, it may be regretted, not from Christianity. Even for pacifism, even for love, a crusade is militant—hence the paradox of the "Christian soldier." In one year, 1882, in England, 669 members of the Salvation Army were knocked down or brutally assaulted, sixty buildings were virtually wrecked by mobs. The Salvation Army toughened its members at the baptism of children with these words: "You must be willing that the child should spend all its life in The Salvation Army, wherever God should choose to send it, that it should be despised, hated, cursed, beaten, kicked, imprisoned or killed for Christ's sake." Evangelists see their life as a fight. The crusader knows that even with a relatively innocuous message, the course of his work is likely to be stormy, so the crusade calls for valor and excludes or rebukes the cowardly. The reason for this storminess is that the crusade rejects things-as-they-are and works without a consensus for which it must fight; it always threatens somebody's peace of mind. At the heart of conflict is not merely a practical but a moral issue—an impasse which usually cannot be solved by merely rational methods persuasion and education because it is a value conflict. Unable to persuade and negotiate successfully, the movement takes up arms for a fight, physically or symbolically. Were the values of this movement acceptable to the public, or demonstrable by mere argument, then it would have no motive to mount a crusade.

2. Righteousness. Although a crusade requires a fight in some sense, every fight is not a crusade. A strike or a feud is no more a crusade than is a fight of two bears for a salmon, unless justifying the militancy is a sense of the absolute rightness and worthiness of the cause. This sense of right keeps the crusader from conceiving himself—even when he creates serious disturbances—as a mere troublemaker or criminal. The sense of right must be absolute enough to withstand contradiction and challenge, and make the fighter unwilling to compromise. A crusade is not pragmatic in spirit, so opportunism and Machiavellianism are inappropriate to it. Likewise, self-interest always endangers the crusading spirit, which is noble in self-conception, sacrificial, grateful for the chance to labor, wanting to do good. A self-interested person is not comfortable with the crusader label. The goal of the crusade is noble, not merely good. Bread-and-butter values are not enough for a crusade—in an abundant society, at least. Grander purposes must be stated in abstractions to justify sacrifices; that is, the crusade draws on resources of idealism, not just on animal energy. This ideal makes possible the crusader's noble conception of his own

role—as saviour, defender, knight, fighter for the right; it makes him, as Howard S. Becker says, a "moral entrepreneur" who wants to revise morality to a higher level. So crusading spirit, whenever it enters, inevitably introduces morality into politics. It produces differences serious enough to fight over, hard not to fight over. It brings in not merely reformers, but puritans, idealists, utopians, saints, and martyrs. It aims not merely at victory but a triumph of right, a new scheme of life where men can be better. in short, a crusade—whatever its practical aims—is a moral battle, an effort to change the social order morally. So the crusader is a cousin of the evangelist: the latter preaches his message, but the former carries it into battle.

Sense of Uphill Struggle. Unlike mainstream movements, a crusade has a sense of an uphill fight against odds—a minority group outlook. Typically there is a rigteous minority versus a recalcitrant or complacent majority. However right abolitionists, feminists, prohibitionists, civil rights fighters, anticommunists, or World Federalists may feel, they also feel it is natural to suffer misunderstanding, opposition and ridicule, even go to jail, for what they believe. Even when a crusade is numerically a majority and the battle is practically won, it still keeps alive the feeling that there is a tough job ahead. This is rather a paradox in that, though a crusade starts from a righteous moral base which gives it a claim to represent the majority interest—and perhaps it does represent the majority interest—it is in the psychological position of thinking of itself as a moral minority trying to awaken, rally, rebuke, and force its will on a reluctant majority. The crusade benefits from its sense of uphill struggle and does not want to give it up. It has the morale of determination; its will is hardened and it is ready for prolonged struggle for victory—if not today or tomorrow, then the day after tomorrow. Without this dramatic sense, a crusade would deteriorate into a mere practical movement. Thus crusades are unlikely to arise within the mainstream of society or in the achievement of goals that are so practicable or easy that they do not require struggle. In this sense, a certain short-run despair is part of the mystique of a crusade, helping to stimulate its spirit. In this sense, too, a crusade is inherently radical, even when its symbolism is conservative; it thrusts against the majority and benefits from the tension, whether its direction is progressive to a "new era" or back to a "golden age"—in either case, a status quo which we do not have now, which will take some doing to achieve.

4. Image of Evil. The goal of a crusade is to defeat an evil, not merely to solve a problem. This gives it the sense of righteousness, of nobility, of the good sword, and of an unfair fight; thus the crusader may think of himself as a hero and define his opponents as villains. Indeed, the crusade classifies as a kind of vilifying movement (Klapp 1959). A crusade without a villain would be as unlikely as a murder mystery without a corpse. Even nonviolent and pacifistic movements have a hard time avoiding hating people they fight so hard, picturing them as aggressors or persecutors. How much easier it is for those who have no objection to making villains to see those who oppose their sacred cause as devils. So William Jennings Bryan, in his famous attack on Darwinism, did not criticize it as a scientific idea but condemned it as an evil and called for a kind of war on it:

> There is that in each human life that corresponds to the mainspring of a watch—that which is absolutely necessary if the life is to be what it should be, a real life and not a mere existence. That necessary thing is *a belief in God.* . . . If there is at work in the world today anything that tends to break this mainspring, it is the duty of the moral, as well as the Christian, world to combat this influence in every possible way. I believe there is such a menace to fundamental morality. The hypothesis to which the name of Darwin has been given—the hypothesis that links man to the lower forms of life and makes him a lineal descendent of the brute—is obscuring God and weakening all the virtues that rest upon the religious tie between God and man. . . . Taxpayers should prevent the teaching in the public schools of atheism, agnosticism, Darwinism, or any other hypothesis that links man in blood relationship with the brutes.

From a very different perspective, Mario Savio, leader of the Berkeley "free speech" movement, defined his enemy as bureaucracy:

> In our free speech fight at the University of California, we have come up against what may emerge as the greatest problem of our nation—depersonalized, unresponsive bureaucracy. We have encountered the organized status quo in Mississippi, but it is the same in Berkeley. . . . In Mississippi an autocratic and powerful minority rules, through organized violence . . . in California, the privileged minority manipulates the University bureaucracy to suppress the students' political expression. That "respectable" bureaucracy masks the financial plutocrats; that impersonal bureaucracy is the efficient enemy in a "Brave New World."

It is also true that, whether or not one feels a moral need for the image of the villain, it helps a crusade to "sell" its program to the public. For example, much of the effectiveness of the propaganda of the Anti-Saloon League, says Odegard (1928), came from making a villain out of the saloon:

> The League directed its propaganda not so much *for* prohibition as *against* the saloon and its evils. This was an effective device because even drinkers who balked at the idea of absolute prohibition were willing to admit that the American saloon had become a noisome thing. . . . (According to the League's publications) "The saloon is the storm center of crime; the devil's headquarters on earth; the schoolmaster of a broken decalogue; the defiler of youth; the enemy of the home; the foe of peace; the deceiver of nations; the beast of sensuality; the past master of intrigue; the vagabond of poverty; the social vulture; the rendezvous of demagogues; the enlisting office of sin; the serpent of Eden; a ponderous second edition of hell, revised, enlarged and illuminated."

Beneath this "sales value" of villains is a social function: that the morale of a crusade is based upon the hope that the trouble can be simplified to one root that can be lopped off or eradicated. In other words, a purgative function is part of the mystique of a crusade. Were it not for this hope of finally defeating an oversized villain, there would be little dramatic interest in a crusade and little climax when its practical goal was achieved. It may be that the villain draws more people to a cause than those who lead and suffer for it.

5. Unwillingness to Compromise. The above characteristics—militancy, righteousness, determination to win an uphill struggle, and the image of evil—make the crusade unwilling to compromise and give it a tendency to go to extremes. The crusader's attitude is illustrated by the intemperance of Garrison's statement, previously cited ("I am aware, that many object to the severity of my language . . . I will be . . . harsh . . . and . . . uncompromising . . . I do not wish to think, or speak, or write, with moderation"). The crusader tends to view half measures and concessions as treason to the cause, and to penalize those who wish to bargain. This may be called fanaticism or sincerity, depending on how one likes the goals. With all this contributing to the head of steam, it is easy to see why crusades develop an overdrive which carries them past set objectives to actions they did not contemplate—as did the original Crusaders, as did Cromwell, as did Robespierre, as did Fidel Castro and other revolutionists. It just seems you cannot fight so hard for so long for anything so "good" against anything so "bad" without some tendency to extremes when the ball finally gets into your hands. How can you set limits on something that is good, or stop fighting something that is bad? A

crusader really does not know where he will stop. He drives as far as he can go. So William Booth, in building the Salvation Army, was not satisfied with success in England, but took the world for his parish, personally traveling by ocean liner, motorcade, even bullock cart—he never stopped trying to reach people with his message. In sixty years he traveled five million miles and preached 60,000 sermons. A good soldier, a real crusader, just because he did not know when to stop!

6. Implied Evangelism. In offering members an opportunity to re-define themselves, by gathering and witnessing, the crusade has an emotional payoff not unlike what happens at revival meetings. Because of its emotional rewards, a crusade has a spirit of evangelism. Take this example of a meeting of the John Birch Society when its founder, Robert Welch, was still active. A person present reported on Welch's speech to about 500 members in a packed convention room in a California hotel. An over-life-sized photograph of John Birch is displayed on the platform beside the American flag. The meeting begins with a flag salute and prayer invocation. Then, after some business, Welch begins. This is obviously the "big moment" the crowd has been waiting for. He apologizes at the beginning because he "doesn't want to talk too long." A member in the audience calls out, "Go ahead and talk for five hours! We'll listen." Indeed, he does give a long speech. The crowd hangs on his words, drinking them up as though it cannot get enough. His speech is a ranting, rather bad-tempered, but not humorless, tirade against the whole of American society as an "insane asylum" going to pot morally. He gives vivid examples of corruption and bad behavior. Americans are insane because they cannot see the communist menace in all this. Drastic measures are needed. In his talk, Welch makes no specific action proposals, reminding his audience that the John Birch Society is not a political party—indeed is nonpolitical as an organization though members as individuals may be political. The crowd enjoys the tone and the feeling of his speech, as one would a sermon that makes one feel good; they are not disappointed that specific action proposals are not made. On this occasion, at least, evangelism is enough. Welch has enbodied in his words and living presence a role model for them. The meeting ends with discussion and testimonials from the floor; a man rises to tell how his life has become more meaningful since he joined the Society: "I'm a new man since joining, life has started over for me."

Unlike an evangelical meeting, however, nobody comes forward to be saved; most were apparently already converts. But the emotional ritual of such proceedings shows that its function is like that of a church service for the faithful. They come away confirmed and uplifted, feeling that life has more significance.

Such elements give the crusade an implied evangelism even when its goals are practical. William Booth had a doctrine to help make him a missionary; yet even when there is no explicit doctrine, as in the work of CORE and SNCC for civil rights in the South, the fervor and symbolism keep the issues from being mere "bread and butter" or political rights issues. The implicit evangelism of civil rights can be seen in the mystic fervor of a slogan like "We shall overcome"; it can also be seen in the sacrifices of the martyrs. This implicit evangelism is the crusade's mystique. At the same time its message to outsiders and emotional payoff to participants go beyond the practical results—and, indeed, practical results may be a mere fringe benefit, since the real reason a fighter is in the movement is for what it does for him personally, in terms of emotional intensification, moral confirmation, proof of manhood, and so on. A crusade is like a cult in having a mystique, beyond a practical program, consisting of those things outsiders do not readily see and appreciate (beliefs, assumptions, sacred values, meanings, sanctifications, redemptions, visions of millennium or Armageddon, devils, myths, Grail symbols, prophecies, perhaps cures and magic) which provide an emotional payoff for members.

In this light we should view the following: the satisfaction Woodrow Wilson got from sacrificing himself for the "lost cause" of the Versailles Treaty and World Court; the notion of "manifest destiny" that inspired the American wars with Spain and Mexico; the chivalric imagery by which Winston Churchill thrilled the English in their fight against Germany; and Hitler's turgid fantasies about the Jewish conspiracy, the purity of the "Aryan" race, and his own Siegfried-like infallibility.

With such things going for the members, it is no surprise that crusades carry on even when leaders die or their practical efforts are temporarily a failure. From the mystique comes not only the motivation to carry on, but to sacrifice beyond what real, day-to-day results justify. With Grail symbols, salvation, image of evil, or demonic threats, and millennium reached or golden age restored in the reckoning, it is quite impossible to say when a movement has failed from purely practical considerations. Its goal is more exciting and dramatic than anything that can be reduced to mere programs of social welfare, higher wages, minority rights, military victory, or restored capitalism—nothing less than a realization and purification of self and society, a purgation of basic evil from the world, and institution of some eternal and absolute form of good. Thus, it is quite possible for a temperance fighter to carry on while the rest of the world guzzles liquor and puffs cigarettes.

In this section I have tried to explain how a crusade is different from a movement aiming at only practical results and in what sense a crusade is a movement which carries both a cross and a sword. When a movement develops moral fervor from a mystique which offers something to get excited about and sacrifice for, it tends to become a crusade. Reform and welfare movements become crusades when they begin to aim at some absolute good or sweeping away of evil rather that merely a gain in the balance between good and bad in human society. Likewise, political control movements become crusades when, beyond passing a law or changing an administration, they promise to "save" society. Finally, any movement becomes a crusade when in a conflict for what it wants to achieve, it begins to demand personal commitment like that of a cult, or to ask a person to take risks beyond what immediately tangible rewards justify, or to change himself as a person. The crusade offers a person the opportunity to change himself by fighting for a good cause.

Contribution of Crusader Role to Identity

Beyond the general values of emotional revivalism, let us note more specifically how the crusading role contributes to identity. What is it that it gives that workaday life usually does not? I wish to point out here the contribution to identity of: (1) the feeling of return home; (2) the test by which to prove oneself; (3) the break with normal life; (4) reorientation of life; (5) the opportunity for a heroic role; (6) the purgative function of the image of evil; and (7) the vision of the good.

1. The first thing to note is that the crusader role has an unusual capacity for giving the feeling of "rightness"—more so, even, than rational certification procedures, such as court decisions, licensing,

conferring of diplomas, or professional promotions. The crusade's power of conferring rightness resembles that of a cult in giving a deep moral, rather than a merely technical, sense of rightness, and in making life more exciting. An "urban populist" tells how he got involved in a movement:

> I got involved in raising money for the International Brigade, for the sharecroppers down south, helping stop the evictions of city people who couldn't pay rent, fighting for public housing. Wherever you turned you saw injustice. The issues stuck out as clearly as they did in a prison. You knew what was good and what was evil. Life was very exciting. . . .

A civil rights crusader tells how his sense of rightness was strengthened:

> At first, when I joined CORE, it was really to get away from home and be somebody on my own, I guess; but when I saw how things were I really got interested. When you go through someplace like Mississippi, you really feel identification with the Negroes and you get so mad at the way things are you really don't believe it can really be like that. . . . I don't have any religious reasons for what I'm doing. I just feel that if you think something is right, you have to do something and not just talk.

It may be that something in early life sensitizes a crusader to "wrongness" which makes him want to respond to make things right. A SNCC crusader said:

> In early life I saw great injustice in my own home. My grandparents on my father's side dominated my mother and made her very unhappy. My mother took me and left when I was eight years old. Ever since, any injustice or domination of people that can't fight back makes me angry. We moved to Virginia, and I was aware of Jim Crow laws but didn't pay much attention at the time. Then I entered college, I became interested in civil rights through reading and listening to the professors. I admired Dr. _____ and this has a lot to do with it too.

Malcolm X tells of the wrongs he experienced as a child, culminating in the murder of his father by white men, which prepared him to be an antiwhite crusader. The straight laced upbringing of Harriet Beecher Stowe doubtless sensitized her moral indignation and helped prepare her for the role of crusader. She had a keen sensitivity to wrongs and esteemed moral indignation chief among the virtues. But, however the leader acquires the "overactive superego" which helps him to see wrong, he, in turn, helps stir the sensitivity of others by the situations he provokes and the example of his role. The sense of rightness that a crusade gives might, I think, be summarized by the following statement: "After all the things that I have done in my life, many of which I was not particularly proud of, *this is right!*" This is what I mean by the feeling of a return home morally. A person may live much of his life with programs, institutions, ideas, and people he has no heart for; he is not even sure they are moral. The crusade allows him to return home. Bandages, scars, and jail time can further signify the sense of right, what William Cameron calls "status-through-militancy".

2. The crusade offers not merely a freshened perception of right, but the kind of thing one can *do* to actualize that feeling and prove oneself. Actions vary greatly in their power to confer rightness. A public demonstration or testimony is likely to do more than a private resolution or deed. A Christian crusader who had for the first time professed his faith publicly said, "Through this experience (of witnessing) I now find a joy. I went with real fear in my heart. Now, my life has taken on new meaning." Donating blood is symbolically more significant than money to buy the same amount of blood; somehow it gives an "in" feeling, bridging the alienation of man from man in a mysterious way. Work "beyond the call of duty" gives one a sense of right by its sacrificial element (whereas much modern work not only gives no sense of rightness but actually makes a man feel wrong, as in "deals" or sales in which he has to compromise morality). A fight involving risk and sacrifice has the mystique of the donation of blood, multiplied by the gravity of the danger. A crusade offers some kind of test by which a person can prove himself morally, a moment to "stand up and be counted"—an occasion that may never have come before, especially unlikely in a bureaucracy. The most common forms of this test are, perhaps, the "baptism by fire", an ordeal with risk in which one conquers fear. A Negro girl member of SNCC said: "Now I've been down there (the South) I'm not scared. I really don't mind if they kill me." Another member of SNCC said:

> I felt that I had to do something to help, so when the student Y sponsored the trip to Virginia I went along. At first I felt guilty about the, because there really was no danger there and I really felt like I was making no sacrifices. The second trip, to Atlanta, was better because I really felt that we were helping and it was dangerous. We stayed at a Negro college, and even though there were only four

Negroes out of twenty students, we seemed to get a sense of identification—at least when I was in a white area. Even when I was alone, I had the funny feeling of being afraid and careful as if I were Negro; it was so real I could feel it in my skin.

Getting arrested for the cause had double significance, as personal test and message to the public:

Sure, we want to get arrested when we demonstrate. We want to make it clear to the public that we are serious. And we want to show our immediate concern toward our neighbors. Non-violence shows concern, not so much for your friend as for your enemy. When we demonstrate, our non-violence shows that we can disobey and alter without harming the individual. At least I hope that's what we show.

The religious crusade often provides its test through a "formula for witnessing": the member proclaims his faith, tries to convert others, and endures derision and opposition. A college Christian crusader says:

The arguments the crusader has learned to give for defending his faith tend to crystallize that faith in his own mind. . . . I was hesitant about trying to convert someone on the spot. . . . After my first successful conversion, I remember feeling a sense of righteousness and joy, also a sense of oneness with the crusade movement. This feeling was greatly reenforced during a "sharing" meeting the same day.

Such tests of rightness are especially important in an alienated society, because what an alienated person wants is to be home and, once again, like the Boy Scout, to tread the straight and true path of merit badges or, like Galahad, to successfully sit in the siege perilous.

3. Another contribution of the crusade to new identity is that it helps, indeed requires, a person to break with the routines and obligations of normal life and start a new life. With the crucial step, he puts his old life behind him, perhaps renounces friends, job, church—much as does many a sect convert. Family and friends often object to the crusader devoting so much time, effort, and money, which is at the same time inconvenient to them and a sacrifice for him. So, during the time of the famous Sacco-Vanzetti case, men quit jobs and mortgaged their homes to "save Sacco and Vanzetti." The justification for such renunciation is the nobility of the role undertaken, compared with the relative worthlessness of the relationships neglected. The

crusader does not feel any more at fault for leaving old friends than would a monk for devoting himself to begging. Crusades vary, of course, in the degree to which they demand a break with normal obligations. Some, such as Billy Graham's, make less demands than movements like Jehovah's Witnesses or the Communist Party; perhaps this is a fault in the former, namely, that the more truly crusade-like a movement is, the more demands it makes. So the crusader, once he has joined, even if still accepted by his former friends, feels dislocated and set apart. Jail experience, or suffering the status of outcast, of course, greatly helps the break with normal life:

> I wrote my book *Reveille for Radicals* in . . . jail. Sometimes the jailers would tell me to get out when I was in the middle of a chapter. I'd tell them, "I don't want to go now; I've got a couple of hours more work to do." . . . Now revolution ever got off the ground until the status quo performed the essential service of taking the leader or the organizer out of action. He'd never do it voluntarily. Think of what that first jail experience during the Montgomery bus strike did for Martin Luther King. That was when he decided to go all-out for total integration. And he was a very different man after the Birmingham experience, as he has written in his "Letter from a Birmingham Jail." . . . He came to understand that the well wishers who say, "I approve of your objectives but not your tactics" are an anchor around your neck. He saw that revolutionary changes never occur without conflict. (Alinsky 1946)

Though set apart, he does not feel to blame, but may rebuke those who do not join him—as Martin Luther King did churches which "remain(ed) silent behind the safe security of stained glass windows." He feels that others belong on *his* side, not that *he* has stepped out of bounds. If he feels set apart, it is by dignity and dedication to higher calling, rather like Sir Galahad among the sinful knights. So the set-apartness is not a loss of status but a gain. Though judged a heretic, apostate, oddball, troublemaker, traitor by some, he breaks with normal life to embark on a new life—rather like a cultic rebirth.

4. As compensation for dislocation from the social structure, the crusade offers a reorientation of life with a sense of courage and purpose. A Jehovah's Witness, who left his job as a telephone company technician to devote his life to preaching, said:

> Until then, we seemed to have no purpose. We made money and spent it and had fun, but there was an emptiness in our lives. Everything in Jehovah's Witnesses is teamwork. It is a vast family pulling together with the precision of a well trained army.

The crusade converts the "cat on the street" in Watts, Los Angeles, into the young lion (Simba) of Black Nationalism. Its action on the mass is that of a magnet on iron particles: it draws rioting mobs into disciplined regiments, "lost souls" into corps with trumpets and tambourines. This orientation is like a cultic one, except that it is directed toward action upon society—whether by agitation, evangelism, nonviolent pressure, or outright war. When a movement is at the same time religion and crusade, it is hard to tell how much of the identity reclamation is due to the cultic and how much to the crusading aspect. A perfect crusade offers the paradoxical combination of the joy of righteous combat with the promise of perfect peace. Whatever may be its effect upon society, it offers a cure for the individual's anomie.

5. Like the cultic path, the way of a crusader is not ordinary, but heroic. The difference between ordinary life and a heroic role is the difference between climbing stairs and climbing Mr. Everest. It is achievement which sets a person above others—the straight-and-narrow path, the bridge of swords over which the questing hero must crawl with bleeding hands. Defeat allows a crusader to think of himself not as loser but as martyr. Hence, the power of uplift comes from the inherent exultation of the heroic role: the sense of having fought the "good fight," identification with leaders even more heroic, and cancellation of any guilt by merit and suffering.

Therefore, one of the prime duties of a crusade leader is to provide a firm, inspiring model for his followers. He should be the first to swing the axe, begin the march, apply the boycott, go on the hunger strike, and the last to recant or retreat. His personal style should be austere, expressing devotion to the cause. Aggressive, forthright, opinionated, morally courageous individuals who despise compromise make the best crusaders—such figures as Carry Nation, Billy Graham, Malcolm X, Martin Luther King, Gandhi—to all of whom the remark of a Goldwater follower in 1964 would be equally applicable: "What I admire most about him is his absolute honesty and idealism." By his assurance he helps all of those around him to feel like new men: he is clear and they find out where they stand; he is firm and they become resolute; he is opinionated and they become sure of themselves; he "knows" and they understand. Thus a crusade leader refreshes identity; through him a mass can experience an uplift without personal contact, as is true of most symbolic leaders (Klapp 1965).

This does not imply that crusade followers—though they get psychological rewards—have the same personal characteristics as the leader, however much they may identify with him. It would be a mistake to put all "fanatics" in the same mold. He is strong, they are dependent; he has initiative, they imitate; he is authoritarian, they are suggestible. Their strength is a facsimile of his, produced partly by imitation, supported by whatever inner strength they may have. Likewise, what a leader gets out of a crusade psychologically must be distinguished from what his followers get: a mix in which for the former there is a greater amount of realization of abilities, and for the latter more moral confirmation.

6. The heroic role by which the crusade takes a person away from his old life pits him against evils which he now sees clearly, though he may have been complacement about them before. We must, therefore, consider the contribution of the image of evil to identity. A heightened melodramatic image of an enemy at whom to lance, or of apocalyptic evil looming, gives a person not only a sense of battle but an elevated image of himself; he may feel the stature of the heroic role and gird himself to meet the evil. Indeed, the image of the villain changes the aspect of the whole world for the crusader. Thus, as Malcolm X's sister explained, once the "demonology" of the Black Muslims is accepted by any black man, he will never again see the white man with the same eyes. Likewise, the Ku Klux Klan leader complains of the moral menace of "strangers" who have taken over the land, invaded the cities, broken down moral standards, desecrated the Sabbath, and threatened Nordic Americans. If the villain has changed the world for the worse, then getting rid of him will change it for the better. By attacking him, the crusade gains a purgative function, providing a relief rather like that of lancing a boil, both for the individual and for society. So the idea of cleansing or sweeping away evil in order to restore goodness and save society is part of the mystique of the crusade and puts it in the category of the ritual of purity and danger. This is called (I think mistakenly) the "paranoid" mentality of people like Birchers and fluoridation fighters, which may reflect no more than a need for the ritual of a fight for the right and a little romance brought into otherwise meaningless lives.

7. Likewise, the vision of the good that will be achieved after the

fight is over needs to be sharpened for the crusader. It need not be a utopia, but it should be purged of villains and radically improved. So a rebellious university student described the world he wanted after reform:

> What I want is a world where people are free to make the decisions that affect their own lives, a world in which they are not trapped on a vast merry-go-round of concealed power, not forced into situations where the choice is already made for them. I want a "participatory democracy" . . . a nonexploited system in which no one is making money off another man's work. I want people to be happy, too. More than anything else, I want a world where we're free to be human to each other.

Without some such image, however short of pie in the sky, no crusade would have the power to stir people, for getting rid of the villain is not enough unless there is a better world ahead.

As a result of such features—emotional revivalism, the feeling of a return home, a test by which to prove oneself, the break with normal life, reorientation, the heroic role, the purgative function of the image of evil, and the vision of the good—the crusade is able to offer a deeper change of self-conception and identity than would be possible in ordinary life. So people who have participated in crusades tell of the changes that have occurred in their outlook. A university student rebel during the sixties said:

> We're a new generation of people. . . . We have been fairly well off. . . . So it's interesting that while many of us have not gone through a war or had to fight through a long depression, more and more of us are getting very upset about the world around us. Today most people look at students who are involved in protest as though they were still searching for an identity and not yet adjusting to our social situation. They see us as "not quite balanced." My parents, for example, still think I'm going through a phase. This common view . . . completely misses the point. Many of us *have* found an identity. What we are trying to do now is to make our identity realizable. We've found possibilities for a brotherhood—for understanding a lot of things that people kind of feel are corny. Brotherhood is something you talk about in rhetoric, but in everyday life brotherhood and love and understanding are things that people get squeamish if you talk about. . . . The thing for me right now is the movement. That's an interesting word, if you think about it—movement. Because it is people in motion. It's not an end; it's not static. That's a very apt word for what we are doing.

A white schoolteacher tells how he got rid of his habitual mental baggage in the civil rights movement of the sixties:

After a few days you throw out a lot of baggage, your habits and expectations, from running water and inside plumbing to brushing your teeth regularly; and you become "men against the sea"—a small group rowing against odds that are sometimes heavy. . . . you think of yourself as removed from a lot you once took for granted; when I go past a bank or a restaurant now, it's like I'm looking into another world. . . . I guess, in a nutshell, you become an outsider.

An educated Negro tells how the Watts riot, in which he did not actively take part, gave him a renewed pride in Negro identity:

He found himself joyously speaking the nitty-gritty Negro argot he hadn't used since junior high, and despite the horrors of the night, this morning he felt a strange pride in Watts. "As a riot," he told me, "it was a masterful performance. I sense a change there now, a buzz, and it tickles. For the first time people in Watts feel a real pride in being black. I remember, when I first went to Whittier, I worried that if I didn't make it there, if I was rejected, I wouldn't have a place to go back to. Now I can say: I'm from Watts.' "

Colorful changes of name and costume—fezes, hairstyles, Moslem or Swahili robes, white vestments, grand titles, army uniforms, silver shirts, and so on—may make clear the purpose of the crusade to change identity and the effect it is having on identity. Malcolm X tells how a change of style, accepting Black Muslim name and symbolism, helped him to feel a new person:

My application (for membership) had . . . been made, and I received from Chicago my "X" during this time. The X for the Muslim was a symbol for the true African family name that he never could know; it would replace the white-slave-master name which had been imposed upon my paternal forebears by some blue-eyed devil. It meant, the receipt of my X, that in the Nation of Islam thereafter I would be known as Malcolm X. . . . Reginal wrote, "Don't eat anymore pork." I tried it and did it, and for the first time in a long while I began to get a little feeling of self-respect, though I hardly knew even how to identify the feeling.

When a crusading spirit enters a movement, its natural tendency is to change the lifestyle, often in the direction of puritanism and austerity. So one sees how the crusade of Mao Tse-tung changed the identity as well as the politics of China: people uniformly clad, both sexes wearing mannish haircuts and overalls; women's bosoms and legs completely covered up; fancy hairdos, drainpipe trousers, pointed shoes, love songs, painting on handkerchiefs, and other "bourgeois" extravagances condemned; children marching in orderly ranks in the street; physical culture so strong that people shadowbox on the street; nightlife virtually nonexistent, prostitutes "re-educated".

Helping identity change in any crusade is something that any military or athletic organization has too: a comradeship of the elect, the *esprit de corps* of veterans who have proven themselves and feel they are an elite corps. Drawn into and accepted by this elite corps, the crusader begins to feel he has gained something precious, however unsuccessful the fight or the game. He has "earned his letter," and his self-esteem rises.

Changes of identity are not peculiar to crusades, but may be found in many kinds of group activities. Almost anywhere one may meet people who introduce one to a new way of life. Hero worship is a common experience, outside as well as within crusades. Conversion experiences, also, can happen in may sectors of life, without intense interaction, cultic ritual, or ordeals. Still, cults and crusades are likely to maximize the factors which favor identity change. And the crusade has its own special elements which give it immense power to change identity, center a person, and provide an emotional payoff, win or lose. For this reason, crusaders can always say, "It is better to have loved (a good cause) and lost than never to have loved at all."

With such effects on identity, we see how the crusade, even if practical results are meagre, has the capacity to make people feel good, give a sense of meaning and a catharsis to those who, win or lose, have fought or even only watched the good fight. By giving an opportunity to "do something," they help people to define themselves and give a sort of moral redemption of self—a reward, even, for sacrifice. So I see crusading as a route of identity transformation, one of the kinds of movements besides cults that does for its members internally as much as they do or try to do to society at large.

This is, if you please, a kind of inflation—a personal enlargement and raising of the moral level—a kind of moral overstatement. But appreciating it requires a kind of relativism, recognizing the obvious fact that every crusade is right to some people, no matter how bad it is to others.

While we may regret the results of some crusades, such a mentality, in itself, is neither good nor bad, but it *is* righteous, and if you are on its side it is "right". From its rightness and romantic exaggerations comes its power to mobilize and change people and its courage—or presumption—to change society. Without crusading, I dare say, social change would be a rather lukewarm affair of trying to build a better world by piecemeal improvements and pragmatic methods, with minimal disturbance to the status quo. There would be little sense of moral conflict between groups. Major changes would be slow, except where innovations were obviously sensible (as in the improvements of auto design) or "fun" (as in the case of fads and fashions). No one would become famous for stirring up things in the manner of a Margaret Sanger, Carry Nation, or Gandhi. But, because it is so human to crusade, we do not really know whether society should get what it wanted without such activity for whenever we have large changes—as from modernism and acculturation—we have usually had crusading in some form. We do not know whether changes like the Reformation or English Revolution could have occurred without people being thrown in jail and having their heads bashed. But, though we do not know exactly what crusading accomplishes, there is little doubt that our society would be less exciting if there were no people with a zeal for causes.

Just because crusading is a kind of moral overstatement whose morality is relative, we cannot easily reach a final verdict on whether it is good or bad. In the short run, its faults are plain enough: It exaggerates bad into evil, and divides the world into righteous crusaders and their unrighteous or ignorant opponents. It generates a self-righteousness that can easily turn into intolerance, uncompromisingness, and arrogance (the less lovable side of Quixote). It recruits by mass contagion, such as hysteria and militaristic war fever, lending itself to a paranoia to which even normal people are susceptible. It enlarges, aggravates, and escalates conflict favoring counter-crusades, rather than compromise or "winding down." For such reasons, dispite its many contributions to progress, we judge crusading to be a poor instrument for scientific analysis or practical control of problems. Its main value, which cannot be denied, is in the emotional sphere of making people feel better—identities confirmed, passions purged, moral values upheld—to a degree where high costs of sacrifice and even martyrdom feel justified.

But that leads to a main criticism of crusading, that it arouses a moralism in politics which may lead to fanaticism, sectarianism, extremism, even totalitarianism. Who wants to use a weapon that can escalate to such results?

Would society, then, be better off without crusades, introducing changes gradually by piecemeal measures and compromises which do not require fights? The gain, certainly, would be less disturbance to the status quo and less threat to democratic processes. But there would be losses: reform would be intolerably slow for many people; politics would be less interesting and exciting; and one of the psychological bonds giving a mass society a feeling of togetherness would be gone. It is hard to imagine how boring and hopeless a society would be where no one cared enough to crusade about anything.

One thought always lingers behind any evaluation of crusading as a type of moralistic activism. The ancient wisdom of Taoism teaches that if you want something, do not strive, contend, and stir up crises. The battle is rarely won by the "winner." Proceed quietly, seeking a natural and easier "way." Be like water which flows through nets. This is a nugget of wisdom, a basic proposition about life, which no crusader has ever really faced up to—nor, judging by their actions, even understood. The reformer who wants action now—or keener identity from struggle—may not be interested in this point. But for those who want permanent and larger results, and have no burning identity problems to solve, it may be a very important point indeed.

Do crusades work practically? Are they cost efficient apart from their emotional satisfactions? I am inclined personally to say no, having been born during a war to end all wars and make the world safe for democracy; and having grown up during the prohibition of drinking alcohol. Neither of these two huge crusades worked. The Great War, by its enormous human costs, spirit of vindictiveness, and the harshness of its treaty, sowed the seeds of another, bigger war. The Prohibition Law did not much reduce the amount of drinking, and did vastly increase the number of criminals and their wealth.

But then neither did the first or any later crusades save Jerusalem. Has the testing period been long enough?

4

Contagious Communication

Many people have been struck by the mysterious impulse that causes a flock of birds to swerve, swoop, and settle, then fly all at once by instantaneous decision, without an apparent leader telling them what to do and when to do it. While the contagious spread of feeling in a herd or flock is more mysterious than that of humans (at least to us), humans have a wider range of feelings and thoughts that can be communicated. If Saint Francis talked to birds, he had less to say to them than to his fellow humans.

Bees, ants, birds, whales, fish, and apes communicate by vocabularies that humans are only beginning to fathom. There is no reason to suppose that man lacks such natural vocabularies of his own to which he responds without being able to say what it means. The point is that humans communicate unwittingly as animals in addition to all they have to say deliberately by means of symbols.

This range of natural communication is not deliberately sent as messages but unwittingly given off and received—"caught" some might say as one would a cold. I call it *contagion* as it passes unwittingly from one to another—signals which act on us so compellingly that we accept and obey them uncritically and unwittingly, and we label such communication: authority, suggestion, hypnosis, imitation, obedience, persuasion, prestige, fad, craze. And because such signals can spread among millions of people with the rapidity of—even faster than—a disease epidemic, they are called mass contagion. And such persuasive communication comes often not from friends, relatives, fellow students, colleagues, one's own church members, but from people we do not know.

The paradox is that, along with a lack of concern in community and day-to-day relations, we are much affected by mass contagions emanating from media and people we do not know. This is what it is to be a *mass* in the special sociological sense: a lot of people who are little connected with one another in a caring, responsible way, but are much influenced by one another in ways described as crowd-mindedness, herdlike thinking, hysterias, fads, crazes, manias, frenzies, and so on. Unlike an organized group, such as a village, corporation, or army, a mass is a lot of people rolling about like billiard balls, striking and being deflected by one another, often in extreme ways, often in one way.

This interplay of mass contagions produces a kind of emotional weather of popular moods, which come and go like weather fronts, making certain kinds of things (crusades?) likely or unlikely.

As one example of emotional weather, America during the late eighties was seen to have entered an era of flag-waving. Old Glory was flown above suburban lawns and used car salesrooms, as well as banks and government offices. There was extreme sensitivity about respect for the flag, which caused a row over a previous Supreme Court decision permitting desecration as "free speech." This mood helped presidential candidate George Bush in 1988 to defeat his opponent Michael Dukakis by a charge that the latter had once vetoed a bill to make reciting the pledge compulsory in his state's schools— implying somehow that this showed a lack of patriotism. Aside from influencing elections, flag-waving slips easily into extremes like war fever and jingoism—even becoming of use to fascism. So legitimate patriotism needs to be tempered by awareness of extremes to which flag-waving by mass communication is liable.

Another contagion of popular mood observed to be sweeping the nation in 1989 was "lottery madness" ("lotto-mania"). It was stimulated by huge jackpots as large as $69.9 million. People who had never gambled before were suddenly hooked. The explosive growth of gambling cut across race, color, creed, income, and ethnic category. People drained savings accounts, cashed paychecks, even borrowed to buy tickets on the big ones. Typical was an elderly woman who walked into a Philadelphia drugstore and announced that she had "cleaned out" her $700 savings account. She used every available dollar from her fixed income to buy lottery tickets.

A subtler sort of pressure from contagion is found in an unwitting resonance noted by Harold C. Schonberg (1981, pp. 64–5) in the programming and performance of classical music by various artists over the world. "A sort of mystical intervention . . . makes an awful lot of musicians turn up with the same work during the course of a season." For example, there was a rage for Prokofiev's Seventh Sonata during 1950–51. Pianists from France, Austria, Germany, England, Mexico, America, "simultaneously decided that their lives would be an empty mockery if they did not immediately program the Seventh." A year or two later it was Schumann's *Etudes Symphoniques*; not long ago the Franck Violin Sonata. Taking the example of Beethoven's *Appassionata*, Schonberg wrote, "musicians all over the globe stir uneasily and get the message. Sure enough, like sheep, they come to town the next season with Beethoven's Appassionata." It was a sort of unwitting consensus, which Schonberg compared with "subliminal advertising." That comparison is fair enough, but many more signals than advertising are subliminal. The entire array of subliminal signals is our emotional weather, affecting arts, sports, politics, social movements, and fashions of all kinds. Is this our flight of a flock of birds all over again?

Vast or small, this sort of thing—a country being swept by mental contagions—violates our rational ideal, bequeathed to us by Plato. It is the Emersonian ideal of being independent-minded:

The great man is he who in the midst of the crowd keeps with perfect sweetness the independence of solitude.

By all signs, we are far from the rational ideal—very much swayed by signals of many kinds, interpersonal and mass mediated, conscious and unwitting. Nor does advancing civilization reduce emotional contagion (after fascism who could doubt it?); media generated tensions have made us more vulnerable than ever to unwitting and seemingly irrational influences.

The connection of all this with inflation is that it gives many examples of more becoming less—symbols losing value as their supply increases. Contagious communications spread rapidly and thoughtlessly, and lead to extremes and exaggerations that are later often seen to be follies. In this sense they make much out of little, magnify little into seeming much. After which, they fade or burst like bubbles. This is what we denote when we speak of rumors, stampedes, panics, hysterias, mobs, riots, fads, crazes, manias, booms, bubbles. Their time is brief but their curve of growth is exponential, as with disease epidemics.

Let us look over briefly some of the facts about contagious communication that psychologists, sociologists, and historians have learned from their studies.

If anyone deserves to be called the founder of the study of contagious communication, it is Gustave LeBon, whose book *The Crowd* (1895) endures as a classic. He saw the crowd as an enemy of the rational mind. It was he who pulled rationalists forcibly to the idea that majorities are not wise if they are crowds (an idea also expressed by Alexis DeToqueville as the "tyranny of the majority"). The crowd has ideas of its own, wrote LeBon, which are clear and forceful, but also simple and stupid, if not worse, in reducing a congress of learned individuals to a crowd of fools, by the power of vivid hallucinatory images to overwhelm rational thought. LeBon's crowd idea was the very opposite of Rousseau's "general will," supposed to be a rational decision about what was truly good for all.

For the first time, a major historical event—the Reign of Terror—was attributed to the "madness" of crowds, or as Wordsworth put it, "the crimes of the few spread into the madness of the many." Historian Robert Darnton (1989) describes the excited popular mood that prevailed in Paris in and following 1789—an extraordinary agitation and permissiveness that made it easy to do new and shocking things. Darnton writes:

> Although the spirit of '89 is no easier to fix in words than in mortar and brick, it could be characterized as energy—a will to build a new world from the ruins of the regime that fell apart in the summer of 1789. That energy permeated everything during the French Revolution. It transformed life, not only for the activists trying to channel it in directions of their own choosing but for ordinary persons going about their daily business.

During that era, 1400 streets in Paris were renamed; fads in dress included exposed breasts, diaphanous gowns, the liberty cap, exotic hair styles; and there were political and legal changes, and a new calendar and metric system adopted.

To see the bizarre and powerful effects of contagious communication, much is owed to that fine old book by Charles MacKay, Extraordinary Popular Delusions And The madness Of Crowds (L. C. Page & Co., 1932, 1941, 1952). It gives fascinating accounts of contagions such as The Mississippi Scheme, South Sea Bubble, tulipomania, alchemists, fortune telling, magnetizers, crusades, witch manias, popular admiration of great thieves, and relics. MacKay wrote:

> Men . . . think in herds . . . they go mad in herds, while they only recover their senses slowly, and one by one.

Many people overrate their own resistance to such "madness" coming from the suggestions of others. They claim to be able to stay calm and self-possessed in even the most excited crowd. Yet many watching hypnotism demonstrations have seen subjects, when asked, deny they are hypnotized; then go into a trance at a snap of the hypnotist's fingers. This is the point of Ionesco's play, "Rhinoceros": that any or all of us are not immune to contagion of "madness" but can be transformed into snorting beasts.

Let us look further at varieties of contagious communication that draw men into herdlike behavior.

Some of the most striking examples come from the crowd itself, in its various forms, riots, mobs, or religious revivals, (a crowd might be defined as a dense interactive gathering of people who do not know one another). A crowd moves people not by numbers but its unanimity and types of interaction that prevail. According to sociologist Herbert Blumer, crowd contagion develops from circular interaction (often called milling), in which interaction by speech, applause, yelling, shoving, escalates movement into joint action or expressive behavior. A key point is that circular interaction is by automatic responses which are quick and similar, rather than by "interpretative" responses that are deliberate, take more time, and make people different. The crowd attains unanimity, not the diversity of public opinion. In an excited crowd, people reinforce each other by feedback, causing emotions to escalate. Anonymity also helps release behavior from normal restraint. Another point to reiterate is that contagious communication not only informs but "catches" you because it contains arousal stimuli, subliminal perceptions, and hypnotic suggestions that evoke responses that one is not able easily to control. Usually people do not choose to be, but are swept into the crowd spirit. For them, the saying (paraphrasing Oliver Goldsmith) is apt: "those who come to scoff remain to pray."

Cathartic audiences are those in which people are expected and permitted to get excited and let themselves go emotionally. To be swept into the crowd spirit is the purpose of cheering at sports contest; to get spectators as excited as possible over the game—even to enter it. In the following case, as the crowd overflowed into the football field after a game, a student recalled:

> I don't know what got into me. I seized a staff, improvised a banner by tying a piece of the school colors onto it, and led a chanting, raving snake dance of students onto the playing field. Then the most incredible thing of all: a student was standing by watching the dance. I knocked his hat off, yelling "Salute the flag!" He looked abashed, did not challenge me but kept his hat off, and soon joined the dance. Where this idea of saluting the flag came from I have not the slightest idea. It is totally unlike my regular self.

Religious revivals give even better examples of being carried away by circular interaction into expressive behavior. A witness observed the audience of evangelist R. C., the "fireball" from Chattanooga, Tennessee:

> As he speaks, the fire from heaven seems to descend upon the audience. Men, women and children begin dancing with jerks. Women begin speaking in tongues. A youth dances for a long time by himself, eyes closed, bent sideways. A girl about twenty years old stands in the aisle beside me, her eyes closed, teeth chattering, and talking to herself in a high voice. A woman gets up with a shriek and rushes out. People stand and give impromptu sermons and testimonials. The evangelists sing and beat on little drums with cymbals. One little girl about eight years old watches the scene with open-mouthed wonder. The children begin imitating. Now the climax is reached. The whole crowd flows down in front to meet with the evangelists, singing, praying, crying, hands raised, embracing, receiving holy touches. Women fall unconscious, stretched out on the floor, trembling and twitching. Miracles, miracles, miracles seem to be in the air, according to all kinds of testimonies. Some women are so excited they can't control themselves, and return to their seats with difficulty, like a sailor clutching a rope against heavy seas.

An extraordinary height of religious crowd frenzy was illustrated by the behavior of mourners at the burial of Iranian Ayatollah Khomeini.

> At the first attempt to bury Khomeini the crowd seized the body and tore pieces from the shroud, leaving the corpse, its unhealed operation scars cruelly revealed, rolling in the dust. Groups of Hezbollah chanted and rhythmically beat their close-cropped heads and chests with their hands. Khomeini finally was buried six hours later in a shallow grave. Lorry trailers were place on top of the grave to protect it from the faithful. Undeterred, holy men handed out bowls of dirt scraped from the dry earth at their edges. Followers regarded this as sacred and ate it. (*Times*, London, 11 June 1989)

But that frenzy was not all that different from the frenzy of sports crowds, which, too, can approach the ecstatic level, such as the frenzy of baseball fans at the unforgettable triumph of the underdog New York Mets in the World Series of 1969. The delirious fans ran out of the bleachers and began to pull sod from the infield as souvenirs. A mother and son climbed the fence and joined the sod-pullers. She explained:

> I have a shopping bag full of sod from the infield of Shea Stadium. On hands and knees I pulled it up right after the Mets won the World Series. The getting of the sod was an unlawful but joyous thing. And even the law was on my side for a while—as evidenced by the policeman who helped me off the fence . . . when I headed for the sod. . . . In the pulling I felt a little funny. Down on hands and knees, ripping that nice grass up. I felt more comfortable when I saw a very dignified gentleman doing the same. . . . I was still on my hands and knees . . . when an officer came and ordered me to go. . . . Reluctantly we left—most of us holding our sod with the cautious manner reserved for newborn babies. . . . The . . . important thing was that each of us being shuffled into subway turnstiles had a hunk or bag or suitcase or armful of sod. "Just touch it for magic anytime," my son said. . . . A woman with white hair and an armload of sod said: "I'm going to plant mine. I am going to put a fence around it. I won't let anyone walk on it. It has the Mets' footprints on it. (UPI, 17 October 1969)

Pearl Bailey, who sang the national anthem, was observed to be embracing a piece of sod as she entered the New York clubhouse to congratulate the team.

It would be hard to argue that this example of sod mania, as it were, was a collective ecstasy altogether different kind from that felt by devotees about saints' relics.

But all mass contagions do not require the milling (circular interaction) of crowds to set them in motion and keep them spreading. Those contagions called "mass," carried by imitation, rumor, and media, may reach uncounted numbers of people over a nation, even the world. In the broadest sense, we include those popular moods that drift in and out like weather fronts, making certain events likely and hopes and fears plausible.

A demonstration of the scale of mass contagions and how fast and far they can spread, was the urban ghetto riots of 1966 and 1967, in which rioting, looting, and vandalism spread to many American cities (eighteen in 1966 and over thirty-nine in 1967). The trigger that started this contagion was a comparatively trivial incident in Watts, California: a tussle of police with a teenager and his mother, which let loose a volcanic eruption of hostility and rebellion, under the motto, "Burn, baby, burn!" and threatened to divide the United States into two nations (as it was said).

Contagions of fear involving distorted beliefs are commonly called hysterias. Scores of cases have been reported in the literature. Some were circulated by rumors that dangerous agents were working, then picked up by the press. To recall a few of the more colorful and best known, one might mention: the Phantom Anaesthetist (also known as the Mad Gasser) of Matoon, who was said to be spraying a mysterious gas into women's bedroom windows; the Phantom Slasher of Taipei, who was supposed to be attacking children with razor blades; the "windshield pitting" epidemic in Seattle, in which there was mysterious damage to automobile window by metallic particles (Medalia and Larsen, 1958). Some hysterias involve symptoms of bodily illness which spread contagiously, such as the "June Bug" epidemic among women workers in a textile mill (Kerckhoff and Back, 1968). Then there were doomsday fears produced by various cultic groups prophesying that the end of the world was at hand.

The prototype of American hysterias from evil agents supposed to be working in the world was, of course, the Salem witchhunt, in which fear found scapegoats in some score of victims, including a dog. A similar paranoid mentality was displayed in the great Red Scare of 1920 in America, as eloquently described by Frederick Lewis Allen in *Only Yesterday*.

Ironically, one hysteria in America was spread by public education: The Fallout shelter panic of 1962–63, provoked by instructions about what to do in a nuclear emergency, which set people frantically digging in their backyards for what later turned out to be rather expensive wine and mushroom-growing cellars.

Such fearful contagions illustrate social magnification of few to many and little to much—as Chicken Little said, "The sky is falling!"

Need contagious communication be unpleasant? Plainly not. It may be hopeful, enthusiastic, optimistic, ecstatic, wish-fulfilling— one could say happy. This is the spirit of contagions called rushes (gold or uranium), booms (the stock market of 1929, the Florida land boom of 1925), bubbles, crazes, and manias. Lottery fever has already been mentioned.

Among the pleasant sightings are those which illustrate hallucinatory results of contagious communication—that people tend to see what they fervently agree they want to see (that wishes are self-fulfilling). One example is crutches and prosthetics piled up in shrines where miracles are said to have occurred. Religious apparitions often seem to promise benefits, such as the "miracle of Sabena Grande", a vision of the Holy Virgin that many in a crowd of over a hundred thousand Puerto Ricans thought they saw (Tumin and Feldman 1955).

No less pleasant are some visions of flying saucers (UFOs), which also show the wish-fulfilling side of contagious communication. In 1966, in one event, flying saucers were sighted by at least twelve policemen and forty other persons at Ann Arbor, Michigan, who said they saw a weird flying object, guarded by four sister ships, land in a swamp. Hope and optimism were the prevalent mood (not the fearsome memories of Orson Welles' radio news hoax). One man brought his fiddle to the scene and began playing, hoping the phantom pilots would hear and come to earth; another man sat in his car blinking his headlights hoping to communicate with the visitors. Numerous multiple sightings of flying saucers have been recorded and the extraordinary agreement in some cases (like that about the Loch Ness monster) seems to require explanation either by the truth of the observations, or by contagious communication among observers made suggestible by hope.

By a small stretch of imagination, war fever also can be counted as a happy form of contagious communication, because, in early stages, at least, it is characterized by glee at what one is going to do to the enemy, and eagerness to be in the conflict (in Britain in 1914, young men clamored to have a tilt at the enemy, afraid that the war would be over "by Christmas"). When the American Congress succumbed to war fever and declared war on Germany in 1917, it was not with deliberate debate but with a feeling of a stampede that few could resist. Congressman Fred Britten, Republican of Illinois, in a statement to the House, 5 April 1917, described the mysterious power of war fever:

There is something in the air, gentlemen, and I do not know what it is, whether it be the hand of destiny or some superhuman movement, something stronger than you or I can realize or resist, that seems to be picking us up bodily and literally forcing us to vote for this declaration of war. (Millis 1935, p. 454).

War fever seems also to have helped passage of the Gulf of Tonkin Resolution by the Senate by a vote of 98 to 2. Senator Dale Bumpers recalled the "herd instinct" against which Senators Gruening and Morse were the only ones to vote no: "the two who today stand out in history as two men who, had they been listened to, would have saved 57,000 lives . . . in what everyone admits was the most debilitating war the U.S. ever fought" (The Washington Spectator, 15 September 1987, p. 2).

Another extraordinary product of contagious communication that could be called ecstatic or happy was the famed and still unforgotten festival at Woodstock, New York, in 1969, a mammoth concert of electronically amplified rock music, which drew four hundred thousand youths (estimated by *Time* to be the largest crowd of people ever assembled). It produced a phenomenal traffic jam stopping cars for miles around the area. But the behavior was not violent as police expected. A peculiar euphoric mood developed, which enveloped police too, who, charmed, gave way to sentimental expressions like "a swell bunch of kids." Many observers agreed that something new had happened: the rock movement, and in a broader sense youth itself, had acquired a new collective self-awareness and sense of mission as a movement. *Time* hailed it as "History's Biggest Happening". Two decades later it was still being recognized and commemorated as a major consciousness-raising in the history of the nation.

Finally, we end this review of events of contagious communication by taking note of fads, an unending series of which, imitated briefly, add spice of variety and relieve boredom from the standardization (redundancy) of modern life. Fads inflate by rapid oversupply and glut of things only momentarily wanted, which soon add to the boredom they were supposed to relieve. We defer treatment of the inflationary nature of fads to chapter 9 on fashion.

Aware of this historical and social background, psychologists have long been concerned with what it is that makes some communication contagious. They studied hypnosis in clinical and laboratory settings, and various conditions, such as anxiety and extraversion, that made some people more suggestible than others. A subfield of social psychology grew up concerned with "conforming behavior" in laboratory and clinical settings, which threatened individual autonomy. Early studies by Clark Hull, seeking to understand and measure suggestibility, found that most people unwittingly imitate what they vividly see

or imagine. He called this "ideomotor action." For example, a standing subject connected with a kymograph will unwittingly sway if
faced by a person who deliberately sways in front of him. Muzafer
Sherif made a historic study of social norms: how they form and how
people change judgments unwittingly to conform when they heard reports of others about seeming (autokinetic) movement of a light in a
dark room. People were unable to avoid conforming because they
didn't know they were doing it—and leaders obeyed the group norm
rather than setting it. This research has profound implications for
such things as jury decisions and peer influence. Another historic
study, by Solomon Asch, concerned what happens to judgment when
one is contradicted by a unanimous group. He found that about half
of the subjects gave way and changed their report of a plain matter
of fact when contradicted by, say, four others—a comment, almost
needless to say, on the power of crowds. Stanley Milgram in ingenious studies found startling—even shocking—facts about obedience,
e.g., that most people will obey a stranger (in a white coat) who
commands them to do something objectionable, even to inflict pain
on another subject.

So there is great suggestibility in human behavior—more willingness to agree, obey, and go along—than had been suspected before
these studies. Note, also, that such conforming effects occurred with
strangers (not the tribe, military corps, peer group that one trusts and
shares background with).

Such findings about conformist behavior came as a surprise to social scientists (even remembering LeBon) who believed in the rational autonomy of man. Some resistance to recognizing the full
scope of contagion comes, I think, from the fact that it violates our
image of an independent, rational mind. Indeed, contagion invites a
metaphor suggesting that people are like tenpins waiting to be bowled
over, their suggestibility being attitudes that make them lean or tilt in
certain directions. Following such an analogy, the "tilt" is partly in
the floor itself (as culture, status, and social class); and some is in
the individual, as prejudice, suggestibility, anxiety, tension, prestige
(in the eye of the beholder), and so on.

The other analogy we have used concerns the spread of popular
moods, which make certain specific contagions likely. The analogy is
with weather; popular moods drift like storm fronts, which leaders
try to sense and, if possible, predict, so that action can be taken. The

analogy with weather helps understanding of the role of agitators and demagogues, who lead by catching a mood at the right time. Here, the analogy is with cloud "seeding." Rainmakers "seed" the clouds with particles especially attractive to moisture, such as silver iodide. As water condenses, particles unite into drops so heavy that they fall as rain. Leaders who draw on popular moods—Thomas Paine, Harriet Beecher Stowe, Martin Luther King, Gandhi, Saul Alinski, Senator Joseph McCarthy—are like the particles because they have the sensitivity to pick up and formulate moods that are "in the air." Then people gather about them, repeat what they have said, and organize thought and action.

By the 1990s, it was impossible to ignore a new kind of contagion which loomed on the horizon. It was the computer "virus," whose spread threatened to infect whole systems, electronic files, and pools of information. The "virus" was a program that copies itself and spreads like a contagious disease from computer to computer through disks and computer bulletin boards. Virus programs "develop a life of their own, like a chain reaction in an atomic reactor." The greatest threat is the enormous propagation speed of the virus (Burger 1988, p. 29). It does damage by destroying information—making it irretrievable from disks, files, and bulletin boards—thus threatening to erase files, clog memory, and otherwise wreak havoc with personal computers as well as the great systems of banks, businesses, libraries, and the military. The damage yet to be done by computer viruses remains to be assessed. It could cause human social systems to fail, and play its part in mass contagions of the sort described by MacKay, helped by the latest communication and computer technology.

Having looked at such cases, few can doubt that America is subject to epidemics of contagious communication--and, hence, to the inflations implied. Our main point here is that all emotional contagions, from crowd and mass to rumor and fad, are important forms of inflation by social magnification. They are exaggerative. They spread uncritically by imitation and suggestibility, and may be passed on to millions. They increase responsiveness to certain stimuli. They overvalue, magnify, and distort their objects. They make things that are small and trivial seem large and important. They tend to extremes by multiplication and reinforcement of stimuli. They spread in an epidemic (exponential) pattern for a time, then collapse, or burst like a bubble (history is littered with dead fads and costly infatuations). While in vogue, they produce a feeling of euphoria and rightness until they pass away. Every crowd mood and crusade is self-righteous to the point of arrogance. After they have faded, they are felt to have been regrettable, irrational, and foolish. They foster uncritical judgment, credulity, emotionalism, rhetoric, and other kinds of poor thinking. Hence, social contagions are highly inflationary. They create a transitory, ephemeral world of fantasies, expectations and feelings that cannot last, and are bound to be disappointing when they burst, or fade of their own accord.

5

Emotional Hitchhiking

Americans visiting England are so fond of royalty with its pomp and pageantry, that one would never guess they fought a war to get rid of a king.

The British attitude toward their own royalty is not one of unmixed delight. They grant the value of royalty for tourism, but question whether it earns its keep. Indeed it may be conceded that celebrity does not cost as much as royalty, comprising mostly as it does ordinary people overblown into superstars by media publicity. But justifying the expense of royalty are deeper meanings. It is often said that the Queen serves as a symbol through which, as General de Gaulle said, the English "perceive their own nationhood, the person by whose presence and dignity the national unity is sustained." She could be said to be a sort of group superself. De Gaulle might have said the same of himself, as a symbol for the French.

Yet another advantage of having a royal family is that it is a sort of soap opera, which pays its way by entertaining the public with its loves, marriages, births, deaths, escapades, sports, hobbies, vagaries, eccentricities, and very real human problems.

This function they share with innumerable other celebrities, news of whom serves an important psychological function in modern life. *People*, the magazine of celebrities, has a circulation of three million, all hanging on the doings of rock stars, movie stars, sports champions, jet-setters, billionaires, showgirls, and the like. Attesting to the importance of such celebrities, one can often see crowds of people hanging about doorways from which celebrities are likely to appear, just for a glimpse of one. Such appearances mean much to people who, not having real pomp of royalty, are eager to salute the glitz and glamor of celebrities.

We wish here to look at the extent to which people use the roles of celebrities and media characters to enlarge themselves and live borrowed lives through a sort of inflation I call emotional hitch-hiking.

What do people nowadays want from celebrities and royalty? I would say they seek not a tangible service, but a free ride in some-body else's life. Celebrities are especially sited for emotional hitch-hiking, furnishing a vehicle by which fans can enlarge themselves by vicariously living through the career of the celebrity.

The interest of sports fans goes beyond mere interest in sport. "They want a love affair," said one owner of a leading professional football team. By that he meant, I think, that fans draw psychologi-cal gratifications that go beyond whether a game is played well. He meant that fans also want to follow a team, be loyal to them, be proud of them, identify with them—loving them in victory or defeat might not be too strong a term.

This gratification occurs through what psychologists call identifica-tion. It is identification which gives us the ability to enter and rejoice in others' lives—bidden or not. Such experience is often called vi-carious. The special charm of vicarious experience is that it allows one to enter another person's reality very cheaply, without risk of being shot at, impaled, or otherwise endangered by reality. In *The Old Curiosity Shop*, Dickens wrote,

"A bullfight is found to be a comfortable spectacle by those who are not in the arena."

What is identification, what kinds are there and how do they func-tion? Broadly viewed, identification has many aspects and goes under various names.

Viewed positively, it is a gift that makes us human. It goes beyond intellect to a freer range of imagination. As sympathy, empathy, com-passion and concern for others, it enlarges our minds. Sociologists often prefer to call this gift role-taking or role-playing, but one should be careful to note that it is not mere copying or imitation of the behavior of another (which could be done without identification). Role-taking requires putting oneself imaginatively in the shoes of another—seeing things his way—and, especially, looking at our-selves through the eyes of others and judging oneself by this reflec-tion. Charles H. Cooley termed this the "looking glass self," and George H. Mead called it "taking the attitude of the other"—the basis, both Cooley and Mead held, of fairness, justice, conscience and all moral conduct. Children learn adult roles and attitudes by play-acting or make-believe as a sort of rehearsal.

A distinction is made between role-taking and role-playing. Role-*taking* is imaginary or covert (such as daydreaming, sympathy, audience experience and reading. S. I. Hayakawa tells how our lives are enriched by role-taking in literature (impossible to the illiterate):

> In a very real sense, people who have read good literature have lived more than people who cannot read. . . . It is not true that we have only one life to live; if we can read, we can live as many more lives and as many kinds of lives as we wish. (S. I. Hayakawa, quoted in *The Writer's Quotation Book*, ed. James Charlton [New York: Penguin Books, 1986], p 12.)

Role-*playing*, by contrast, is overt and includes role performance required by status (for example, a priest), theatrical drama, and legitimately faking identities as in masquerades and carnivals. Illegitimate overt role-playing is found in psychosis (acting out), masked banditry, and imposture. In a classic study, sociologist Daniel Lerner (1959) took account of differences in role-taking and playing opportunities in traditional versus modern societies. Traditional (we might call them closed) societies restrict what one can identify with, as in caste barriers, censorship, authoritarianism, and illiteracy. On the other hand, in modern societies, especially to the literate, media open a huge window of role opportunities, a showcase or cafeteria of choice of what to be. Lerner called "psychological mobility" the modern ability to imagine oneself in another caste, occupation, culture, and so on. So, peasant Turks had low psychological mobility, but in Ankara it was higher. In such a view, how many roles one can take and how many identities one can conceive for oneself are a mark of modernization. Open and closed societies are also distinguished by the scope of their role-taking and playing: open societies have high access to roles, overt and covert, and little restriction. Closed societies have low access to roles, and high restriction.

Even if unable to actually move, a person can still enjoy benefits of identification with those who do move. When the mighty Sultan of Swat puts it "out there" for you, he gives a thrill, first, to those who identify with his batting role; and second to those who imagine themselves belonging to the team for which he bats. When the Great Lover takes the girl into his arms, he gives a thrill, first, to those who imagine themselves kissing; and, second, to those who imagine themselves being kissed. I venture to say that the popular success of any drama or contest depends on identification. Whether we really enjoy a contest, stage play, movie, story, romance, or adventure, depends very much on how much we identify with the central character whose fate momentarily becomes our own. The first thinker to recognize the benefit of what I call emotional hitchhiking was Aristotle, who wrote that audiences get a catharsis by identifying with a tragic hero. And no small benefit of identification is its economy, the fact that there is no limit to how many people can identify with one hero; any number can "climb aboard" the same vehicle.

"Hero" is our commonest name for people we enduringly admire and strongly prefer to identify with, on account of their achievements (which we vicariously share) or attractive personalities. Identification with a hero may be momentary or lifelong.

To illustrate such degrees of identification, we might take the example of a football game. In the grandstand or among those watching television at home, we can distinguish: (1) those watching without identification, without caring who wins; (2) partisan cheering for one side, sharing emotion as a team wins or loses, but not imagining oneself to be a player; (3) imagining oneself to take the role of a player (e.g., as quarterback making pass); (4) enduring, habitual commitment (e.g., as fan following a team loyally from game to game).

So we see that identification allows us to enlarge ourselves-escape from the boundaries of our own life, enter many others' lives, and be many kinds of persons. It gives unlimited scope within which to roam and dream. It is hard to set boundaries for a human because he spends so much time outside himself. A secret life is possible, as shown by James Thurber's character Walter Mitty. Mass media offer an ever greater range of roles to modern man than ever before. Soap opera shows people entranced by watching others' personal problems not all that different from their own, except for being intensified and compressed to fit television time slots. The social function of the battery of fan magazines, tabloids, and gossip columnists seems to be to feed this demand, give people images to identify with, and to keep them abreast of the latest.

The oft-heard remark, "Everybody's a little bit Irish on Saint Patrick's Day," inane though it would be if strictly applied to persons, illustrates that people do enlarge their identities by identification with collectivities—family, tribe, nation, race, class, team, gang, profession, gender. The advantage is obvious: the individual is alone, the collectivity is numerous; the individual is weak, the collectivity is strong; the individual is mortal, the collectivity is potentially immortal. Embodying the collectivity, the hero is brave, moral, noble (sacred, said Durkheim)—a head taller than others and so might be called a group superself. In short, identification with collectivities and their heroes is a sort of inflation of the individual who thus makes himself psychologically larger without having changed his actual traits, poor though they may be.

Perhaps the first time people realized the extent and intensity of popular identification via media was the emotional following that developed for Dickens' character Little Nell. It was discovered that 100,000 readers of Dickens' weekly magazine, at home and abroad, were following the doings and tribulations of this heroine as though she were a real and dear person. Her death was a major public emotional event. Crowds gathered at the quayside in New York awaiting the next issue telling news of her fate. Critics confessed weeping over her. A similar surprise, showing the unsuspected extent of vicarious living in heroes, occurred when some 50,000 overwrought people (including men as well as women) showed up to create a mob scene at the Great Lover Rudolph Valentino's funeral.

In all this emotional hitchhiking on the careers of stars and celebrities, it is important to recognize their compensatory function of doing for people what they cannot or dare not do for themselves— winning prizes and trophies, getting rich quickly, squandering riches, sexual prowess, lush and rapid love affairs, multiple marriages, robbing the Bank of England and making the Great Getaway. They give us in imagination what we do not actually do (and perhaps would not want to do) in real life.

This compensatory function explains why *ordinariness* is such an important feature of heroes, however sensational their deeds may be. Ordinariness invites people to identify, to feel "I could be like him." This helps to explain why so few popular favorites are great men and women (geniuses, supermen, saints) who are just too extraordinary for the common man to approach, too far out of the ballpark, so to speak. Far from being a great man, the ordinary popular hero is one whose success is not so much due to great abilities and virtues as to luck, which encourages us to feel that any of us could do or be the same. It is celebrities, not great men, that are generated in an enormous crop by the media of today.

This raises the question of whether emotional hitchhiking has a special function in mass society, of compensating for what isn't there. Mass society could have people spend more time hitchhiking than living their own lives. The stereotype of the "couch potato" gives a picture of one who is giving up his own life to watch what is happening on a TV screen. Should we so wish, by emotional hitchhiking, everybody might escape into someone else's problems. There would be nobody at home, so to speak.

What are these functions? At the very least one can say that vicarious experience of heroes adds romance and excitement to life. So it can compensate for emotional deficits of mass society, such as boredom, loneliness, family instability, anonymity, and personal insignificance—the meaning gap. The more boring, humdrum, and routine life is, the more people need vicarious experience to compensate. Here is where soap operas and Harlequin novels make their special contribution to the housewife, while her husband follows sports teams from bowl to superbowl.

In more sociological terms, we might say that emotional hitchhiking remedies anomie, fills gaps of decaying solidarity, substituting imagined fathers, mothers, sons, daughters, spouses, friends, counselors, comrades, and heroes for ones lacking in real life. So it compensates for defects of social structure, lack of opportunity, rewards of interaction lacking, or goals unrealized. Desk-bound Mittys live dangerously and ride to adventure with Louis L'amour. Harlequin readers find true romance. Seekers of the American dream find success-stories. War and shoot-outs in the media offer imaginary outlets for frustrated would-be Rambos. Lottery players wait hopefully watching a few others win the big prize. It seems that expectations of self-fulfillment are arising precisely when features of modern mass society and bureaucracy defeat them: bureaucracy shutting the door on self-realization in work; technology closing the door on work itself; mass society filled with the faceless crowd and the audience watching celebrities achieving identities not possible for the man on the street who hankers for a place in the limelight but never gets there.

These compensations of emotional hitchhiking are not remedies giving a more mature and settled identity but are better described as placebos (Klapp 1986, pp. 131–154) masking discontent and leading to a kind of shopping for vicarious identities as people go from one to another seeking meaning (part of the religious marketplace previously described). Having such a rich array of choices, modern man is not simply "there" but has an identity composed of many roles and in no required combination. Rootless in terms of community and free to imagine himself as who he pleases, his identity consists of a number of identifications, diverse, dispersed, shifting, transitory, by no means consistent—in that way inflated. Widespread, unsatisfied hunger for identity is expressed in some quarters as obstreperous behavior—drug abuse, gang fights, wheel-screeching, graffiti, ghetto-blasters—of "nobodies" yearning to be "somebody." Ego-screaming, I called (1969) advertising oneself by eccentricities that attract attention, the cry of the nameless voices of mass society, "Listen to me," "Pay attention to me!"

Hunger for vicarious identity also explains some of the mass behavior toward celebrities and stars. People hang about them, begging for souvenirs and autographs, hoping for some more intimate contact, and reading about them avidly in fan magazines.

The person who has found what he regards as his true identity by enthusiastically following some activity or hero is often called a *fan* (though in the religious marketplace he might be called a devotee or convert). We get a sharper picture of how people use emotional hitchhiking by looking at fans and their behavior.

Because they seek to live in somebody else, they engage in rather curious behavior. They make nuisances of themselves, swarming all over the place, invading privacy, swiping souvenirs. Let us look more at some of this curious "hero worship."

Fans are devotees who make visible their enthusiasm by caps, sweaters, T-shirts, emblems, bumper-stickers, or other insignia; and who follow an activity or the career of someone for the sake of desired vicarious experience. Because of such identification, it is not at all necessary for a fan to be an actual performer or practitioner in the field of his interest. That is, he doesn't have to be a rock musician, or to have played baseball or football, to be a fan of that activity. The reason is that living vicariously is the function—as attainable by non-performers (women, children, amateurs, novices) as by performers.

It was in the Lindbergh era that Americans first realized how sud-

denly and how many heroes could rise from being unknowns to national—indeed world—popularity and fame. It was through striking
roles embodying a sort of success that many yearned for, but only the
hero got. From the twenties to the sixties, dozens of popular heroes
emerged in fields like sports, movies, popular music—wherever the
media cast their glamorizing glow. One would be hard put, though,
to think of a more unanticipated set of heroes than the Beatles.

Were there a Richter scale for fan fever inflated by social contagion, "Beatlemania" in England and America in 1965 would rate
about eight. It was one of the most startling expressions of mass hero
worship in modern times, a frenzy of fans to see, touch, hear, and
collect souvenirs and images of the heroes. It began when Beatles'
recordings began to sell extraordinarily; and crowds followed them
about and gathered wherever they were made visible. It became apparent that they had a "secret army of fans" much bigger than anyone
had suspected—mostly hysterical screaming girls and gyrating rock-
and-rollers. It was a daunting experience for the Beatles, flanked by
security guards, to face 10,000 screaming, chanting fans who were
frantic for a touch or any sort of memento from the heroes—a shred
of clothing snatched with some risk; a piece of Ringo's chewing
gum, popped into the mouth of a fan; sheets the Beatles slept on cut
into one inch squares and sold as souvenirs by hotels (the analogy
with saints' relics is too pointed to ignore).

In his enthusiasm a fan may make himself over in terms of his object of devotion. I mention the striking example of a fan of Gene
Autry, the singing cowboy, who became himself another Gene Autry,
wearing a ten-gallon hat just like his hero's, and making a huge collection of almost everything connected with his idol—Gene Autry
shirts, hats, boots, holsters, six-shooters, guitars bearing Autry's name,
ashtrays, record albums, tapes, photograph albums lovingly mounted
and protected by plastic—in short, anything that will bring to living
experience what it is like to be Gene Autry—to have an existence enlarged by that much beyond one's everyday identity—and perhaps to
share that with innumerable other fans. If this man is yet alive, I do
not doubt that he is still wearing the 10-gallon hat. The devotion of
fans may last a lifetime. In 1988 the worldwide club of Beatles' fans
was still holding its annual Beatles Convention in Liverpool, England, and burning page-by-page a biography by Albert Goldman critical of their idol John Lennon.

One of the most striking expressions of the devotion of fans is an intense curiosity, which might be described as a hunger for anything having to do with the hero. Even a touch is a precious memento to a hero worshipper. "I touched him! I touched him!" is the familiar cry that every celebrity hears when he is buffeted and bruised by crowds (the Duke of Windsor reminisced, "If I were out of reach, a blow on my head with a folded newspaper appeared to satisfy the impulse"). Since souvenirs are what is wanted, something more than a mere touch is highly desirable. The celebrity is likely to have his clothing torn off and pieces taken as souvenirs. This is not theft but expression of an attitude which is almost proprietary. Along with it goes an intense curiosity, a hunger for information. Jack Dempsey recalled, "They want to look at your eyes and your ears to see how badly you have been injured. They want to pick up a word here or a gesture there which, later on, they can relay, magnified, to their own little public." Albert Einstein remarked wryly, "I often feel among crowds like a prostitute who is under constant police surveillance." A respectable-looking woman of middle age tried to peek into Charles Lindbergh's mouth while he was having dinner at a New York hotel to see whether he was eating "green beans or green peas." Kahn (1947) describes how fans kept watch over Frank Sinatra, invaded his privacy, and chased him in packs:

> They pin club buttons not only over their hearts but also on their socks . . . inscribe his name on sweaters and coats. A girl whose arm he had accidentally brushed while trying to escape from a pack of fans wore a bandage over the spot for two weeks, to prevent anybody from brushing against it. Another became the envy of her gang, when, after Sinatra had checked out of a hotel room, she got into it before the maids did and escaped with a precious cigarette butt and a half used packet of matches, both of which she assumed her idol had touched. . . . Whenever Sinatra emerges from his hotel and hops into one of the limousines he engages while in any town, any girls who are lucky enough to be near a vacant taxi swarm into it and take off after him. Others light out on foot, but . . . lose track of his car after a block or so. Then, breathing heavily, they try to guess where he is eating or—since he almost always goes to the theater after dinner—which of the shows is on his agenda.

Such "nonsense" makes more sense when one sees it as a kind of hunger for identity and a form of cultic devotion which reaches a competitive frenzy.

Other features of mass society make more sense when viewed in this light—for example, the institution known as celebrity watching.

The function of many restaurants, nightclubs, and discotheques known as "celebrity hangouts" is not to provide food or entertainment but to allow people to watch celebrities (who, themselves, may be subsidized for their patronage). Celebrity watching is a major preoccupation of a mass society with countless people nourishing themselves vicariously by watching the famous. Likewise, television quiz shows, "guest appearances," and so on are thinly disguised forms of celebrity cult—institutions to feed celebrity hunger. Most of the time fan magazines, gossip columns, fan mail, and a farflung organization of fan clubs provide the pipeline of information about celebrities.

The fan club, even when commercially inspired, is not a mere association but basically a form of hero cult. They collect their idol's recordings, see all his films, read everything printed about him, write him applauding his successes and thanking him, treasure his autographed pictures and especially letters, and send him get-well cards when he is ill. As an organization they put out a bulletin to keep members up to date, also pictures and sometimes mirrors and pins with the idol's picture on them. They work as a pressure group to thank publications which praise him; and defend him, even trying to boycott or have banned publications which criticize him. They say, "We are proud of him and wouldn't want him changed."

Such examples show how the fan club serves its members. It brings celebrity-watching to perfection: not just occasional treasured glimpses but a constant pipeline of information and communication to devotees; and psychological support through the feeling of relationship with the hero—sometimes, in fact, mutual; in any case, fellowship among devotees sharing a mystique of "loyalty."

The supreme consummation of any cult is personal contact with its central value—in this case the hero, who appears to the faithful to validate the ikons (pictures, souvenirs, relics) which represent him symbolically. The thrill of such personification can hardly be much less than that of Pygmalion seeing his statue come to life. Such behavior as celebrity-watching, the touching mania, fan clubs, and the personal appearance arousing ecstasy in followers shows that the role of the hero is, in a sense, psychologically nutritional—people hanker for him, he provides for them a kind of feast—and that his service to the mass is vehicular, in that he allows a lot of people to take an identity voyage all at once—not in a canoe but in an ocean liner, not on a motorcycle but on a bus.

Returning to the central theme of this book, how does emotional hitchhiking contribute to inflation? One way is by the sheer amount of it. Vicarious experience is an enlargement of self—psychological mobility—to include many identities. We can have millions of people hitchhiking on one character, be it a soap opera character, political leader, guerilla fighter, evangelist, or film star. Vicarious experience gives people a free ride, an opportunity for identity voyages into strange territories. For this hitchhiking, media offer a cafeteria-like choice of identities. The combinations and permutations are astronomical.

It may be useful to apply the term inflation to cases where the amount of vicarious experience increases while its quality does not, or declines into a "wasteland" of trivia, gunplay, giveaway games, and the like. This kind of roving into new identifications is a "more" that is not necessarily better. Look at the magazine racks in supermarkets and faces on the TV screen to see what kind of people our celebrities are and what they are doing. They are not group superselves and bear little resemblance to either historic great men or traditional supermen. Yet they are enlarged. Is this not enlargement of the mediocre and less? As distinguished from group superselves, which do supply worthy dreams, celebrities are used today by the masses for individual dream realizations, supplying a type of psychic mobility. Their function is not so much to play the big role, but to supply fulfillments of great significance to "nobodies" who live vicariously in these celebrities (themselves former nobodies) as playboys, great lovers, love queens, sports stars, singers, rock and roll musicians, successful writers, disc jockeys, TV stars, and so on. Thus the celebrity has, one might say, a kind of office to perform, to supply vicarious success to those who cannot make it. In such use of celebrities, the "Mitty" function predominates. This is because the odds against success are very high, so the identity problems modern life accentuates are compensated by heroes. From dreams of realization one wakes to a different, or more limited, reality. When identity problems are prevalent, there is perhaps more of a leaning on what the hero does and less on what a man does himself.

So what is wrong with freedom in modeling? Using Gresham's

analogy, one might say that celebrities and emotional hitchhiking are "cheap money" displacing the gold of great men and real deeds. Media are like printing presses running off celebrities like money. Is it not a melancholy fact that, as with money, oversupply degrades social symbols? Is it not a fact that media and the cult of celebrities enlarge persons with the hype of the flashbulb? And just because media are so open and inviting—one might say voracious for personalities and faces—there is in the public mind a curious sense of entitlement to fame, that it is available to everyone, like a lottery ticket, part of the dream of success. All this encourages the egalitarian ideal, the magical rise of a Cinderella, by a lucky picture on a magazine cover, by sports performance, by a hit recording, by looks alone. Entitlement to fame is encouraged by talent contests, charm schools, modeling jobs, work in the media, the roving eye of television, interviewers in the street, which seem to be looking for someone on whom to bestow fame. You never know when the eye of the camera will rest on you.

So, with all these opportunities and magnifiers working, it is not surprising that the hall of fame gets crowded, with newcomers pushing in through the revolving door before previous occupants have come out, Andy Warhol making his well-known remark that the time is coming when everybody will be famous for fifteen minutes. Does it matter that, with all this hospitality to fame, the message is that almost *any* kind of person can be famous, that it does not matter about merit or talent beyond the ordinary. So celebrities cannot be conceived as an aristocracy. On the contrary, they signify fame achieved by nobodies, coming through the open door of ordinariness— mediocre people magnified by media, in which luck is a large factor.

Such abundance of celebrities can be described in quasi-market terms as an oversupply that inflates fame. We shall later consider how oversupply can be thought to inflate credentials, medals, ovations, smiles, kisses, greeting cards, and religious and other symbols by making them too abundant and too cheap to command value in a market. In our kind of society, which places such emphasis on striving and winning, abundance making symbols cheap may erode the very meaning of success, which, after all, is having something that the other fellow hasn't got. It is no surprise, then, that watching the parade of new faces in the media fading into has-beens, a sense of hollowness pervades the ideal of success. Too much celebrity is as bad as none when it leads to leveling differences between better and worse—a race without losers, and therefore without winners, recalling that line from Gilbert and Sullivan, *The Gondoliers*, "When everyone is somebodee, then no one's anybody!"

All this celebrity worship has an odd look from the Carlylean and Emersonian perspective that the function of great men is to enoble and elevate mankind by their own virtues and real achievements. This cannot be said of modern celebrities—that sorry lot. It seems obvious that those receiving the most adulation and fan mail by the sack are not, as a rule, the most important and meritorious men and women in our country. Persons doing the real work—in business, politics, education, science, technology, religion, social welfare—receive little attention unless they hit the public eye in a very special way which generally has little to do with their practical contribution. Popular interest is in celebrities—mostly in the entertainment and communication fields—who have a talent for capturing audiences, managing publicity, and showmanship tactics. So the white knight of the flashbulb not only steals the show from those who are doing the real work, but displaces from the pedestal traditional great men; George Washington, for example, is not half so interesting as any of a dozen singers, playboys, athletes, movie stars. Even the success story of making good by hard work has lost much of its glamour since success is so often epitomized by celebrities who have made good the easy way by showmanship or entertainment gimmicks, and who present a shoddy image of living it up rather than the comparatively rare one of service and ethics as seen in a figure like Albert Schweitzer. If we take the view of Carlyle that heroes should be great men, then the prospect is depressing. While it is hard to find a historical baseline by which to prove that there has been a deterioration of heroes (did the Puritan of the seventeenth century have higher models, on the whole, than the white-collar worker of today?), it is fairly easy to convince oneself of the mediocrity of current celebrities just by taking a good look at them—any collection, in the newspapers or on television, will do. Indeed, it is not implausible to suppose that if a hundred celebrities were chosen at random from the *Celebrity Register*, or from persons drawing the largest crowds or getting most space in popular magazines or time on television, they would prove no better (by any defensible criterion, whether of real achievement or personal, moral, or intellectual merit) than one hundred persons taken at random off the street. If reliable ways could be found for measuring merit—wisdom, virtue, even plain honesty—it could probably be shown that most celebrities are just what they often admit they are: the boy or girl next door—with a little luck. The "luck" might be no more than the "sound" of a voice, a fortunate film vehicle, a good press agent, or a dimple in the right place.

The character lesson that celebrities do seem to teach is not merit but a kind of roulette philosophy, that magic is in the media, you don't have to be good to be a hero: luck is enough. The celebrity himself is often rather apologetic for this aleatory factor, the first to accept what Walter Winchell called the "roulette" philosophy of success, whose proponents included Perry Como, Frank Sinatra, Bing Crosby, and William Holden who said:

> My success is just luck. I'm the kind of guy, I guess, that any other man can identify himself with. If Holden can do it, the man in the audience thinks, then I can do it too—slug the villain, get the girl, anything.

He is often the first to recognize that "imperfection" is an important part of his popular appeal—because of the filip it gives to the imagination of the average man to say to himself, "If he, who is so ordinary, then why not I?" This is leveling down rather than measuring up. Public relations experts themselves sustain this picture of luck and mediocrity by proclaiming their power to build anybody into a celebrity. A whole profession of "image makers" has grown up; and, if they are half so powerful as they think they are, one wonders what creations will yet come from their pygmy-pygmalion brains. After being built up, or succeeding by sheer luck, we find the celebrity living it up according to popular standards of consumption, again with the help of a public relations agent, who coaches him and disseminates press releases. So the celebrity is seen to be of ordinary stuff; and the knowledge of the buildup and image behind his success do little to encourage the idea that fame is based on merit, or that popular interest is focused on merit that makes "heroes" superior to ordinary men. The voyage of identity offered by celebrities is soon seen to be a train that really does not go anywhere but brings people back to the same place—or, just possibly, leaves them off someplace they had not intended to go, worse off than before.

But the Carlylean perspective on celebrities is bound to be disappointing. It is like trying to weigh shrimps in a scale designed for tuna fish. It may be asked, what right have we to expect the mass heroes of today to measure up to the great man? Most of them are little people like ourselves, whose attempts to find a lifestyle, whose little victories, whose dramatically simulated emotions or interesting "looks" have caught the imagination or warmed the hearts of people, many of whose lives are so much poorer that these seem rich. Once we abandon the Carlylean perspective, the celebrities of today stop being merely disappointing and become interesting as experiments in identity, some pathetic, some brave. Like fads, they are efforts to find an exciting and victorious way of living under modern conditions of bureaucracy, impersonality, and push-button comfort, which work so powerfully to defeat the heroic spirit. If these triumphs are largely compensatory and vicarious rather than real for the mass, amid obstacles to heroism so great, why should we depreciate them in a world which is relatively poor in identity? It is rather like complaining about having to use a candle when there is no electricity.

My conclusion is that, although the power to identify—to emotionally hitchhike with others—is one of the great strengths of a human being, in some circumstances it goes wrong, fails to function and becomes a weakness when inflated by too many unworthy models. Not only does emotional hitchhiking provide unworthy models but it might be said to increase the entropy of social modeling. Random and indiscriminate adulation of ordinary celebrities leads to a variety that is not enriching but lowers standards by losing discrimination of better from worse.

6

Social Market Inflation

So far we have looked at four sources of inflation in which symbols lose value by oversupply. They are: overstatement, crusading, contagious communication, and emotional hitchhiking. There is, however, a fifth form of inflation which stresses market processes of supply and demand as a reason why symbols lose value—more becoming less.

Inflation is here broadly conceived as a loss of value that could occur not only to money but to almost any cultural symbol: a medal, a certificate, an article of clothing, a style, a word, a work of art. Market inflation is perceived when people find they cannot redeem tokens at expected value, that tokens have lost "purchasing power" in terms of prestige or other sought social response, because there are too many of them.

It could happen to stone axes in an Australian aboriginal culture. A case well known to anthropologists (Sharp 1952) tells what happened to social relationships among the Yir Yaront when missionaries introduced steel axes into their stone age economy. The polished stone axe was the most prized material possession of adult men, obtainable (because of scarcity of suitable stone) only by trading relationships at fiesta-like tribal gatherings. It was not just a tool but a status symbol of masculinity and prestige of age, which women and children could not own but only borrow according to rules of kinship asserting the authority of a father or older brother. It was also a totem for some clans and used by men to make secret paraphernalia for religious ceremonies.

When the missionaries arrived, all this changed; for they brought with them a good supply of steel axes, and gave them away at Christmas parties and other mission festivals "indiscriminately" to young men, women, and even children. This greatly increased the number of axes per capita and the cheapness and ease with which they could be obtained. But so many axes in circulation also reduced their value either for trade or asserting male prestige. They became so easy to get that no special status could be claimed by owning one. The men owning stone axes found themselves in the position of people ruined because the currency in which they had banked their savings was devalued.

Such a collapse of value resembles inflation in which money loses some or even all of its value by oversupply. The analogy hinges on the fact that the axes were serving not only as a commodity but a sort of money, in two ways especially: first, they served as a standard with set value in the primitive market, by which wealth and social importance could be compared, measured, and accumulated; and second, while axes could be loaned to a woman or child, *ownership* brought deference, prestige, and credit for ascribed qualities such as age, wisdom, masculinity, and leadership. In this sense, axes might be said to purchase such values for their owners when offered, exchanged, lent, or sold. But they lost such purchasing power when axes became so plentiful that one did not have to pay deference to get one. The chief point of resemblance to inflation is this: increasing supply of a money-like commodity in circulation brought not prosperity but ruin. More became less.

Preconditions of Symbolic Inflation

How does more become less? Such a paradox occurs in two ways familiar to economists. One is diminishing returns from more of the same kind of investment, say declining crop yields from adding more and more fertilizer. The other is falling price when supply outstrips demand in a market.

Monetary inflation is a special case of the latter, where that which loses value by being oversupplied happens to be money.

Now, we hold that monetary inflation is a subset of symbolic inflation, of which there are other sorts, such as will be described in later chapters. If symbols other than money can inflate when their supply increases, it raises the question of what are the minimal preconditions of symbolic inflation? I see three: (1) there must be a market in which values are exchanged; (2) tokens must be used to represent values exchanged; and (3) there must be some sort of pricing, though not necessarily as exact as that of money.

Let us, then, first try to specify what is essential to make a social market.

Social Market

Exchange goes far beyond economic trade. In the broadest sense, life itself involves exchange between an organism and its environment, in ways like breathing, eating, and excreting. Goal-directed behavior is exchange in the sense that work is invested for the sake of reward. Symbiosis, e.g., insects fertilizing flowers, is a sort of exchange between species. Likewise domestication and training of animals. Sociologist George Homans (1958) held that even a pigeon in a laboratory pecking at a target for which a psychologist feeds it corn, is engaged in exchange, paying the "cost" of his input to get the corn; likewise, the psychologist pays for the pigeon's behavior by laboratory work and corn; so a relationship exists between them because each perceives some sort of profit. A relationship stabilizes, at least in the short run, at the point where each is "doing the best he can do himself under the circumstances."

Such a notion of exchange is a little too broad to specify where symbolic inflation begins. Within that circle, let us define a smaller one: *social* exchange occurs when members of the same species voluntarily trade things they both recognize the value of. Depending on a two-way flow (of information, matter, or energy) that both want, such a relationship is reciprocal. It rules out cases like artillery exchange, catching a disease, a smoker polluting air, theft, parasitism, or use of sheer power to control another without reward for compliance.[1] On the other hand, it does not have to be deliberately accepted or bargained for, but could include reciprocity like the flow of blood between Siamese twins. However, whether natural or formally contracted, social exchange is a *quid pro quo* of some sort valued by both parties that holds them together.

Within this circle, let us distinguish a smaller one, those exchanges which arise by some sort of *bargaining* or *negotiation*.[2] These require: the freedom[4] of choosing or shopping among at least two alternatives; some calculation regarding such things as preference, or whether behavior achieves a goal or a relationship is worthwhile; representations by both parties to each other of offers and terms acceptable; and, when the outcome is successful, a new consensus (deal, contract). Bargaining, of course, is restricted to humans; animals exchange but do not bargain (e.g., a predator may "invest" in pursuit, but the prey, for all its maneuvers, does not bargain).

Bargaining need not be explicit and verbal. When a performer tries to get his audience to applaud harder; or changes his act to get bigger hands from succeeding audiences; he is negotiating without saying, "Please applaud me"; and they, by more or less enthusiastic applause, are negotiating with him without words for better performance, or an encore. Even in conversation, much negotiation is non-verbal, as when parties watch each other for signs of interest, change topics, display animation to encourage each other, or decide enough time has been spent and find a courteous excuse for moving on. Blau (1955, pp. 50–51) analyzes implicit bargaining in consultation of law enforcement agents. Asking and giving advice is not just a favor but an exchange of values in which "both participants gain something and both have to pay a price." The questioner pays respect to the superior knowledge of his colleague, at cost of acknowledging inferiority; the giver of advice gains prestige at cost of time and disruption of his own work. However, Blau (1969, p. 315) holds that, unlike economic transactions, in most social exchanges there is no contract and no exact price. The giver of a favor may act on the general expectation that it will be returned, but must leave the exact nature of the return up to the judgment of the receiver, and if not satisfied has no recourse except to stop doing favors.

Bargaining ranges from intimate to international; but, on any scale, and whatever its tactics, requires a certain amount of freedom[4] within which parties maneuver by offer and counter-offer to get closer to what they want.

Maneuvering includes not only negotiation but *shopping* among parties with whom to negotiate. That is, there is freedom not only to negotiate, but to look for another who might offer a better deal. Courtship and seeking advice provide ready examples.

When shopping is added to bargaining, interaction becomes marketlike, i.e., it is possible to think of what "they" (all sellers and buyers) offer and accept, how much supply and demand there is, and so on. Some sociologists do not hesitate to apply fairly sophisticated economic reasoning[5] to social behavior, even when commodities are not exchanged and values are not monetarily priced. It is in *market* as a structure of bargaining and shopping that we find the first precondition of inflation. One rose does not make a summer, nor does one negotiation, however complex and prolonged, make a market. A market is a situation where *many* parties exchange, bargain, and shop competitively. From shopping and bidding against one another, they are able to reach a general consensus as to worth or price; and they can see aggregate supply and demand as distinguished from the wishes of particular parties. Above all, a feedback loop conveys information to all parties regarding such things as outcomes of bargaining, terms, prices, supply, and demand, so that they can plan their participation accordingly. Even a primitive bazaar does this.

A developed market is far more than just an arena of trade; it is a super-channel, a remarkable feedback mechanism telling how trade is going. Paul Samuelson (1970, p. 38) describes it as a "communication device for pooling the knowledge and actions of millions of diverse individuals," solving, without a central intelligence, "one of the most complex problems imaginable, involving thousands of unknown variables and relations," finding an equilibrium between supply and demand by pricing, through a "vast system of trial and error, of successive approximation; and determining what will be produced, how it will be produced, and for whom." Whether merely by gossip or by a centralized tote-board or price-listing, a market gives a reading of many transactions in a diffuse network, telling traders far more than they can see in direct exchange.

In sum, a market is made not just by exchange but by feedback delivering information about their own and others' experiences of exchange, comparative worth, going values (whether or not monetary), supply and demand conditions, and so on, that can be used to reckon one's further input to the system. Such feedback might come from a gossip network, public discussion, observation of an auction, stock ticker tape, computer printout, ballot count, social rating, applause meter, opinion poll—any way of gathering and abstracting information about what is happening in exchange to make a social pricing process.

Do any aspects of social exchange fail by lack of feedback to become public knowledge? Strauss (1978, pp. 224–33) notes that much bargaining is silent and implicit; as when in the hospital people avoid talking about the fact that a patient is dying, or elderly patients reduce expression of pain for the sake of good relations with the staff. Such bargains may never be talked about enough to enter pricing feedback. Likewise, there is doubt if very subtle negotiations at the Freudian unconscious level, or what Eric Berne (1964) calls games, become recognized, unless the psychiatric interview itself supplies the feedback. So also for what ethnomethodologists call indexing: such signification and fine tuning of relationships with little or no public feedback is rarely able to reach the status of an objective, a-greed-upon social price ("account"). The same goes for much body language (as contrasted with the hand signals of traders or race bookies): it is given off and reacted to unwittingly.

On the other hand, even body language can get into public social pricing. For example, an arrested traffic offender's appeasing gestures might persuade a cop to let him off without a ticket. Such feedback could enter the pricing process in terms like public consciousness that "if you are nice to a cop, he'll let you off"—that conciliation is part of the recognized social price of avoiding a traffic ticket.

Tokens

The second precondition of inflation is that tokens be used to represent values exchanged. Then, when the supply of tokens varies in proportion to the supply of values, we can speak of inflation or deflation.

Of course one can have a market without tokens, as in primitive barter or collectors trading stamps. Then there is nothing to inflate. But, wherever a market forms and many values are exchanged, it becomes inconvenient if not downright impossible to hand over values at the moment of a deal; so tokens come into use, if only to help parties say and remember what and how much they have promised. Tokens circulate more easily than the values for which they stand. They can even circulate when nothing is behind them (as in the case of counterfeiting, or when the agency that issued them has gone out of business). They can also be offered when there is nothing for them to buy. This applies not just to money but to the broader range of tokens defined as anything exchanged that signifies and promises something of value. So a smile can betoken friendliness, a wreath mourning or honor, a uniform official function, or applause recognition and approval—each a value to be expected when the token is offered. Expectation is what gives the token a sort of purchasing power: assurance that the value is available and will be delivered if the token is presented properly. By this definition, all sorts of things, tangible or intangible, can become tokens of values tangible or intangible. For example, an automobile (purchased by money) can betoken, besides its cash value, an intangible value such as prestige associated with owning or riding in it. A smile can betoken friendliness or willingness to do a tangible favor. A beard is a token of remarkable significance. Working as does a theatrical prop, it casts a person into a character, whose purchasing power, so to speak, is the response he gets while wearing it (in Aldous Huxley's novel *Antic Hay*, a fake beard vastly helps the hero's amours; he embarks on a career like that of Don Juan). A mask held before the face and passed from actor to actor, as in Greek tragedy and comedy, signifies an entire role. Likewise for Santa's whole outfit—beard, cap, red suit, boots, sleigh, and reindeer—material tokens of intangible values like generosity and good cheer, which can be put on by anybody.

The transferability of tokens shows they are not merely natural expressive signs (such as fidgeting, sighing, hiccuping, frowning, shrugging, staring, raising eyebrows—"kinesic markers," as Birdwhistell (1970, p. 103) calls body movements accompanying speech), which are ordinarily given off as symptoms, one might say, without deliberate control. On the other hand, there is nothing to keep such natural signs from being produced at will by actors and mimes, or, indeed, anyone. Ekman and Friesen (1975) have identified "blueprints" of emotion in facial photographs of people displaying six emotions: anger, disgust, fear, happiness, sadness, surprise, which are reliably identified and can be simulated with practice; among many rapid facial expressions conveying moods, there are "emblems," i.e., "signals the meaning of which is very specific, the nonverbal equivalent of a common word or phrase," for example, a head nod, eye wink, hand wave.[6] Such gestures are no longer merely natural expressions but have become symbols that can be used as tokens. So body language can graduate from natural sign to cultural gesture (symbol), and from that to token when delivered in exchange regularly with a certain value publicly recognized. The smile has evolved all the way from natural expressive sign to token, and the kiss (a conventional sign used only in some cultures) from symbol to token.

Token character is especially marked in standardized expressions that diffuse rapidly, such as fashion "looks," facial emblems, hand gestures (salutes, auction signals, "V" for victory, "soul brother" up-thumbs handshake, and the like); and verbal expressions—sayings, vogue words, clichés, and catchwords—that Sumner (1906) aptly called "coins of thought." Added to this, of course, are physical objects uniformly displayed ("wearing the green," sprig of holly, carnation in buttonhole) or distributed (gifts, trophies, greeting cards, cigars at fatherhood). All such are like money in the sense that they are part of a common stock of tokens that are exchanged, and passed from person to person, whether as objects or imitated patterns, hence, in that sense, circulate like a currency.

All the same, I would not argue that most tokens are as uniform and physically convenient as money. They are not standardized in form and value-base, abstract in summing up different values, quantitative, precisely equivalent, and symmetrical (worth the same to giver and receiver). A Hindu and an American might exchange deference by different tokens. Equivalence can be recognized in non-monetary tokens, for example, Ph.D. to M.D., colonel to navy commander, Cadillac to Lincoln, academic regalia of various universities. On the other hand, Ford is not equivalent to Buick, nor is muskrat to ermine; it is equivalent to seat a bishop beside a general, but not beside a lieutenant. My point is that rough equivalence and difference in social tokens are discriminable enough to allow calculation, bargaining, rating, and measuring deference and indebtedness.

The overriding fact is that many tokens are as highly prized as money, some buy values that money cannot ("pricelessness"), and it would be hard to make sense of social exchange without taking them into account. So, instead of thinking only of money from mints and credit from banks as currency, we should be thinking of a huge store of gestures and objects serving as tokens; and of the entire symbolic output—media, entertainment, art, literature, education, science, universities, research, computers, think-tanks, fashion designers, commodities, and so on—as feeding such a supply of currency.

The scope of possible inflation is large indeed when one recognizes that all of culture is symbolic in some way and therefore presumably capable of acting in a money-like way when presented as a token in a social market situation. Lands, vehicles, education, championships, medals, pronunciation, breeding, battleships, buildings, and tombs are all capable of being presented like money in exchange for values like honor and prestige. All the same, in arguing that many symbols are enough like money to inflate as money does, let us not exaggerate such a similarity to the point of losing sight of the special characteristics of money as an abstract, standard medium of exchange whose purchasing power is established as legal tender (though that does not prevent inflation). On the other hand, emphasizing the special characteristics of money should not go to the opposite extreme of ignoring its rich symbolic meanings, such as (1) the status of millionaire; (2) the prestige of the "big bankroll" displayed by gamblers and such; (3) the numismatic meaning of rare coins to collectors and hobby enthusiasts; (4) the philanthropic meaning of alms, bequests, and donations; (5) the meaning to the miser of his hoard; (6) the sinfulness of usury and greed; (7) wealth as an obstacle to religious salvation; (8) the fate of Midas; (9) venality; or (10) the power and threat of money ("I won't sue you, I will ruin you," said J.P. Morgan). Such meanings embroider the role of money as a standard medium of exchange and may be far more important that its cash value. In such ways, many layers and levels of symbolic inflation are possible.

Social Pricing

The third requirement for inflation is that there be some sort of pricing, though not necessarily as exact or explicit as monetary.

When people see prices of goods on store shelves rising week after week while their income does not, they know well enough that their money is being inflated. But it is not so plain that social values which do not carry price tags are also being inflated. Yet people do (without waiting for a markdown of money price) become aware when status symbols are not worth so much, especially fading fashions. A kind of markdown is the basis of such awareness even when money prices are not visible. Social pricing can occur when people using tokens compare and rate one another in such terms. When tokens are consciously used for social pricing, they are often called status symbols.

Everyone knows that pursuit of status symbols is unremitting in most modern societies, and at least as keen as that of money. Thorstein Veblen (1899) was first to draw economists' attention away from money market transactions to invidious display, of not only tangible but intangible wealth, as in higher learning. He described business as a sort of trophy hunt, and wives' duty to "conspicuously consume" in costume and leisure wealth for which their husbands worked so hard. This fitted Europe and even more aptly, America with its open market of status.[7] Cleveland Amory (1957, 1960) analyzed the rating system of the proper Bostonians maintaining their rank by carefully preserved genealogies and manners; and how the pillars of old "society" gave way when the flashbulb of news and show business created the even more desirable status of "publicity." Vance Packard (1959), summarizing over 150 sociological studies, reported that, contrary to the American Dream, abundance had not wiped away class boundaries, but striving for status symbols was more strenuous than ever.

> With the general diffusion of wealth, there has been a crumbling of visible class lines now that such one-time upper class symbols as limousines, power boats, and mink coats are available to a variety of people. Coincidentally, there has been a scrambling to find new ways to draw lines that will separate the elect from the non-elect.

In the scramble for new ways to draw lines, almost anything that can be displayed can serve as a status symbol if its value is right: a white collar, shined shoes, a certificate, an old school tie, a carpeted office, a label on clothing, a motorcar, a skill, the "look of success," attained in good part by clothes (Malloy 1978). All this would make little sense if objects had no value as tokens, were merely commodities to be consumed. In the latter respect, a Volkswagen might be as useful as a Mercedes-Benz, a stainless steel fork as one of sterling silver. Now merchandisers of everything from bubblegum to bathroom fixtures, skateboards to real estate, assume that shopping is not just for consumption but that goods bought with money are to be displayed in some further "purchase" of intangible values referred to by words like prestige,[8] glamour, esteem, approval, rating, or, in Veblen's phrase, invidious distinction.[9]

But the race for status hinges on some general and reliable notion of what tokens are worth. It is fair to assume that, for the sake of that game, people have an interest in setting and preserving the worth of tokens (rather than blurring it, which would be like erasing the faces of a deck of cards). By *social pricing* I mean any process that rates people or tokens according to their worth—whether asserting equivalence[10] or ranking pejoratively—and makes this generally known by feedback. Social rating might occur in ways such as selecting people to be on committees; or a professor grading students from "A" to "F"; or a personage sorting invitations received into piles of "must attend," "attend if time permits," and "regrets" (the number of invitations being a measure of his social worth, just as his ranking of the invitations is a measure of the worth of those occasions and the people who invited him). Individual ratings are not the whole social price, but are better thought of as bids or "asking prices" that go into a more general conception of the modal, realistic "going" price in social exchange—modal because as similar transactions become known, expectations seen to be "too high" get trimmed down, and those too low are allowed to rise. For example, a person from a small town visiting a big city might "bid" to strangers by saying "hello" with a friendly smile, but find from a number of such experiences that this bid was too high for the few smiles, to say nothing of coldness and rudeness received; so he would trim down his expectations as to what a smile is worth. Indeed, in such a market, a person might conclude a smile is worth nothing; he might even discount it into negative value, as meaning "someone wants to take advantage of me." On the other hand, the smile might be such standard coinage that it is, like a subway token, required for all rides. In short, feedback from exchanges gives rise to a general notion of what a token or person is worth, in comparison with other tokens or persons. This is all I mean by social pricing. (The term rating is taken as synonymous with pricing.)

Such social pricing, though not as exact as monetary, is no less real. It ordinarily functions along with monetary price, as a sort of penumbra. C. Wright Mills (1951) had social price as well as wage for labor in mind when he described the "personality market," where the salesgirl's "smile behind the counter is a commercialized lure" (p.183); where one puts oneself (not just one's skill) on the line, in salesmanship, show business, interviewing, negotiation, diplomacy, media, teaching, and so on. Both monetary and social prices have appropriate indicators. Monetary prices are compiled and stated publicly by devices such as auctions, catalogs, price listings, financial and commodity exchanges, tote boards, computer printouts, and so on. Such quantitative accuracy is not to be expected in social pricing; but parallel devices can be found in such things as tournament rankings and seedings, prizes and trophies, batting averages, expert judgments (as in horse, dog, or beauty shows), popularity contests, applause meters, poll ratings, vote-getting ability, star-billing, theatrical and book reviews, best-seller lists, honorary memberships, listing in *Who's Who*, and the ranking inherent in academic grades and degrees. As I have already suggested, even the number of invitations received is a measure of social worth. All such things enter into social pricing insofar as the community is aware and takes account of them.

The most universal social pricing institution is gossip, compiling news out of hearsay and establishing reputation. Rosnow and Fine (1976) analyze telling of rumors in terms of exchange between teller and hearer of values beyond that of information itself, such as prestige and relief of anxiety. On the scale of the community, as it circulates (Blumenthal 1932, Firth 1956, Evans-Pritchard 1937), it is plain that it earns its keep by social pricing, i.e., rating people and what they do and own.

An especially clear example of how gossip prices people socially is found in Willard Waller's (1937) study of social rating and dating on the campus of a midwestern university. He found students were rating each other according to a scale of social desirability (personality, looks, conversation, behavior on a date, participation in campus activities, status of fraternity or sorority or other club membership, and so on). In competition for dates, top-rated men (Big Men on Campus) sought top-rated girls: a class A girl must date a class A boy or suffer loss of rating, and so on. Ratings were set and revised by discussions, e.g., fraternity and sorority bull sessions after proms, in which dates were compared by frankly expressed opinions. This flow of information continually determined status on campus. It does not take much of a stretch of imagination to see such a competitive dating market as a sort of pricing system. All the essential elements of social pricing are there: competition of bidders and askers, and comparison of worth in bull sessions supplying feedback to establish a generally accepted rating or rank order—a public price list, to which a boy seeking a date might refer much as an investor looks at the board to see how much stock he can afford. A later study (Rubin 1973, p. 68) found university students in dating tending to pair off with others of approximately their own level of "social desirability," such as physical attractiveness and occupational prestige, generalizing that one of the trading rules of the "interpersonal marketplace" is that attractive women and successful men are likely to become paired with one another.

Such pairing helps establish both equivalence and non-equivalence of social worth. It asserts equivalence by the "birds of a feather" principle. It ranks people pejoratively when it becomes a statement of who does *not* associate with whom, *not* sit at the head table, or *not* rate a red carpet or place in a news picture.

Objects used as tokens become graded for equivalence or nonequivalence of social worth, as in determining the expensiveness of a wedding gift on the basis of one's relationship to, and the social status of, the person being married. Social engagements are graded as tokens, for example, that dinner is a closer relationship than lunch, and lunch is closer than a cocktail party (where attention people give one another is diluted by numbers). The way anthropologist Mary Douglas (1979, pp. 142–43, 145) describes "standardization" of possessions and consumption styles is close to what I mean by social pricing: Sabo housewives are ranked in status according to the number of bowls they possess, and bowls in daughters' dowries become a measure of their marriageability. Douglas asks:

> What is the point about this tendency to standardize? It seems likely that it would not arise except where close comparisons of value are required. At the fringes of a market system, where turnover is slower, where knowledge is incomplete, and big profits riskier, discrepancies in standards can pass. But where competition is hottest, standardization emerges. . . . Relative value can be established since everyone in the circle is a connoisseur. (p.145)

Though monetary pricing is more exact, such comparisons—social rating or reputation, equivalence in pairing, pejorative ranking, and standardization of tokens—seem precise enough in equating and differentiating values to be spoken of as social pricing. We need not insist that price be expressed as an exact quantity in a single medium of exchange,[11] but may understand it to be merely a generally understood "going value" of what something will bring if offered, or how much is owed after receiving it, payable in various roughly equivalent ways. The main requirement is that social pricing be accurate enough to help people decide practically about such matters as to whom to give deference, or whether a relationship is, on the whole, worthwhile or fair.

Social worth is not closely related to monetary worth. For example, one could not tell the value of a clergyman by comparing the monetary price expressed by his salary with that of the contractor who repairs the church. One would have to reckon deference, gratitude, and other sentimental values, to guess what the clergyman was worth to his congregation. The important difference remains between the two kinds of pricing: that social pricing does not hold so broadly for the world at large, but is more specific to a particular context and set of raters, whose knowledge and judgment may not be shared by another set of raters. Social pricing is relative to reference groups, especially peers, who share special knowledge and cultural values; also are most keenly competitive, hence making sharper judgments than the general public. An obvious example is the rating of a tennis player by other players, versus public opinion of his performance. The monetary price of either a tennis player or a clergyman is more abstract and universally valid in *its* terms than is the social price, but it is at the same time more superficial (expressed in the saying, "he knows the price of everything and the value of nothing"), leaving out most of the qualitative and attitudinal components of social pricing. So it cannot be said that monetary pricing is equivalent to social pricing, nor better or worse. Both have shortcomings, and both are indispensable.

Exogenous symbols become more money-like than those which are indigenous,[12] because they are abstract, defined, and not rooted in local cultures with, perhaps, unique meanings untranslatable to the world-at-large. Almost every culture—even that of the seclusive Amish—has some exogenous symbols by which to exchange information with the world outside. Pluralistic American society, being a mixture of cultures, has a high proportion of exogenous symbols; so its social tokens easily become money-like a—a currency—without yet being money.

This difference reflects the sociological fact that the feedback of the market of social pricing (in terms like gossip, peer judgment, and community reputation) comes from a different and richer set of networks than those pricing commodities in terms of money. A soccer star like Pele is priced by both markets: on the social side, the worship of his fans over the world; on the monetary side, his salary depending on promotional facilities and the number of paying spectators he can draw. The social market is larger than the monetary: all the players, fans, and habitual audiences watch performances and know the rules and ratings of major players. It is more enthusiastically knowing and feeling than the money market, which might price a ticket without even knowing what the game is about. What is the range of this social market? It is not economic *Gesellshaft* at large, but, within that, might be called the world of soccer. So we choose the term *social world*[13] to designate the network supplying feedback for social—as distinct from monetary—pricing, whether within a small community or everywhere else. Many in the monetary market have no notion of the social pricing (other than monetary demand). People who belong to the same social world focus on the same arenas of action, share the same interests, and talk the same lingo— be it of sports, art, hobbies, business, rackets, or whatever. It is within a social world—not the city as a whole—that certain status symbols become fashionable, that is, high enough in social price to be sought eagerly and command an exaggerated monetary price. The market in which inflation occurs may comprise such a special social world with its own style of life, or the entire worldwide market of information and popular culture.

How Tokens Inflate

If the social market goes beyond money, there seems no reason why inflation must be confined to money. Why cannot it happen to any tokens, the supply of which increases in proportion to the supply of values for which those tokens stand? I would like to try to translate economic thinking about inflation as a loss of purchasing power of money to the rest of the supply of tokens of values that are not for sale. Then we might get a picture of how, in spite of having more tokens, one could get less of what is promised by the tokens—a prosperity that people do not realize is false until they try to cash in.

Let us, then, first look briefly at how economists apply the idea of inflation to money before transferring and adapting it to symbols other than money.

Inflation of Money

Inflation is a familiar fact of modern life. We are all accustomed to finding our money buys less this month than it did last. As economists see it, it is a rise in the general price level that reduces the purchasing power of money. Such erosion of purchasing power, whether creeping or galloping, is involuntary, as distinguished from *devaluation* (a government reducing the amount of gold backing its currency), and *debasement* (using cheaper metals such as nickel and copper in coinage), which are deliberate. So inflation is hard to blame on particular parties.

The main reason no one is ready to take blame for inflation is not only that it is not a result of any person's choice; but, like pricing, it is due to a *systemic* relation of supply and demand, laws of which, first glimpsed by Adam Smith, now appear in economists' statements about price equilibrium, elasticity of supply and demand, diminishing marginal utility, Gresham's Law, and so on. Such properties are systemic because they are not a simple summation of intentions of individuals; and they are social because they go beyond strictly economic to other sectors of life and culture. Indeed, rather than calling them economic ideas, it might be better to say that some are general truths about social systems that appeared first in economics.[14] With this assumption, I extend the idea of inflation as something that could happen to tokens in any social market. But, first, the case of money.

Economists see demand inflation as an erosion of purchasing power from too many dollars chasing too few goods (otherwise put as spending outrunning production, or the supply of money growing faster than the supply of things money can buy). Such loss of purchasing power can come from declining productivity while people spend just as much; or from an increase in the money supply in proportion to the supply of goods, which, increasing demand for goods, drives up prices (hence down purchasing power). A standard formula[15] expresses the relation of prices to the money supply:

$$P = \frac{MV}{T}$$

where P = prices (average), M = amount of money supply, V =

velocity of circulation, and T = number of transactions. The rise in prices can come from many things that enable people to want and buy more, such as easier credit, lowered interest rates, demand stimulated by advertising or education, slower rate of saving, or printing more money (including bank paper and even counterfeiting). Monetarists such as Milton Friedman and Frederick Hayek consider governments the chief cause of inflation, through deficit spending and printing of money. Huge purchases, as in war expenditures or American oil imports, throw so much money on the market that they lower its ability to buy either goods or foreign money, according to familiar laws of supply and demand. (Another sort of inflation is called cost-push inflation, because it comes from elements of supply, such as rising wages and costs of raw materials, that go into prices of goods on the market.) Whatever the causes of inflation, they are interwoven and looped systemically. Economists recognize that inflationary spirals come from positive feedbacks of elements of money supply and costs into one another; for example, labor demands—higher wages—higher demand for goods and higher costs of goods—higher prices—labor demands; or higher prices—higher costs of government—printing more money—higher prices. Economists also recognize rising expectations, many coming from non-economic sources, are a powerful factor in inflation, as in the case of raising prices or purchases or wage demands in anticipation of inflation, which then aggravates it.

An excellent example of how increasing money velocity and supply produce demand inflation is the way speculation in real estate drives up home costs. A study by the California Public Interest Research Group (Polis 1980) found that housing costs in San Diego rose 23 percent (roughly twice the general inflation rate) during 1978–79. This was attributed to the fact that one sale in five involved speculators not interested in the goods *per se* but "out to make a fast, easy buck." Telltale signs of speculation were: multiple transactions involving the same property (averaging about one a year), low purchase and high resale price (33 to 112 percent profits), and lack of improvements. Such speculation adding to money supply and velocity pushed up not only prices of property, but also taxes (through appraisals), interest rates, points, and rents, making home-seekers' dollars able to buy less.

Two other ideas from economics will help much in extending inflation of money to that of tokens in the social market. One is *elasticity*, i.e., the amount of variation of supply or demand in response to changes in price. Elasticity of supply can make goods quickly more plentiful, hence keep prices lower. But elasticity of money supply can mean more inflation as more dollars printed, easier credit, or lower interest rates or taxes, allow more dollars to chase the same amount of goods. We shall extend this idea of elasticity to increasing the supply of social tokens.

The second idea from economics having something to do with inflation not only of money but, as I hope to show, social tokens is known as Gresham's Law.[16] According to this law, if two kinds of money in circulation have the same denominational value but different intrinsic values, the money with higher intrinsic value (called good) will be hoarded and eventually driven out of circulation by the money with lesser intrinsic value (called bad). So, for example, when in 1980 the price of silver went up, silver coins were hoarded, became collectors' items, and virtually vanished from circulation. No longer had a paper dollar the purchasing power to buy a silver one, as it had in 1960. In Gresham's terms, the bad money (paper) had driven out the good (silver). At the same time, the supply of paper was increasing. So one could say that a double inflation had occurred, of poorer quality compounded with larger quantity. Another Gresham's effect in paper money is merely the fact that people tend to pass on soiled or torn bills and keep fresh ones. This, without hoarding, speeds circulation of poor dollars until withdrawn. On the other hand, if a paper bill were given as a gift, say, to a child, it would undoubtedly be new. Such differences of social value may be immeasurable monetarily, but are no less real and appreciable.

That Gresham's effect applies to things happening outside the realm of money is suggested by the fact that it has caught the fancy of writers on such topics as degradation of language, or popular music, where shoddy and vulgar values seem to prevail because public taste is indiscriminate or even prefers them. As we shall see, the analogy is imperfect because in such cultural degradations demand is for the *poorer* rather than the better—the opposite of the case with money in Gresham's Law. All the same, the term is useful for conceptualizing something that happens to tokens in a market system. I shall use the term Gresham's effect for any case where a social market is flooded with inferior tokens replacing better ones—any degra-

dation in quality, as distinguished from quantity, of circulating tokens, for whatever reason (e.g., whether due to sharp perception by
the public of poor quality of tokens, or poor public discrimination in
accepting poor tokens). Such an idea helps us to distinguish degradation of quality of tokens that might go along with increased supply,
making inflation even worse. So, one might say, Gresham's effect
turns the screw on inflation.

Inflation of social tokens

Extending these ideas to the social market, it seems reasonable
that, if too many dollars chasing too few goods lessens the purchasing power of the dollar, then too many tokens chasing too few values
can lessen the value of any sort of symbols playing an important part
as tokens in social life.

Let us here try to state a few hypotheses about factors favoring social market inflation.

1. The most obvious factor is that of supply. Inflation occurs when
the supply of tokens in a social market outstrips the supply of values
for which tokens stand. There are two sorts of supply to be concerned
with, first, increase in supply of tokens, second, decrease in values
tokens can get in exchange. In either case, tokens fall short in exchange value or "purchasing." This is a simple demand concept of inflation. To avoid inflation, there must be a balance between the supply of tokens and that of values, not a disproportionate change in
either. According to this conception, elasticity of supply of tokens
favors inflation, and inelasticity of supply of values supposedly obtainable by those tokens also favors inflation. To take a case to be
dealt with shortly, if an army wished to give out more medals as an
incentive to heroism, and the material from which medals were made
were cheap, it would be easy to greatly increase the supply of tokens.
But since heroism is a rare thing, and calls for extraordinary courage,
the supply of *that* value is inelastic, so increasing the number of medals given out will not "purchase" more heroism but only cheapen the
medals, i.e., that is, inflate them.

As it happens, the supply of many important values—love, courage, intelligence, altruism, honesty—is inelastic, much in demand
but not easy to increase even when high rewards are offered for
them. Equality, for example, is much sought and talked about; but

most social systems deny it in one way or another, the fact being that status is constricted at the higher levels, and the distribution of status little matches the distribution of abilities as described by the normal curve. That is, the supply of equality is inelastic regardless of how many tokens there are for it.

2. Another general hypothesis is that loss of value of symbols (tokens) by inflation occurs mostly in their display value (a type of exchange value) rather than in their use value. We consider display value (called by Veblen conspicuous consumption and invidious distinction) to be a success a symbol has in impressing somebody or getting social credit, as might be achieved by a diploma, a credential, a medal, a badge, or a stylish hat. When a symbol is unable to evoke the desired reciprocal response from people (e.g., failure to return a military salute) it may be said to have lost its display value. "Social price" is the generally recognized display value of a symbol—what one realistically expects to get from others in exchange for displaying it. Money per se has little display value of its own, despite its purchasing power in economic goods, because it is abstract and not attention-getting other than by what it purchases. But in cultures where a "big bankroll" is "flashed," or women wear coins as ornaments, it does have display value. In any case, our hypothesis is that increasing the number of times a symbol is displayed in exchange tends at some point to reduce its display value. For example, as more graduates hang diplomas on the wall, people are less impressed by them.

3. Our third hypothesis is that mass affluence, by abundance of cheap consumer goods, favors inflation as loss of display value of those consumer goods. Will Rogers said that Henry Ford fixed it so the poor could go as fast as the rich. But as fast cars got cheaper, more and more drivers could go as fast as the law permitted, so it was harder to gain distinction by the speed of one's vehicle. A similar leveling could be expected in power boats and personal aircraft. In the same way, one could expect that too many synthetic diamonds, emeralds, and pearls, displayed by virtually everyone, would become glitz. And likewise for coats made of captive mink. As consumer goods become cheaper and more abundant, they lose scarcity—an important component of display value. So abundance of consumer goods makes it easier for the common man to attain the ostentation that was once the preserve of upper classes.

4. Advertising and puffery contribute to inflation of tokens. They do so by overstatement, and by stimulating "keeping up with the Joneses" rivalry and rising expectations, encouraging more and more people to present the same symbols for display value that may not be forthcoming.

5. It seems reasonable to hypothesize that rising expectations—a feature of most of the modern and modernizing world—favor inflation of social symbols, though the exact process needs further study. At least it can be argued that rising expectations, engendered by abundance of consumer goods and advertising, create an optimism about what one is entitled to—a false prosperity—that multiplies claims which cannot be fully met at the "cash window" of experience, disappointment of which widens the want/get gap (Lerner 1959), frustration from which is so potent in civil disorder the world over.

6. Inflation of symbols is favored by masslike conditions, as sociologists understand this term. A society is masslike when a large number of people from varying walks of life, who do not know one another well, are crowded together in an urban setting (some 40 percent in shantytowns), to make an aggregate that is without community in the sense of a village or tribe or extended family—just a lot of people with fluid and fragile relationships, living mostly for themselves and not wanting to get involved—but often involved in aggregates like street crowds and traffic jams, without choosing to be, and without feeling anything in common—essentially strangers (as described by George Simmel) in spite of physical closeness. This is a paradox of the mass, that, however crowded physically people may be, they are not close in relationship and there is little sense of reciprocal obligation. If there is likeness (as in fashion imitation), it is without social bonds. In that sense people are free, mobile, and rootless. For this reason, the mass is said to be atomized.

This leads to the first consequence of masslikeness for inflation of symbols. When people are strangers, they must bargain and calculate to get what they want from others, since they cannot count on strangers who feel no sentiment or obligation to help (as explained by Ferdinand Tönnies describing *Gesellschaft*). It follows that the more masslike human relations are, the more market-like—the more based on *quid pro quo*. And the more based on impressing others, by sales talks, cajolery, hype—lies if need be. Thus, a social market forms, in which politics, even human relations, become like marketing tactics. In the social market innumerable tokens—offers to buy and sell, sales talks, advertisements, credentials, fashions, greeting cards, gifts, promises, emblems, trophies, membership cards, labels, trademarks, patents, contracts, rhetorics, ideologies, slogans—must be displayed and negotiated to mediate relationships. In this negotiation, fashions, "looks," and "images" become ever more important.

But awareness of hype, puffery, and other bargaining tactics causes competition to get better and more sophisticated devices to beguile and dazzle the public. And not long after that there grows up a certain cynicism in discounting tokens. Here is where a loss of value of tokens seems inevitable, as people begin to discount what is recognized as hype. Perhaps this is better called a vicious circle, as ever more sophisticated devices are used on ever more resistant audiences.

In such ways, the bargaining, calculating, and maneuvering of strangers in a masslike market increases the elastic supply of symbols and contributes to loss of value of those symbols.

A second way in which mass living contributes to inflation is by vicarious experience—emotional hitchhiking—already treated in chapter 5. By identifying with the careers of others, such as stars, celebrities, soap operas, and Rambo-exploits, huge numbers of people are living in borrowed lives, bubbles of fantasy that have little connection with their real lives. Massness, as we said, generates emotional and meaning deficits that are compensated by such bubbles. But the compensations do not really solve problems nor do they last long (how long does elation from winning a World Series last?), though it may readily be granted that certain television series of soap operas, such as "Upstairs Downstairs," seem to have immortality, which argues for the durability of the emotional deficits served.

Yet a third way in which masslikeness favors inflation of symbols is that it generates loneliness and anxiety, which increase suggestibility and thus make people vulnerable to emotional contagions (as described in chapter 4). Part of the paradox of the atomized mass is that in spite of living for themselves—indeed, because of being isolated—people are prey to anxiety and loneliness, which make them more vulnerable to contagions. Lacking roots and moorings of community and tradition, people are more easily swept off their feet by hysterias, panics, crazes, slogans, hype, catchwords, propaganda, speculative bubbles, demagogic appeals, charismatic heroes, cults, and the like. So anxiety of massness makes people more herdlike.

So we find in the masslike social market three hypotheses, that inflation increases by increase of symbols appealing to strangers, compensation for emotional deficits of the mass, and anxiety increasing suggestibility. Because of these three factors, tokens tend to outstrip values. There can be an actual deficit even where symbols are most abundant. When tokens outstrip values to which they refer, tokens lose "purchasing power," because not enough values are forthcoming from exchange in the social system to honor all tokens. The average value of tokens must fall, which people feel as disappointment. It may come to the point where there is so much symbolic froth that the world itself seems full of hype and glitz.

7. A seventh hypothesis concerns a Gresham's effect in popular culture—that of kitsch. It was first stated by Dwight MacDonald (1957, p. 61), who put it this way:

> Good art competes with *kitsch.* . . . . There seems to be a Gresham's Law in cultural as well as monetary circulation: bad stuff drives out the good, since it is more easily understood and enjoyed.

Displacing authentic culture and fine art, kitsch is a sort of cultural crabgrass which spreads over the world because it is cheap and gaudy enough to sell easily to people with poor taste. It circulates easily because it is not deeply rooted but adopted and discarded as are fads, and commercialized and imposed from above by technicians hired by businessmen (McDonald 1957, p. 60). Seeing the homogeneous character of mass culture in widely different parts of the world, one becomes aware that the world's popular culture is becoming a soup with the same noodles floating in it.

What, then, is inflationary about popular culture—especially kitsch? One factor is sheer quantity, a huge supply of identical products that can glut any market, just as any commodities become cheapened by oversupply in a market, according to the familiar principle of equilibrium price set by supply and demand.

Beyond that market effect, there is an inherent "badness" in kitsch, which critics have variously tried to define. Of what does this "badness" consist? They agree on phoniness. Schrank (1977, p. 18) calls it "phony art—masquerade, packaged pseudo-culture."

> Something is kitsch if it is made to appear cultured or artistic or profound or something it is not when in reality it is intended to appeal to mass tastes and the mass market.

Dorfles (1969, p. 221) says:

> Kitsch is essentially the falsification of sentiments and the substitution of spurious sentiments for real ones.

A case of the falsity of kitsch (Dorfles 1969, p. 135) is Forest Lawn Cemetery, where death is a "great ally of kitsch . . . . a candied affair, swamped in sentiment and pathos."

There is also a tendency toward degradation in kitsch. Copies of great art, Dorfles (1969, p. 32) holds, "only apparently encourage culture and taste: what they really do is put the authentic masterpiece on the same level as the mediocre or even obscene copy. It is reasonable that, if a symbol is both false and degraded, people, finding themselves fooled, might hurry to pass it on to others, so giving it a more widespread circulation, while prized objects are withheld."

8. Our last hypothesis concerns the effect of egalitarianism on inflation of symbols. It was the Dodo, in *Alice in Wonderland*, judging the caucus race, who enunciated the spirit of egalitarianism: "Everybody has won, and all must have prizes." In market terms, the question can be put, does egalitarianism increase the supply of symbols in relation to the demand for such symbols, and thereby cheapen them? It seems apparent on the face of it that an ideology stressing equality of men will favor as many as possible having (at least access to) the same number and kinds of valuable symbols. This is to be expected especially where supply of symbols is elastic, that is, the social market is quick to supply whatever is wanted (as in the case of credentials and diplomas, generously issued and even counterfeited, to be considered in the next chapter). There are also cases such as military medals, where the supply is inelastic—restricted even though the ideology is egalitarian, because profligate issue of such medals would destroy their value for honorific distinction (also to be considered in the following chapter).

Here we summarize eight hypotheses about how oversupply inflates symbols in a social market:

1. Inflation of social tokens occurs wherever tokens outstrip values, i.e., the supply of tokens is more elastic than that of the values.
2. Inflation of social tokens especially involves display-value rather than use-value.
3. Abundance of cheap consumer goods favors inflation of social tokens.
4. Advertising favors symbolic inflation.
5. Rising expectations favor symbolic inflation.
6. Inflation of social tokens is favored by four conditions of mass society:
   a. mass-mindedness and imitation,
   b. appeal to strangers,
   c. compensation for emotional deficits of mass society,
   d. anxiety increasing suggestibility and vulnerability to contagions
7. Popular culture is inflationary because it homogenizes the world with a sort of Gresham's effect.
8. Egalitarianism favors symbolic inflation.

I shall draw on these hypotheses as they prove applicable to cases following. Let me hasten to add that the purpose is not to test the hypotheses (which would require more data than I have) but to illustrate and explore them—to see what inflation could consist of in contexts that are not monetary.

Notes

1. Some exchange theorists include coercion and intimidation as part of social exchange; e.g., Boulding (1970, p. 9, 21) sees threat as a basic part of society's "ratio of exchange." William Gamson (1968), pp. 83–91) treats power as an exchange relationship in which benefits are obtained at "cost of influence," mainly "resources committed to an influence transaction."
2. Anselm Strauss (1978, p. 1) defines negotiation as: "to deal or bargain with another . . . to confer with another so as to arrive at the settlement of some matter." He includes the following as synonyms of negotiation: bargaining, wheeling and dealing, compromising, making deals, reaching agreements after disagreement, making arrangements, getting tacit understandings, mediating, power brokering, trading off, exchanging, and engaging in collusion. However, agreement is distinguished from negotiation in that the latter always implies some tension between parties, "else they would not be negotiating" (1978, p. 11).
4. Heath (1976, p. 115 ff.) goes extensively into the importance of bargaining freedom to market. Rules and norms may preclude bargaining in social exchange. A notable example is Kula-trading among the Trobrianders (Malinowsky, 1922, pp. 82–83). It is so governed by tradition that parties have little choice as to terms or with whom they trade; indeed, Kula is not so much bargaining for the highest bid as a partnership between two men in "a permanent and lifelong affair." Likewise for traditional exchange of gifts at Christmas in our own society.
   Bargaining is inhibited by obligations of *Gemeinschaft* (community). Ferdinand Tönnies (1887) first described *Gesellschaft* (society) relations with strangers in

which one is free from obligations of Gemeinschaft. Exchange is calculative; each must offer the other something to induce him to give what he would not otherwise out of obligation or sheer sentiment (natural will, as Tönnies called it).

5. Blau (1969), for example, treats such topics as supply and demand, marginal utility, and indifference curves.

6. The meaning of twenty emblematic gestures for a randomly chosen sample of European subjects has been empirically studied by Morris et al. (1979).

7. Veblen first analyzed conspicuous consumption as an economic phenomenon, but he did not theorize about a loss of value from the very abundance and inflation of those symbols. Great ironist though he was, he did not see that irony of affluence.

8. William Goode (1979) has analyzed the "market of prestige" and its social functions.

9. However, we need not suppose that status symbols are used only for vertical distinctions; they also distinguish roles among people of equal rank, such as boy-girl, soldier-sailor, monk-nun, team A-team B, specialist X -specialist Y. More generally, sociologists hold that what a status token obtains from another is an appropriate role.

10. Tönnies' (1940, p. 74) description of exchange in *Gesellschaft* included equivalence of social pricing: "nobody wants to grant and produce anything for another individual, no one will be inclined to give ungrudgingly to another individual, if it be not in exchange for a gift or labor equivalent that he feels at least equal to what he has given." I would say that any rating of equivalence also implies that what is *not* equal is of more or less value.

11. Sociologists are not agreed whether it is possible to have pricing less exact than monetary. Blau (1964, pp. 94–5), for example, doubts it: "In contrast to economic commodities, the benefits involved in social exchange do not have an exact price in terms of a single quantitative medium of exchange, which is another reason why social obligations are unspecific. . . . The actors themselves cannot precisely specify the worth of approval or of help in the absence of a money price." Yet Blau admits that "in the long run" a balance of some sort occurs as participants realize the rough equivalent of what each has received from the other. He also admits (pp. 104–5) that "The entire exchange transaction in a group determines a prevailing rate of exchange, and this group standard puts pressure on any partnership whose transactions deviate from it to come into line." Varying values put on the same exchange come not from lack of a recognized standard but seeking approval of different significant others, varying reference groups (p. 105).

Another exchange theorist, William J. Goode (1973, pp. 108–10) sees the possibility of social pricing, however different people and their viewpoints may be, in the following terms: every relationship has a standard of performancce reached in a role-bargain, which sets a "going price" on what individuals do and expect to get out of a relationship. This price is set by the interaction between three supply-demand factors, which can cause a party to "pay high" or perform perfunctorily, depending on how strong are: (1) norm commitment, desire to carry out the performance; (2) how much the role partner will punish or reward; and (3) approval of reference groups and social networks.

12. "Indigenous signals are familiar, high in redundancy, local in reference, communicated from people one knows; so they are immediately understood without definition and trusted; whereas exogenous signals (strange in origin, referring to

things with which one has had little direct experience, coming from people one does not know) require continual definition, calculation, and testing if one is to know what to make of them, so they carry a greater decoding burden while contributing less to any particular identity" (Klapp 1978, pp. 21–2). Marketing, then, is one way of testing and decoding exogenous symbols in terms of what they bring.

Collins (1979, pp. 60–2) has made a similar distinction between "indigenous" and "formal" production of culture. "Formally produced culture operates more nearly as a monetary currency," because it is "widely negotiable" as a "medium of exchange" among status groups competing for such currency in order to "improve or consolidate their position" (p.64).

13. The concept of social world is more specific in locating social market than the view that all of social life is a sort of marketplace (Kapferer 1977), or a view like that of Deutsch (1961) treating the city as a marketplace of communication, in which signals directed at strangers become strident and sometimes overload people with noise—accepted as part of the bargain for the sake of the economic and cultural advantages of living in a city. To be living in a social world perceived selectively cuts down considerably the load of negotiations of any shopper in the market of the city. The concept of social world stems from the social interactionistic theory of sociology, which holds that reality is subjectively defined by interactors (G. Mead 1934, H. Blumer 1969). (A compatible view among psychologists is that all perception is selective.) The view of the city as a congeries of social worlds was implicitly stated by H. Zorbaugh (1929), a student of Robert E. Park. It was explicitly stated by T. Shibutani (1962), who emphasized that in the city social worlds interpenetrate but do not blend; e.g., persons living next door might be in quite different social worlds. For theorists of communication, an equivalent, and perhaps more precise, term for social world is "epistemic community."

14. All sociologists are not comfortable with extending economic ideas to other sectors of social systems. Blau (1964, 1967) boldly borrowed refined concepts from economics, such as diminishing marginal utility (for example, the more advice or praise received the less will be valued another unit of it), indifference curves (showing various quantities of two commodities that a consumer values equally), and elasticity of supply and demand. Others (Skidmore 1975, Heath 1976) criticize such extension on the ground that actual social exchange does not come close enough to ideal conditions of an economic market to allow precise mathematical statement and prediction, with which economists have difficulty even in money markets. But does it, then, follow that no transfer of economic ideas to social behavior is allowable? In my judgment, lack of mathematical statement does not rule out the working in a crude and less predictable way of factors like supply, demand, and social price, even though rarely exactly reckoned. In the case of inflation, I see no reason why the supply of tokens, and velocity of their circulation, should not fluctuate in proportion to values in a way that could be experienced as a sort of inflation when tokens obtain less in exchange. I take, then, economic as a synechdoche for social market; and generalize that money is parallel to tokens, monetary to social pricing, in terms like prestige, and monetary to symbolic inflation.

15. According to conventional monetary theory, growth in the supply of money versus real wealth causes inflation. Inflation arises to the extent that spending outruns production, or to the extent that the supply of money grows faster than the

supply of things that money can buy. If money grows faster than production (say 8 percent versus 3 percent respectively), the difference (5 percent) is the rate of inflation. Money growth raises demand, which raises prices, which in turn lessens what money can buy. This relationship of money supply to inflation is expressed by a formula known as the Fisher equation (from the American economist Irving Fisher):

$$P = \frac{MV}{T}$$ (where P is the price level, M is the supply of currency and credit, V is the velocity of circulation, and T is the number of transactions). Banks using this formula distinguish between M_1, basic money supply (commercial bank demand deposits plus cash and checks in circulation); and M_2, a larger aggregate including savings deposits as well a M_1.

In 1989 the Federal Reserve Bank used as a measure of long-run inflation a formula developed by economists Richard D. Porter, Jeffrey J. Hallman, and David H. Small:

$$P = \frac{M2 \times V}{Q}$$

In this formula, P is the general level of future prices, M_2 is a measure of money in the economy, V is the rate at which money is the economy changes hands, and Q is an estimate of GNP growth (Kilborn 1989).

16. Expounded by Sir Thomas Gresham (1519–1579) English financier.

7

Inflation of Tokens of Approval

Credentials

Credentials may be a good place to start in seeing how the social market can inflate tokens. Although they cannot be passed on and do not circulate, credentials resemble money in being certificates which bestow a specified amount of exchange value on the person who displays them—social credit for authority, education, skill or other merit that can be used to get jobs, assure competence, or entitle a person to a certain position. Their exchange value consists of what they are worth in social credit when displayed. Is a Ph.D. worth more than an Ed.D.? A karate black belt than a brown belt? It depends partly on face value of the certificate, and partly on how people actually respond.

How, then, can credentials lose their value in a way that resembles monetary inflation?

We expect here that the main answer will be that, like money, credentials can suffer oversupply, a glut that destroys their value because they are so easy to get that they no longer guarantee that the holder has the full competence or merit or expertise or right claimed. Thus they lose their "purchasing power" in terms of respect and other social credit from clients, employers, colleagues, or the public at large. When too many of such pieces of paper are circulating that do not deliver the social value claimed, the average value of the token declines. The decline can even go from zero to negative, when a certificate's loss of credit actually impedes the transaction in which it is offered—as happened to the MBA (Master of Business Administration degree) during the 1980s in America. It is literally true that a student of a business school wrote on his job application, "I have an MBA, but don't hold that against me." He was expressing the fact that his credential had become inflated to the point of having zero or even negative display value, and not giving as much prestige, respect, deference, status, as formerly when MBAs were fewer, calling to mind those happy days when the high school diploma had a display value comparable perhaps to that of a Bachelor of Arts now.

Can we have too many credentials? This seems possible in the United States, which Collins (1979) described as the most credentialized society in the world. He foresaw the possibility of inflation of educational credentials to a point where one might have to have four years of college for a labor job (p. 197). It does not seem altogether fanciful that a time might come when credential inflation could affect every certificate from a Ph.D. to a dog pedigree.

Whatever the token—diploma, license, hero's medal, or champion's cup—we expect it to inflate when increasing supply of that token is followed by a loss of its display value, i.e., "purchasing power" in getting prestige, honor, legitimacy, employment, from other people—"too many tokens chasing too few goods."

Why should there be an increasing supply—and consequent inflation—of credentials and diplomas? Perhaps the most obvious reason is increasing size and massification of population. As people move from rural, traditional, and communal societies into urban life, they need to certify themselves to people they do not know except for that all-important piece of paper. When people do not know others well, it is easy to make claims—even IDs, passports and green cards—that cannot be readily verified. How many "Doctors of Divinity" are there preaching and collecting money today, from schools no one has heard of and are not listed among accredited colleges and universities? A mass society needs credentials, inadequate though they may be as guarantees of identity, just to find out who people are and what they can do. The mass society hypothesis also favors the view that people who are uncertain of identity and thwarted in careers (where acceptable positions are fewer than applicants) will spend more money on certificates to tell the world what they can do—to compensate for identity problems of the mass society.

A second reason that credentials are inflated is that it is so easy to increase their supply—inherently more elastic than that of values referred to by the tokens. A piece of paper saying one is educated is simply easier to create than an education. One could decide, "Tomorrow we shall have twice as many certificates," but it would not be so easy to double the jobs and amount of education available. Sheer profitability with low costs adds pressure to increase the supply of certificates. It is hard to beat the profitability of selling an attractively engraved piece of paper. During the 1970s and 1980s, degree-granting institutions sprang up like toadstools. One could buy a D.D. degree for $20 no questions asked. Such fabricated certificates were like "printing press money," costing the issuer no more than printing and paper. Asked the director of one university, "Do you know any other business where you can sell three or four pieces of paper for $5,000?" ("Sixty Minutes", 27 August 1978). Degree mills flourished in the United States and Europe, offering the Ph.D., Doctor of Divinity, law degrees, MBA, and other degrees, with advertisements like this:

> DOCTORATES. Fully-accredited doctorates with less than a month on campus. Good, respectable Ph.D.s entirely by correspondence and home study. Doctorates from lesser known but wholly legal Bible schools, virtually by return mail.

To control such inflation, we have no regulation of the supply of certificates comparable with that of the Federal Reserve and Secret Service over money. Short of counterfeiting and fraud, a group can issue just about any credential it wishes to whomever it wishes without running afoul of the law (outside of specific areas such as truth in advertising, pure food and drug regulation, medical licensing, and perhaps academic accreditation).

A third reason for credential inflation is slipping academic standards and downgrading requirements, which make degrees easier to get but worth less when one gets them. The thesis for the Ph.D. and Ed.D. was one of the requirements often downgraded; adding to the flood of credentials, many graduate schools conferred doctorates without completion of a thesis. Some schools upgraded the title of a degree, as did Harvard Law School offering for a small fee and no further training to exchange its Bachelor of Laws degree for a Jurum Doctor (Berkley 1976).

Part of the slippage of academic standards in the last few decades was due to "cafeteria" curricula allowing great freedom in electives to satisfy requirements for degrees, including an increasing number of "Mickey Mouse" courses (cosmetology, theory of basketball, etc.). Helping relax standards was the fact that teachers' promotions rest in good part on student evaluations, which create a pressure for easier courses and entertainment for the sake of popularity—as one college professor said, "We used to hear a lot about the 'publish or perish' syndrome. Now it's please or perish" (Goldman 1979). Another factor lowering educational standards was physical education programs admitting athletes who did not come up to entrance requirements—some even illiterate; and nursing them through easy courses for the sake of their performance on the playing field—highly profitable to the university. For such reasons, apart from sheer oversupply, a B.A. degree may come to mean less and less.

Yet another slippage in academic standards was a drift upward of median grades due to easier grading (which often established B as the median for upper-division and even A for graduate classes and even abolished the D and F grades)—an inflation that has been going on for decades in even the best schools. At Harvard, for instance, 82 percent of the class of 1974 graduated *cum laude* or better, while at Vassar for that year 81 percent of all grades were A's and B's. (It was embarrassing that the rise of grades in high schools and universities coincided with declining average scores on the Scholastic Aptitude Test (SAT) for over ten years.) At one university, the graduate committee in a department of sociology reported the following grade distribution of graduate courses: "half our grades are A's; almost 100 percent of our grades are A's or B's and it seems almost impossible for a graduate student to get a grade below 70 percent; there are several classes where the number of A's is more than the number of B's."

In such a situation, professors who wished to "hold the line" often succumbed to pressures, both from students and administrations. One, for example, reported that the higher the grades he gave out, the higher his evaluations by students: when he failed 40 percent, he was rated "average"; then he failed only 20 percent to see what would happen, and was rated "above average"; finally he failed only 5 students, and his evaluation became "excellent." Another professor wanted to fail six out of forty-eight, but the dean told him it would be hard to attract students to the university if he did so; taking the hint, with its implications for his tenure, he changed his F's to D's.

But such rampant grade inflation slowed somewhat in the 1980s. In 1985 a survey of 1,600 colleges and universities by James Quann, Registrar of Washington State University, Pullman, sponsored by the American Association of Collegiate Registrars and Admissions Officers, found that the pendulum was swinging back from the grade inflation of the 1970s toward more traditional grading standards, discarding the more lenient grading systems. A department of sociology, finding that its average grade for all undergraduate students was B, was reported to be cautiously trying to make C the average grade again. The chairman explained: "It's unfair to start grading too severely because other schools aren't trying to do the same thing, and everybody's trying to get into graduate school. We can't reverse a national trend overnight." As a result of such efforts, some lowering of average grades was perceptible; but officials were cautious, one committing himself so far as to say, "I think we've stabilized the situation somewhat. But we haven't gone back to the levels of the '60s." From such modest efforts, it appears that grade inflation had better be regarded as a continuing battle than as a trend that can be reversed so long as demand for credentials is so high.

The inflationary pressure on educational credentials was not all in the schools. Much came from popular demand in society at large—what might be called the fad factor, of "keeping up with the Joneses." People claimed degrees who had not been within miles of a university. It became fashionable to pretend to be attending, or to have attended, various universities. Thousands wore T-shirts of Harvard, Yale, the Sorbonne, outnumbering those who had actually attended such schools. Banners, bumper stickers, and decals aided the spurious claims. Judging by the number of claims, the educational level had never been so high.

Even the highest professional and academic degrees were not immune to credential faddism. By the seventies, to meet the popular demand, a "doctor fad"—a rage for doctorates—was noted to be sweeping law and professional schools that did not usually or previously offer doctor's degrees. An oversupply of degrees—especially Ph.D.s—became noticeable. During 1975-79 there were 125,000 new Ph.D.s for which no jobs existed. Two new Ph.D.s, with grim tenacity, wrote 2,000 letters of application for teaching positions and received 2,000 rejections (Goldman 1979).

The rage for higher degrees led to an inflationary effect commonly called overqualification. There were simply too many people with advanced degrees unable to find jobs in their levels and fields. Horror stories abounded of Ph.D.s doing stoop labor, working as waiters and filling station attendants, and the like. Such "overqualification" be

came part of the disappointment which told people of credential inflation. So, as one article caption asked, "CAN'T SOMEBODY
TURN THE DAMNED THING OFF? The U.S. educational system has loosed a flood of Ph.D.s which the market cannot absorb.
And the situation is getting worse" (Kathleen Wiegner, "Can't Somebody Turn the Damned Thing Off?" Forbes, 7 August 1978, p. 47).

No small factor swelling the supply of credentials was outright faking and counterfeiting of certificates. Yale's files contain the names
of more than 7,000 persons who have claimed to be alumni but are
not. Almost any degree of any university is purchasable by mail
(Editorial Research Reports, 1978).

Because of their high prestige and market value, medical doctors'
degrees are faked despite the high technical standards and vigilance
of the profession. In 1984, the U.S. Inspector General's Office of the
Department of Health and Human Services and the U.S. Postal Service began a wide-ranging investigation, involving fifteen states, of
the extent to which people with fraudulent degrees—possibly bought
for only a few thousand dollars—were being licensed to practice
medicine. The probe began with a list of 164 names of suspected
buyers of fraudulent medical degrees, often from medical schools in
the Caribbean (such as the Universidad Centro de Estudios in Santo
Domingo), who obtained degrees merely by writing for them
(Turegano 1984). Continuing investigation of medical degrees turned
up four fake doctors in New York hospitals, which led to "priority investigation" of 60 more suspected cases, and examination by the
state Office of Mental Health of another 200 medical residents in
training at 31 facilities, with plans to review records of 800 more
doctors working in state psychiatric hospitals. In California, officials
said that of 5,500 who applied to take the test for a medical license
in the past year, 325 were rejected because of suspect credentials. An
official of the California State Board of Medical Quality Assurance
said his agency alone had identified 2,500 individuals with suspi-
cious credentials to be investigated. A former president of the American Medical Association also expressed concern about a substantial
increase in cheating on medical examinations. He blamed the situation on lack of a uniform national policy or law controlling such
fraud, and the fact that verification of medical credentials was so
complicated and time consuming that officials could concentrate only

on people applying for licenses and not on those who already had them (Lyons 1984).

Another sector of credential falsification was lying about qualifications in job resumes. The lies included listing degrees not earned, colleges not attended, degrees not finished, and honors never received. The most common lies concerned college credentials. According to an expert of the National Credential Verification Service, "We find about 30 percent of the people misstate college records" (Watterson 1982).

Phony religious credentials added to the flood of certificates in America. Anyone who could convincingly call himself a minister received exemption, under the First Amendment, from taxes on property and operation of a "church". As a result, the market was deluged with divinity degrees purchasable for a few dollars. With real estate operators, accountants, stockbrokers, counselors, teachers, and psychologists calling themselves ministers, and their incomes a "pastor's fund" (the use of divinity degrees and "church" charters for tax avoidance was fully reported by Krier, 1980), the situation in faith became like that of everyone printing his own money, the chance of getting full value from a token sinking lower the larger the proportion of counterfeits circulating.

An added reason for inflation, pointed out by Collins (1979), is "credential radicalism," a paradoxical effect of status groups and lucrative professions trying to restrict their own credential. By monopolizing their status, they stimulate outsiders to open wider the gates by policies such as open admissions or no grades, and by founding and attending new schools that supply "non-elite" credentials. All of this leads to "galloping inflation" (Collins 1979, p. 196). Thus, trying to close the gate opens it.

Does anything especially encourage credential inflation in America? I would say that behind all such pressures to increase the supply of credentials is the laudable democratic ideal of egalitarianism: to give everyone the same chance of education and as much schooling as possible. To restrict the supply of credentials, even to protect their value, goes against this ideal. What is wanted by egalitarianism is increasing school output: more people going to higher levels of education than ever before, and more people going to school to learn what they formerly learned informally. The institutional machinery meeting this demand is not inaptly characterized as a huge cafeteria, in which everyone freely enters a line, picks out what he wants, receives a student number, and finally receives certificates accordingly.

Egalitarianism is particularly hard on the rank system of academics. Their scholarly titles, regalia and plumage, seem grotesquely anachronistic. Some universities call every instructor "Mr." (or "Ms.") regardless of his rank and title and how many degrees he has. Others call every instructor "Professor" or "Doctor" with equal indifference to the actual distinctions. Either way, distinctions are erased. There is also a tendency to equalize scholarly plumage. Convocations are mass graduations of hundreds, even thousands, dressed alike in procedures more mechanized and less ceremonial. There is a tendency to equalize academic plumage—not by eliminating it, but by making everyone equally gorgeous. In one university convocation, the entire graduating class got not only caps and gowns, but hoods as splendid as those of the M.A.s and Ph.D.s. The only way one could tell the difference by robes was that the B.A.s trooped in already hooded while higher degrees got their hoods personally draped on their shoulders in the ceremony. Such tactics may raise the honor to the lower ranks a little, but they do so at the expense of the higher, whose tokens are cheapened by a loss of "purchasing power" in terms like prestige, respect, authority, status, and perks.

Thus we can discern seven factors swelling the supply of, and hence cheapening and inflating, credentials. They are: (1) massification, (2) elasticity of supply, (3) slippage of academic and professional standards, (4) faddism, (5) counterfeiting, (6) credential radicalism, and (7) egalitarianism. Such things swell the supply of credentials, and may make a glut throwing into question the ability of the social system to deliver what the tokens promise. In that sense, credentials, whatever they cost monetarily, are cheapened—i.e., inflated—by the loss of social "purchasing power" of their overabundant display.

Medals

H. L. Mencken (1982:516) noted in 1920 an inflation of decorations among American civilians, when the lust to gleam and jingle got into the arteries of the American people. For years the austere tradition of Washington's day served to keep the military bosom bare of spangles, but all the while a weakness for them was growing in the civil population. Rank by rank, they became Knights of Pythias, Oddfellows, Red Men, Nobles of the Mystic Shrine, Knights Templar, Patriarchs Militant, Elks, Moose, Woodmen of the World, Foresters, Hoo-Hoos, Ku Kluxers—and in every new order there were thirty-two degrees, and for every degree there was a badge, and for every badge there was a yard of ribbon.

Cynics say medals are a cheap way of rewarding people for things they wouldn't do for money. A medal may look like a coin, but it would only cheapen an Olympic Gold Medal, or a Congressional Medal of Honor or a Croix de Guerre to equate it with money. This is because it expresses transcendent values like courage, loyalty, and self-sacrifice which (whatever their cost) are not priced in a monetary market. Another difference between medals and money is that decorations, to have value, must be displayed whereas money works quite well in the dark.

All the same, is it not true that decorations, trophies, and other displayable honors can lose some of their value from oversupply as does money? And as credentials do, as we have just seen. Much seems to hinge on scarcity. Some good things are scarce, others are plentiful. Medals happen to be best when scarce. So making them plentiful is a good way to explore negative effects of abundance in honors. The problem is put by James Jones' *The Thin Red Line*, which tells of pressure of an army administration to give medals, including a Congressional Medal of Honor, after a particularly bloody engagement in which many soldiers had been about equally gallant. The ethical question was, since one may not give the Medal of Honor to so many, is it fair to give to *one* credit that has in fact been earned by many? The administrative answer was not to spread the honor but to almost arbitrarily select one soldier for the Congressional Medal, take him from the front line, and put him to work recruiting by his splendid example. Naturally that soldier felt embarrassed by honors that set him apart from his comrades. He might even feel discredited by arbitrary preferment. But the administration, if pushed to explain, might well have answered that it had a quota system; and that it could damage a medal, especially the Congressional highest honor, to give it to too many at one time. Better it would seem to focus glory on one, as saga-writers have habitually done, creating the myth of the solitary hero. (By contrast, military decorations such as theater ribbons, given out to *everybody* in a whole category, have no capacity to single out the best and bravest; only *scarce* honors can do that.)

The question then can be asked, what would happen if society abandoned scarcity in honors—if medals were given out much more freely, say merely as a bonus for good citizenship, early payment of taxes, biggest corn production, even for having a large number of children (as was done for "heroic mothers" in the Soviet Union)? Might we not find that such generosity did not multiply honors but merely attenuated them, that however plentiful the decorations were, the values they stood for were as scarce as ever?

Such a problem is posed in countries such as England and America that have omnipresent media publicity and which give out large numbers of military and civilian decorations.

In England, the Queen's birthday is occasion for a veritable cascade of titles, as a result of which distinctions, English society is encrusted with honors that help maintain the relative place of each within the social structure.

Who gets the medals? In both England and America, the military have the best of it over civilians in decorations. The United States gives out some seventeen medals and thirty-eight service ribbons for military achievement. The English give out an equally impressive number, with the Victoria Cross at the top. European and British awards are perhaps more picturesque and grandiose than American— the British carrying titles like Knight Grand Cross of the Royal Victorian Order, Order of St. Michael and St. George, Order of the Bath, and Knight Bachelor. Lavish decorations and pomp can lend a certain musical comedy air of glitter and glitz to public ceremonies. Avoiding such overstatement, the Congressional Medal is a demure gold on blue.

On the score of gender, men have the best of it over women with medals. By count of social types (Klapp 1962), several times as many "hero" types apply to men as to women, explainable perhaps by their prevalence in military and risky services. All countries have yet to account for the fact that men far outnumber women in honorary titles, prizes, recognition, championships, and the like. Sports— dominated by men—bestow innumerable championship cups, ribbons, and other trophies to a new crop of winners each year. In sports also, a new way of increasing the number of winners has been found: the use of steroids and other chemicals to surpass the natural abilities of athletes, and cloud the question, who is best? This is obviously a sort of inflation, which, seeming to honor more, actually degrades the sport.

Having sketched the inflation of medals as one in which oversupply destroys scarcity, let us try to understand this paradox that too much honor destroys honor. I see four ways: (1) sheer oversupply, or loss of scarcity; (2) extension to unworthy recipient; (3) proliferation of pinnacles of achievement; and (4) counterfeiting.

1. The first source of inflation, oversupply, refers to sheer quantity. One person wearing the Medal of Honor, or only a few in the same place would be expected to receive maximum attention, respect, admiration as part of the Medal's "purchasing power." But fill a room with holders of the Medal and it would be hard to avoid a sense of diminution of rank—especially if all were seated or standing or treated in the same place or manner. The total honor received from display of the Medal would have to be divided in some way by N, the number of displayers, to find out how much inflation had occurred from quantity. For lesser medals, such as the Bronze Star and Purple Heart, so many are given out (the N is so large) that there is little distinction in displaying them.

To avoid such devaluation, wherever highest honors are bestowed, supply is restricted by various devices—as it is with canonisation of saints in Catholic countries, a severely rigorous procedure that takes over fifty years. In Britain, the decoration of Knight Companion is scarcer even that the Victoria Cross: limited to twenty-four alive at the same time. The sixty-five Companions of Honor are a select company including Graham Greene, Lord Whitelaw, Sir John Gielgud, and the Cambridge astronomer Stephen Hawking.

On the American side, the Congressional Medal, being most honored, is most restricted. For an idea of quantities given out, we may note that in the Battle of Iwo Jima, one of the bloodiest ever fought by the U.S. Marine Corps, 6,821 made the supreme sacrifice, 19,217 were wounded, and 2,648 suffered battle fatigue, totaling 28,686 casualties, all of whom received Purple Hearts—but only two dozen got the Congressional Medal of Honor.

General Jimmy Doolittle apparently did not understand this need for restriction of honors, for, when he received the Medal of Honor from FDR, he claimed it should have been shared by all twenty-one fliers in his mission, since all were in the same danger and did the same work. But one who wishes to give honor should realize that one cannot multiply or divide up heroism without diluting it—for most honor there must be focus on one.

Another example in a different field of restriction required for highest honors is found in the Gold Medal of the Royal Philharmonic Society, which is given only to artists of highest eminence, in some years all candidates being passed over and no awards made. In 115 years, the Society gave its Gold Medal to some seventy artists only, of the stature of Rostropovich, Horowitz, and Segovia.

Thus, whether we are speaking of saints, soldiers, or musicians, one might say a certain stinginess is necessary for highest honor.

The U.S. campaign in Grenada gives an example of lavishness of honors that threatened to violate this principle of scarcity. Apparently the Pentagon was eager to glorify a success and reward the soldiers. According to varying reports, about 7,000 (some said 9600) landed in Grenada. To this force, the Army awarded 8,612 (some said 19,600) medals, some to people who never left the United States. Forty-five Grenadians were killed. Nineteen Americans were killed, and 116 wounded, including accidents and "friendly fire." Taking the most conservative figures, this comes to over one medal per person. Among these medals were 680 Bronze Stars, and 4,581 Army Commendations—but no Congressional Medals of Honor, thus preserving it from oversupply. But do not the rest seem rather a lot of honors to bestow on so many soldiers, few of whom were killed in a relatively minor action? Surely it does not bear comparison with Iwo Jima. Perhaps it came close to the point at which honors lose honor because they carry little distinction.

The main point seems to be that increasing the number of medals cannot increase the amount of available or potential values (such as admiration, respect, valor, self-sacrifice), which remain in limited—inelastic—supply regardless of how many tokens are issued or displayed. The supply of such sentiments is limited and can be exhausted, as people become tired and unable to emotionally give more of that. Parades, ceremonies and honors passing this limit become boring—instead of war fever, war weariness.

Returning Vietnam veterans complaining about the unenthusiastic home welcome they received may have suffered from such inflation of honor, i.e., the supply of sentiment supporting the war (especially war weariness) may have been simply not sufficient to honor all the uniforms, medals, and service ribbons that suddenly appeared on the scene to claim jobs and schooling if not higher honors. A simple arithmetic might prevail; that is, if the amount of sentiment is limited (inelastic), then no matter how symbols multiply they will not increase the honor supply—doubling the number of medals might reduce by half the amount of prestige that those tokens can "purchase" in the social market.

But there is a second way, beside sheer oversupply, that decorations can be cheapened. It is by extending them to unworthy candidates or types of achievement.

Such a thing happened when a retired captain complained about medal-giving policies of the U.S. Army in West Germany in 1986. The captain stripped from his uniform the Bronze Star and three Purple Hearts he won in World War II, and shipped them to President Reagan, saying they were "cheapened" when U.S. soldiers, while off duty, were wounded in a terrorist bombing of a West German disco, and for that received Purple Hearts. His reasoning was that the off-duty soldiers had done no voluntary service nor had they displayed bravery, but were merely there by accident—a risk shared with civilians. In other words, the captain felt "civilians" were not entitled to military honors, and the Purple Heart was degraded by being extended to them.

A similar degradation of a decoration by extension to inappropriate parties seems to have occurred when Queen Elizabeth bestowed the Order of the British Empire on the Beatles in 1965, whose huge dollar earnings from record sales and such had helped the English trade balance. As a result of this ceremony, six English war veterans turned in their OBEs, one commenting indignantly, "English royalty wants to put me on the same level as those vulgar nincompoops." Another said, "There is nothing brave about yapping at a howling mob of teenagers with a million in the bank." The veterans turned back their medals because they felt they had been cheapened by equation of real heroes with rock musicians.

Similar in spirit was a complaint about giving a medal to Frank Sinatra, in a letter from Arlington, Virginia, to a newspaper editor, which asked: "I would like to know why Ronald Reagan gave the Presidential Medal of Freedom, the highest award a civilian in this country can get, to a controversial character like Frank Sinatra and yet turned down the late Benny Goodman three times for the same award?" (Walter Scott, "Personality Parade," *San Diego Union*, 1 February 1987, p. 1).

A crime disqualifies a person for the OBE. Thus, a famous jockey in England was jailed for income tax evasion and as a result was stripped of his OBE (for services as a jockey)—a fate of about thirty officers of the order in the past twenty years. Thus the honor of this decoration was protected from degradation by unworthy recipients.

Some of this sensitivity to dishonor is found in British sports in the distinction between amateur and professional. The amateur is thought of as a gallant player who loves the game and holds it above the sordid making of money which degrades the sport. Professionalism is felt to flout the strict standards and tarnish the ideal of pure amateurism. Thus a captain for a British olympic team complained that all the leading professionals of tennis (such as Ivan Lendl, Boris Becker, and Martina Navratilova) had to do to become eligible for the 1988 Games was to "take off their sponsorship logos for two or three weeks while they are living and competing at the Olympics." He made a similar charge about professional footballers. "I fear that their (the Olympics') romantic appeal may be gone forever and with it the public appeal, which has made our medallists household names. I fear the Olympics may become just another one of those TV events that occur every year or two."

During the 1980s, drug abuse by athletes in order to win, offered a stronger threat to the honor of sport, amateur or professional.

Such examples show that laxness in upholding the ideal of the medal and in extending it to unsuitable persons can degrade it by what might be called negative prestige of unworthy recipients, with resulting loss of display value.

A third way of inflating honors is by multiplying the avenues, opportunities, and competitions by which one can win medals, so awarding more of them. I call this proliferation of pinnacles of achievement. Note, for example, the intricate statistics of football recording Superbowl achievements. Innumerable achievements are given hair-splitting distinctions (for example, Most Valued Players, most points, most yards gained, 100-yards rushing, longest runs from scrimmage, longest pass plays, longest punts, longest field goals, longest punt returns, longest kickoff returns, most passes completed, most touchdowns). Such distinctions are celebrated in "halls of fame" where athletes gather to congratulate one another. Many of these distinctions would not even be noticed by the public without the statistics, pointing to one, then another, star. Note also the *Guinness Book of World Records* telling of records in all sorts of things, from flying around the world to goldfish-swallowing. With all those records to beat, it would seem that almost everybody could be a champion of something—if only of a sport he has just invented.

For those seeking further pinnacles, a reference book, *Awards, Honors and Prizes* (Detroit: Gale Research Company), lists over 10,000 prizes offered in the United States and Canada. (We have already noted that the San Diego telephone directory lists forty businesses producing and selling trophies, awards, and medals.)

Such things proliferate pinnacles of achievement until hardly anybody need be left out. Essayist Melvin Maddocks writes, "Out of a kindly democratic instinct that nobody should be left out, The Best has become a mass-produced category" (Melvin Maddocks, "Nothing But the Best," *World Monitor,* January 1989, p. 12). The effect, however, is not distinction but mediocrity, as trophies become inflated, Maddocks argues: "Nothing signals mediocrity like the excessive awarding of prizes."

Yet a fourth way in which decorations can be oversupplied and so cheapened is by fabrication or counterfeiting. We have already noted that the San Diego telephone directory lists forty businesses producing and selling trophies, medals and awards. Trophies can be engraved to order; and, in every large city, there are antique and numismatic shops where one can buy an Iron Cross, Croix de Guerre, Victoria Cross, or even a Medal of Honor. A Distinguished Service Cross can be bought for $9.95, a Purple Heart for $10.25, a Navy Cross for $10.50, and a Bronze Star for $8.25, ordered by mail.

This means that the supply of trophies and medals is potentially quite elastic. Authentic or fake ones are easily purchased (as noted also with credentials). So they easily outstrip whatever supply of real merit there is. Especially, in a mass society like ours, where people do not know others well, who knows who is the hero? It is easy to appear at gatherings, ceremonies, banquets, etc., as a "hero" or "champion" with a medal dangling on one's chest. Many people also have identity problems of yearning to be somebody, which might be assuaged by a medal or two. Mass society is also eager to greet celebrities and to build them by media publicity, phony or not; and gives hearty welcome to audacious poseurs like Fred Demara and "Prince" Mike Romanoff, in whatever decorations or costumes they might assume.

So, in such ways—sheer quantity, extension to the unworthy, proliferation of pinnacles, and counterfeiting—society, if it does not hold the line of restriction, sometimes multiplies distinctions that become cheaper and less distinctive the more there are of them.

Applause: What Comes After the Standing Ovation?

During the late 1970s and early 1980s a curious fad was observed to be sweeping audiences of the performing arts in America, England, and Europe. The highest accolade, to stand while clapping, was being given so often as to become commonplace. "Today everybody gets standing ovations," said the actress Eva LeGallienne. For a while it seemed that anyone who fiddled, sang, or kicked with verve deserved a standing ovation.

Early in the period of this fad, I saw a surprising example in the reception by a collegiate audience of the flamenco guitarist Carlos Montoya. After his first offering, everyone in the packed hall rose and remained standing while applauding. This went on after every number. Plainly Montoya was surprised, and rather overwhelmed, by the acclaim. Was it some kind of delayed gratitude for previous artistry elsewhere? Perhaps there was a difference between the East Coast, from which Montoya had just come and the West Coast with its known hospitality to extremes.

But, flattered though he might be, Montoya's professional judgment was too keen to be fooled by that enthusiasm into thinking he had suddenly become an immortal descended to earth. Was the standing ovation truly a measure of his performance, or merely a sort of catharsis for the audience? Critical reviews following gave no sign that anything extraordinary had happened that night.

This poses the question of how critics and performers are to read the feedback from audiences—ranging from stony Boston to faddish L.A. (known as the "city of the standing ovation"). They have to discount polite as well as hysterical adulatory applause—each veering from the truth—in order to tell how well performers really did. Our question here is whether overproduction of applause can blur its message, fail to discriminate better from worse, as we have seen in over-easy academic grading and in awarding too many medals and trophies.

The trouble was that the standing ovation as a comment on performance seemed to have undergone an extension which included "good" and "very good" in the same category as "superlative." There was no way to tell by applause alone which performance was superlative—indeed, there was no superlative any more. So a critic (Beaufort 1976) concerned about the state of the arts asked, if ovations become standard, how is society to recognize from applause a truly outstanding performance? How can the artist himself tell when he has done supremely well? Society needs measures of excellence. What new measure, then, comes *after* the standing ovation; what is to be the ultimate accolade?

The new accolade would have to restore scarcity which made possible discrimination between very best and merely good, for without scarcity there is no discrimination. Equal applause for every performance conveys no more information than no applause for any performance. The indiscriminate ovation becomes no more informative than those inane "canned laughter" tracks used by radio to make jokes seem funnier than they actually are. Politicians, too, have found use for the indiscriminate accolade, in clacques which follow speakers around on campaigns to give automatic enthusiastic applause whenever they pause in a speech. A British journalist complained about artificial standing ovations and their contribution to the meaninglessness of politics:

> The first rule of the . . . Party conference is that any statement followed by an expectant pause from the speaker is vigorously applauded. Lose your place for more than three seconds and you earn a standing ovation. (Craig Brown, "Pushing Hot Air to New Heights," *Times*, 9 October 1987)

Why do people overuse applause in such indiscriminate ways? One reason seems to be kindness coupled with a well-intentioned ignorance. Americans, for example, are well known to be kinder than Italians in judging grand opera—and know less about it. An opera critic notes that in Italy, judgment of singers is notoriously severe, expressed by boos, jeers, laughter, and even thrown vegetables. But in America booing is considered poor sportsmanship, and most often the harshest negative feedback is silence. On the favorable side, American approval is too generous, reports an opera critic. With so many more people attending opera who know little about it, they "wax understandably enthusiastic about just about anything. . . . Performances that even five years ago would have been tepidly received nowadays garner rousing cheers." Standards of opera have "eroded alarmingly." Knowledgeable operagoers feel frustrated "when a singer who has spent much of the evening in search of accurate pitch, high notes, or even just the correct notes, receives a bevy of bravos at curtain call" (Eckert 1983).

Egalitarianism also probably has something to do with handing out too many and too high rewards and awards, already noted in academic grading. Somehow, it seems unfair—undemocratic?—to set some so much higher than others, to reserve the charmed circle for the select few. Why not let others in? At least it seems more generous to give everybody, who is not absolutely terrible, a standing ovation in his turn. Why not, since we rotate offices that way, anyway?

Such good intentions are doubtless coupled with a powerful force in all collective behavior, namely contagious communication (chapter 4), also called suggestibility. Crowds and audiences offer opportunities for catharsis, of which standing ovations might be an outlet. Involuntary imitation is part of a social pressure to conform. It seem churlish to withhold applause and not go along when others are so eager to give it. As a result of contagion, the standing ovation might happen like this: after the performer had taken his bow, a few people (his fans or a hired clacque) would rise clapping persistently. Then more would rise. Finally, those still seated would become aware of a pressure; and, not wishing to seem grudging (perhaps with thought like, "Why not? After all it wasn't a bad performance"), they, too, would get on their feet. At last, all would be standing.

Thus, we have here explored a particular type of inflation, the over-used standing ovation, trying to see how, as a token of honor, it can lose information and become degraded by being too generous and plentiful, rewarding good and poor, and good and superb alike. It does so, we saw, by losing scarcity, becoming too plentiful, becoming less discriminative as feedback, making it harder to tell what its real message is. The main point is that a plentifully bestowed honor can not distinguish unique achievement.

Whatever its causes, the standing ovation now seems to be returning to its proper place on the scale of honor, as a high and rarely bestowed honor—either that or find another ultimate accolade. We have yet to see whether it will continue to greet highest achievement—or is an even higher token on its way?

8

Inflation of Sentiments

We now look at four more examples (after credentials, medals, and standing ovations), to which a market model might aptly apply. The general picture is this: a supply of behavioral tokens (e.g., smiles, greetings, and kisses) are circulating and competing in a social market in which there is an inelastic supply of values for which the tokens stand. If the tokens increase in number versus the limited supply of values, they are worth (i.e., "purchase") less of the value. Such loss of value becomes comparable to that of money in the economic situation of "too many dollars chasing too few goods." I do not mean to imply that the analogy of monetary to social behavioral tokens (smiles, greetings, kisses) is exact and can be simply taken over—only to express the hope that a market model, properly adapted to behavioral subject matter, can help us to understand why so many symbols, heavily produced in modern mass society, lose meaning.

In a mobile mass society, sentiments (however intense) are vapid and shallow, spreading by mass contagion but with little commitment beyond the moment. People are concerned with role-playing and images, not character and sincerity, in a personality market, as C. Wright Mills called it. Images "presented" or offered flow and circulate, and when spread indiscriminately can be cheapened by their number as mass media diffusing images and tokens easily outstrip whatever supply of real sentiment there may be. To this terms like Gresham's effect and inflation easily apply. I hope this will be evident in the following examples, of smiles, greetings, kisses, and religious tokens.

Smiles

The smile has come off faces onto bumper stickers, Yellow Cabs, and bottle caps which read, "Smile. Pass it on." Now it is often no

longer a spontaneous natural gesture but a token with recognized exchange value, deliberately offered to get something, if only another
smile.

When Dale Carnegie (1937) gave his famous prescription for winning friends and influencing people, "Rule 2. Smile," he could
hardly have realized that he was contributing to inflation of a social
gesture.

Inflation as we know it in money is an increase in the supply of
dollars—too many dollars—chasing too few goods. Result, money
buys less.

In the case of smiles, the supply increases easily because they
spread easily and are indeed contagious. The popular song goes,
"Keep on smiling, and the whole world smiles with you." And marketing emotion is now big business, as in the training of airline flight
attendants to give "authentic" smiles to make passengers feel safely
at home (Hochschild 1983), and "use" their smiles as deliberately as
they might a pill to prevent airsickness.

So, in market terms the supply of smiles is quite elastic, and can
outstrip the supply of available friendliness and good humor, or whatever other value is sought by a smile. Then it loses some of its exchange value. The devaluation consists of what the token claims to
mean or offer versus what it actually delivers. Smiles don't always
deliver friendliness. In Thomas Wolfe's *You Can't Go Home Again*,
the boss is a smiling, cheery good guy talking to employees, but
turns into an ogre behind the frosted glass; then, coming out, turns
back into the good guy again. In Arthur Miller's *Death of a Salesman*, Willie Loman operates on "a smile and a shoeshine," until his
friends no longer smile back and his bubble collapses. When smiles
get bigger and phonier, as in gladhanding in politics and business,
then the inflation is perceived by everybody. Such discrepancy between actual feeling and a gesture is sometimes called hypocrisy or
insincerity, but often it is no more than inflation of sentimental tokens, to which we are all more or less subject. In a society where relationships are shallow and uncertain, the more usual policy is to
play it safe and give everybody at least a tentative smile. That is not
usually called hypocrisy.

All the same, this well-meant policy can get a person into a quan-
dary. Take the example of an American girl who entered an English

public school in the fourth form. She tried by generous smiling to make friends and become as popular as she had been at home in California. But the English girls kept asking, "What are you smiling at?" They attached more significance to it, supposing that there must be some reason more specific than a wish to make friends. Finally she stopped smiling so much, and the English girls stopped wondering what she meant by it. Friendship followed.

President Harry Truman made an interesting comment on the smile of President Dwight Eisenhower:

> It's interesting that a single thing, that great smile of Eisenhower's, gave him the worldwide and lifelong reputation of being a sunny and amiable man, when those of us who knew him well were all too aware that he was essentially a surly, angry and disagreeable man, and I don't just mean to me, either. (Harry Truman, "What Makes a Good President?" *Parade*, 3 April 1988, p. 7)

Detecting counterfeit smiles should have about the same effect in reducing inflation as detecting counterfeit dollars: the remaining good gestures become worth more if the false ones are gone from circulation. Just as passing even one counterfeit dollar inflates the money supply ever so slightly (and makes everybody slightly poorer), we expect that one false smile would do the same for the smiles supply. We may also be concerned about a Gresham's effect if false smiles multiplying drive good ones out of circulation.

Psychologists such as Paul Ekman (1975) are studying the difference between facial and bodily expressions of real and simulated feelings. All smiles are not the same: a forced one produces a different muscle pattern from that of a spontaneous smile.

Generally speaking, Asiatics smile often as a way of saving their own, or someone else's, face. Europeans seem to be less inclined to smile. Indeed, they are so sparing with it to strangers that they often seem unfriendly. Maybe it is because they attach more specific meaning to a smile, and so avoid the inflation encouraged by Dale Carnegie in America.

Market theory tells us that inflation can be reduced by having less money in circulation or more goods for money to buy. The parallel with smiles is that aside from trying to detect false smiles we would do well to study how to have more to smile about—a larger supply of genuine goodwill and friendliness on which smiles can draw.

Greetings

The greeting card business has been enjoying a huge increase in sales, according to the *Wall Street Journal* (1986). People are sending greetings to more and more people. Even pets are not neglected: one card reads, "Hello, *Scruffy*. Here's wishing you a dog-gone happy birthday."

Today, greeting cards comprise the bulk of letter mail at holiday seasons, especially Christmas. Flowers, too, are widely used as tokens of sentiment for all sorts of occasions, from birthdays to funerals, cut or potted, wired anywhere. Nor are people any longer daunted by long-distance phoning (which once meant death or crisis or fearful expense) to extend a greeting. Americans exchange more greeting cards than do inhabitants of any other country, an estimated 6 billion greeting cards per year.

Historians say that the practice of greeting cards dates from ancient times, when it was the custom of Egyptians and Romans to exchange symbols of goodwill and greetings among friends. Greeting cards became connected with Christianity by the giving of gifts at the Feast of Saint Valentine (an apocryphal figure who has two putative historical identities as martyrs with the same name). But that religious connotation has been lost, and the symbol has evolved into the valentine as we know it, a slightly cryptic missive of romantic love, that by the mid-nineteenth century had evolved into a frilly masterpiece of handcrafted lace paper, which, if the lace were real, might sell for fifty dollars today. With the introduction of penny postage and envelopes in England in 1840, the exchange of greeting cards greatly increased. Commercial production started in 1860. Today the manufacture and sale of greeting cards are big business. The United States, sometimes called a nation "in love with love," bought an estimated 900 million valentines, and about 70 million roses on 14 February 1989.

It seems reasonable to suppose that such a flow of greetings has a function in a mass society of meeting a need to remind people that fragile relationships still hold, and reassuring them about sentiments (goodwill, concern, liking, kinship, faith) on which relationships rest, and reaching through media, computers, and mailing lists growing numbers of people they do not know well. Nowadays people send greeting cards to people they barely know—if at all—for reasons having little to do with personal regard. No one is surprised to get personalized greetings from insurance agents, auto mechanics, or sales-men whom one does not know. All this has amounted to an explosion of sentimental well-wishing tokens that parallels the explosion of in-formation, of which almost everyone is aware.

But, if there is an explosion of sentimental tokens—if greeting cards are more numerous—dare we assume that there actually *is* more of that sort of sentiment, more genuine warmth and concern? Or could it be the other way around, as we would expect from inflation, that feelings would become thinner, more would become less?

There are signs of loss of sentiment even as the volume of greeting cards increases. For one thing, it has often been observed that holi-day greetings are becoming less specific to the person and occasion, more abstract and generalized ("Season's greetings" instead of "Merry Christmas," "Noel," "Happy Hanukkah," etc., or generalized friendship cards that say little more than a cheery "hello"). A generalized greeting serves more kinds of people, but conveys less to anybody in particular.

A further instance of loss of sentiment is the trend in Valentines al-ready noted, from elegant, handcrafted, frilly masterpieces, to man-ufactured cards little different from each other.

Nor does it deepen sentiment to see Santa Claus on a whiskey billboard, or "Season's Greetings" gleaming every night from the window of a liquor store. Commercialism has its own message, superseding personal sentiment: "We are interested in profits—not you." Crass commercialization may have something to do with a Grinch-like hatred of Christmas by some people. As the flood of im-personal, commercialized tokens increased, it would hardly be sur-prising if people were not filled with goodwill but got a feeling that the spirit of Christmas was not what it used to be. Sociological studies have observed the commercialization of holidays like Christ-mas and Easter (Barnett 1949, 1954). In a survey of college students' attitudes toward Christmas, Klapp (1969, p. 352) found that commer-cialization was the chief cause of complaint about Christmas.

Greeting cards lend themselves easily to inflation theory, because, being physical tokens, cheap and easily multiplied, they are elastic in supply—able easily to outstrip the supply of sentiment—being like "printing press" money able to bring on a galloping inflation in which their value approaches zero as their supply increases. I sup-pose that the volume of greeting cards has no fixed relation to the amount of sentiment referred to by the tokens, and can fluctuate widely, so inflationary disproportions can occur.

Such sentimental inflation would be felt as a sort of emptiness, a lack of genuine feeling in a flood of greetings, and a need for discounting, almost as though the cards were junk mail. How to measure the inflation of sentimental tokens? Unfortunately, we have no price index or Fisher formula to measure the non-monetary "purchasing power" of sentimental tokens. But it should not in principle be impossible to devise a formula that would use a measure of total circulation, or calculate the number of greetings per person being sent and received in a given period, in relation to the exchange value of tokens, determined perhaps by attitude-testing, or even just asking people how they feel about certain tokens. The inflation, then, would be indicated by the finding of an inverse relation between the number of tokens in circulation and the exchange (sentimental) value of such tokens—as we said about all inflation, more becoming less.

One could visualize such greeting card inflation by simply asking oneself how a person would feel if the number of greeting cards he received suddenly doubled. Is he likely to imagine that twice as many people suddenly think warmly of him (not at least until he has looked into other reasons for popularity, such as his name getting on some purchasable mailing lists)? Will he value so many cards more than the fewer he got in the previous year? To decide what they are worth in sentimental exchange value, he might grade the cards by sorting them into piles: (1) from relatives and close friends (probably containing a handwritten personal message, kept to be answered); (2) from mere acquaintances (some of whom he adds to his own mailing list, to be answered next year; (3) from businesses, such as stock brokerages, insurance agencies, and filling stations, reminding clients of their services ("Happy Birthday, ___John___ , from your friendly insurance agent, George"); (4) finally, impersonal, printed "junk" mail, addressed to "resident," to be thrown away promptly. All this batch of cards does not have the same sentimental value. It would range from a few highly valued to many with no value. The average exchange value, then, would be lower as the proportion of cards in category 1 decreased, and the proportions in categories 2 through 4 increased, and the total number of cards circulating in a given time period increased. A lower average exchange value as tokens increase in supply is our definition of inflation.

Kisses

"Say, what do you mean by kissing me?" He looked kind of humble, and says: "I didn't mean nothing, ma'am. I didn't mean no harm. I-I-thought you'd like it."
—Mark Twain, Huckleberry Finn, chap. 33

Lord! I wonder what fool it was that first invented kissing.
—Jonathan Swift.

If kissing were a natural gesture, it would occur in all members of our species (as when cattle moo, birds call) and would mean pretty much the same thing to all members of the species when displayed. But, because kissing is not an instinctive gesture, but a cultural symbol, invented by humans, it can vary widely; there is no guarantee that a certain state of mind will go with it (it can lack meaning or be insincere).

And, if kisses are artificial tokens, it seems plausible to suppose that a market theory could apply to them, as it does to other cultural symbols such as credentials, medals, smiles; and that supply and demand could affect their value when they are freely exchanged in a social market. It might, then, be true that the supply of tokens can outstrip the amount of sentiment or meaning available, which constitutes their "purchasing power" (prestige, respect, honor, affection), and so kisses could become cheapened, diluted, or, I would prefer here to say, inflated.

The supply and value of kisses fluctuate historically and culturally. In Puritan times, all public displays of connubial affection were forbidden. By contrast, in Tudor times, it was customary for a gentleman who went visiting to kiss his hostess full upon the mouth. Kissing of all sorts was widespread among the gentle classes (Plowden 1979, pp. 2–3). This contrasts again with the sparse supply of kisses—indeed, of all displays of affection—we read about in Victorian novels and plays, where, among gentry, a kiss was a breathtaking romantic encounter, assiduously sought and sparingly given (one might almost say rationed) to the courting male, sufficient to legally seal an engagement, and about as far as one could go before crossing the matrimonial threshold.

Statistics of modern kissing are not easy to come by, but in the late seventies and early eighties the supply was plentiful, and an outbreak of social kissing was noted among middle-class Americans and Britons that had marks of a fad. Apparently it began in America, but soon reached the staid Britons; a writer to the Times (London) asked whether the traditional reserve of the English had finally cracked. A lady complained:

> Now at every suburban gathering I find that I am expected to kiss in greeting and goodbye not only my host but my hostess, all guests, female as well as male, already known to me and a few who are not.

An elderly gentleman's reaction to the kissing outbreak was, "I thought by some miracle I had suddenly grown attractive in my old age."

From such glimpses, it appears that kissing is not just a natural impulse but a matter of custom and fashion, fluctuating from epoch to epoch. Were fuller statistics available, it might be possible to chart the inflation of kinds of kisses in various eras in terms of total number of kisses in life and art, versus the sentimental or erotic value per kiss, going back to Neanderthal times when it might be doubted there was any kissing at all.

Along with kissing presumably go other expressions of affection which, when overused, can become inflated (as when a waitress calls every male customer "honey," or a fare-collector on a London doubledecker bus calls everybody who boards "Darling")—and, of course, the boom in greeting cards already discussed fits in here. Were such figures available, it might be possible to appraise the general sentimental inflation of a whole era. Why should it be confined just to money?

Konrad Lorenz (1973, p. 8) has stated an ethological case for limits of affection, which fits well with what we are calling inflation of affection. Lorenz argues that humans are unable to extend affection widely without "diluting" it. We must concentrate affection on a small number of friends, "for we are not so constituted that we can love all mankind." But crowded together in cities, we

> no longer see the face of our neighbor. Our neighborly love becomes so diluted by a surfeit of neighbors that, in the end, not a trace of it is left. . . . So we must select. . . . "Not to get emotionally involved" is one of the chief worries

of large-city people. . . . The greater the overcrowding, the more urgent becomes the need for the individual "not to get involved."

Such "dilution" of affection by a "surfeit" of neighbors states what in market terms would be called a loss of value by excess of supply—a glut, "too much of a good thing."

Another description of limitation on enlarging one's circle of friends or increasing gestures of affection without loss of value comes from *A Lady's Guide to Etiquette* (anonymous, about 1840) which puts the argument explicitly in market terms, so cogently that I shall quote it at length:

> Your particular friends should not be very numerous. My reasons for this advice are the following. To meet all the claims which many intimate friendships would involve, would require too much of your time; and would necessarily interfere with the duties connected with your station in life. You could derive no advantage from having many intimate friends, which would not be as well secured to you by a smaller circle, and indeed just in proportion as the number is extended beyond a moderate limit, you will defeat the purposes which such a friendship is designed to answer. For it is impossible, from the nature of the case, that you should bestow the same degree of confidence and affection upon a great number as upon a few; and as the advantage to be derived is in some measure, in proportion to the strength and intimacy of the friendship, it is obvious that the more numerous is your circle of particular friends, the less satisfaction and benefit you can expect to receive. It is equally true, on the other hand, that the greater the number to whom you proffer your confidence, the less will your confidence be valued in each particular case; for there is no exception here from the general rule that things are cheap in proportion as they are common. Be satisfied, then, with a few choice friends, and be not ambitious to be the confidant of all your acquaintances.

"Things are cheap in proportion as they are common" states a truth from market experience, that whatever is offered too plentifully loses exchange value, whether it be economic goods or such things as kisses and valentines.

To pursue the question of how much inflation of kisses has occurred, it would be necessary to count, estimate, and grade the kisses exchanged by a given population in a given period, and to put that against the amount of affection or other sentimental value received. There seems no reason in principal why such psychological variables cannot be measured or indexed. If the average person received twice as many kisses in one year as in the previous year, does that mean he got twice as much affection—or how much? A zero or inverse relation would indicate inflation. Before deciding how much value kisses carry, it might be well to grade them by sorting them into piles, say (1) deep affection, (2) moderate affection, (3) general friendliness or goodwill, (4) polite or formal gesture, (5) hypocritical pretense (e.g. gladhanding or a "line"). When there is much inflation, one may expect that a greater number of kisses will fall into categories 3 through 5 than 1 and 2. When that is the case, one may feel that kisses don't mean as much as they used to, that they are empty gestures, perhaps of no more significance than a handshake. But that at present is a matter for conjecture.

I hope these three examples—greeting cards, smiles, and kisses—show how the idea of inflation applies to symbols of sentiment. The basic relationship here is of too many symbols being circulated in proportion to the supply of sentiment that can be drawn upon—a shortage of friendliness, goodwill, love, honor, generosity, altruism or other values signified by the tokens. We assume that the supply of sentiments is more limited—less elastic—than the supply of tokens. Such a shortage of sentiments constitutes a loss of "purchasing power" of tokens. The basic idea of such a shortage of sentiment goes back to Ferdinand Tönnies, who held that *Gemeinschaft* had "natural will" to love and cooperate; but *Gesellschaft* (what we today would call a mass society) lacks such sentiment and so must be bargained with to be rationally persuaded to exchange services that within *Gemeinschaft* would be given freely.

So greeting cards, smiles, and kisses, as we have analyzed them, suffer a shortage of feeling to back them up that is simply not there except as "rhetorical" (empty, inflationary) expression. There seems, indeed, in mass society to be a shortage of altruistic love, as pointed out by Sorokin (1950), and of responsibility by Menninger (1973). So we see old-fashioned sentiments like kinship obligation, marital fidelity, and romantic love drying up while their symbols circulate abundantly as slogans and rhetoric. The basic cause of such inflation, then, is not hypocrisy but too many tokens of sentiment being circulated in proportion to the supply of such sentiment (the values) in a particular society.

This illusion of getting more—a false prosperity—is familiar in creeping monetary inflation. Mass media have vastly increased the flow of tokens of sentiment while real roots of neighborly and community involvement have been drying up. So there comes what is often a grotesque discrepancy between the rhetoric and the real supply of sentiment.

On 13 February, 1989, students at a California university celebrated "Condom Week," betokened by a gift with a condom enclosed, to coincide with Valentine's Day. We have managed to discuss kissing without getting into the related subject of sex, its desentimentalization.

Can sex become inflated? I hesitate to get into this lush topic (data being lacking for both sex and kisses), except to note that there has been an enormous change in the value of sex during the last half century—away from its scarcity, protected by ideals of chastity, virginity, and protection of women, to great freedom and plentifulness of sex for women about as for men.

To anyone who has witnessed these last fifty years, it seems to me beyond dispute that there has been a vast increase followed by loss of value, that sex is no longer the unique and ineffable romantic mystery it once was but has become so casual as sometimes to be the proper culmination of the first date.

This fits our definition of sentimental inflation: more followed by less value—desentimentalization. We note it at this time without trying to further pursue its ramifications.

Religious Tokens

It strains our imagination only a little to liken religion to a marketplace, in which churches distribute (sell) religious tokens and seekers shop for things to believe.

Tokens play an especially important part in religion because where the subject matter is esoteric, it is necessary to represent it by tokens that are less sacred and hard to understand, themselves accessible and easily handled, however inaccessible the mysteries to which they refer. Thus, since religion is a spiritual matter, it requires more tokens than do other fields where the values are more tangible.

Churches both sell and freely dispense many kinds of nonmonetary tokens. Sacraments, of course, but also the spread of doctrines by evangelism and propaganda; distribution of books, pamphlets and icons; relics; exegeses of doctrines by prophets and priests; calling up of spirits by mediums or shamans; cures, miracles and blessings; hagiographies (stories of saints). To meet the demand in the religious marketplace flows an inexhaustible supply of tokens (books, pamphlets, pictures, icons, medallions, crosses, mandalas, prayer-beads, charms, mantras, meditation techniques, success formulas, cures, panaceas, diets, regimens, testimonials, decals, bumper stickers; and pronouncements by gurus, astrologers, fortune tellers, prophets, witches, televangelists, therapists and counselors ready to meet any wish in faith.

Our aim is to see how the idea of inflation applies to religion. We ask: (1) when and how do evangelism and shopping for faiths become marketlike; and (2) in such a market, when is increasing supply of tokens followed by loss of value?

In the Christian Middle Ages there was no marketplace of faiths in the sense of choosing what one wants to believe from a sales counter or bazaar. The established church had a monopoly and few competitors. But in "The Pardoner's Tale" Chaucer gives us a glimpse of a market and possible inflation in the sale of pardons, indulgences, relics, and cures by enterprising friars, priests, even lay persons claiming to be authorized by the Pope. The Pardoner in Chaucer's tale tells what he does to swell the supply of religious tokens: he shows a papal seal warranting his holy work with authority to shrive sinners; he brings out saints' relics (including the shoulder bone of a sheep); he promises instant cures from water in which the sheep's bone has been dipped; he dispenses flattery and hypocrisy and preaches a "hundred lying mockeries" to the gathered yokels; he repeats the same text over and over again, that cupidity is the root of evil; he takes in money from crowds wherever he goes, admitting that he preaches for nothing but greed of gain (the very evil his sermons are against). It seems to me that Chaucer here describes not only individual conduct but what must have been, culturewide, a galloping inflation of religious tokens, a few of the particulars being the sheer number of tokens multiplied countlessly (rather like printing one's own money); promises of heaven, pardons, cures and other values; false claims of authority giving credence to preaching; admission of hypocrisy and bad faith; repetitious (redundant) sermonizing.

By his challenge to the priesthood, Martin Luther might be said to have broken the sacramental monopoly, as Max Weber called it, the idea that only the clergy had authority over the channels of grace by which sacramental symbols were distributed, which made possible such abuses as selling pardons. He also attacked "idolatry" conceived as the veneration of icons, relics, and holy images, such as of saints and the Virgin Mary, that proliferated throughout Christendom, until checked by Puritan austerity—and in the Middle East by Islamic countries.

It seems plain that such things as pardons and idolatry constituted a highly elastic, abundant supply of tokens that could be inflated easily, an inflation which Luther might be said to have remedied by restricting the flow of such tokens into the marketplace of faiths.

But that is not all of the story. Though Luther closed the door to one lot of religious symbols, he opened the door to another. Why? Because he opened wider the market of religious tokens, saying, in effect, let no man stand between me and God; let every man be his own priest. He taught the "priesthood of all believers," that is, any congregation may commission any member to perform sacraments. With every man his own priest, the situation became rather like each man printing his own money; the history of Christianity became one long story of proliferating symbols and sects. So it might be said ironically that Luther, having reduced inflation of one set of religious symbols, encouraged it in another.

In modern times, the proliferation of religious symbols is even more marketlike than it was when pardoners sold indulgencies. How so?

Laissez-faire and caveat emptor are slogans expressing the spirit of the marketplace of faiths today. Every purchased "Doctor of Divinity" credential and self-appointed "Reverend" preacher is swelling the supply of religious tokens. In the excitement of a bargain sale, seekers go from one guru or evangelist to another, "shopping" for faiths, seeking "answers," enlightenment, healing, or the experience of being "born again." (In the 1980 presidential election, all three major candidates claimed to have been "born again".) Let us note how apt the concept of marketplace is to describe a pluralistic mass society where there is no established orthodoxy but competing propagandas, evangelists "sell" their doctrines, and seekers (buyers) "shop" from church to church, sect to sect, book to book, and guru to guru, looking for a faith that suits their taste, much as shoppers might look for commodities in a department store bargain sale. In this marketplace, it seems fair to say that those who seek faiths and those who offer them compete in a manner like buyers and sellers, even when non-monetary tokens such as prayer, preaching, and salvation, are exchanged.

Even more marketlike is the crass commercialism of televangelistic churches competing for converts and contributions in ways quite similar to merchandising. They reach a weekly television and radio audience of more than 129 million, undercutting local church attendance much as a supermarket undercuts a small corner store.

They distribute millions of tokens to their audience, some given "free" and others for sale, amply priced in dollars. Analysis of a sample of appeals by television churches to the television audience showed that spiritual messages were heavily freighted with items offered for sale (books, pamphlets, buttons, magazines, tapes, records) and appeals for money. Of eighty-one sample episodes there were fifty-nine offers of materials for purchase; and thirty-eight appeals for various causes, the average request being for $173.93 (Abelman and Neuendorf 1985, pp. 107–8). An idea of how large this income is is given by the fact that one electric church spent $12 million just for air time in one year (Black 1980).

How much of this proliferation and merchandising of symbols is inflationary? Our definition of inflation is symbols losing value following their increase in a social market. Such increase is in relation to a more fixed amount of value to which symbols refer (in this case sentiments such as faith). The inflation of symbols is indicated not just by their number but their lack of "purchasing power" in obtaining the value sought. If religious symbols do not deliver such values as brotherly love, charity, and faith, they are weak in purchasing power. The turnover rate of congregations and drifting of seekers from one faith to another are indicators of loss of purchasing power of religious symbols. It would seem that in its potentially limitless flood of tokens at small cost, religion has great possibility of inflation from oversupply. Its case is like smiles, medals, greeting cards, and kisses. Dispensing their own tokens into the marketplace of faiths, churches are like banks printing their own money.

The presumption is that any large distribution of symbols is in danger of becoming inflationary. The occurrence of inflation rests on three things: (1) existence of a marketlike competition of offerers and takers (buyers and sellers, preachers and believers) in which laws of supply and demand hold; (2) the supply of tokens grows rapidly and elastically; (3) resulting from which tokens lose exchange (display) value. The laws of supply and demand are presumed to be inexorable under proper conditions.

The basic fact—which applies to smiles, greeting cards, and kisses as well as to religious tokens—seems to be that the elasticity of supply of symbols is inherently much greater than that of the supply of actual sentiment. Since symbols increase so easily while the fund of sentiments is limited, a great many symbols circulating become, inauthentic as it were, bad money, bankrupt or bogus, because they cannot be cashed in for anything like their face value. (Such words are hype, schmaltz, corny, lip service, gladhanding, baby-kissing, sentimentality, pathos, rhetoric, slogans, preaching, moralizing, identify such bad symbolic money.) In such proliferation of symbols without emotional purchasing power, it is possible to speak of a Gresham's effect as degraded symbols displace authentic ones in circulation. In the absence of authentic symbols, people will, when called on, display the inflated ones (such as reciting a creed or singing the national anthem at a ball game) whether or not they really feel that way. So it is possible through bogus symbols for a society to be in a state of false consciousness about its own feeling, just as it can be unaware of creeping monetary inflation.

In that development, when too many demands are put upon people for sentiments they cannot display except as inflated, bogus symbols, social crisis lurks, as seems to have been illustrated by the collapse of communism in Eastern Bloc countries in 1989.

Two factors seem to especially enhance the proliferation of inauthentic religious symbols. One is false personalization, a tactic much used by evangelists, as by merchandisers. It is the pretense of friendliness, intimacy, and concern. "Brotherly love" may be only a pretense of feelings that seem to evaporate the moment one leaves the church. False personalization is especially prominent in large evangelical crowds and in broadcasting to radio or television audiences whom the evangelist has never seen but pretends to be familiar with—his "friends" and "brothers" in faith. Analysis of a sample of replies of televangelists to inquiries from the audience showed that most used personalizing devices, such as a facsimile of a handwritten letter from the broadcaster himself, forty of forty-five letters had facsimile signatures of the broadcaster himself, seventeen used personalizing elements in the text, and two looked like telegrams from the broadcaster himself. Almost all asked for financial contributions (Horsfeld 1985, p. 94). False personalization degrades religious tokens just as it does smiles and kissing.

The other factor enhancing proliferation of inauthentic religious symbols has already been treated in chapter 4: contagious communications in crowds and masses. They fill the bubbles of mass hysteria and other forms of herd thinking. They make possible instant baptisms and "conversions." They create trances in thousands responding to the same hypnotic appeal. They induce extraordinary states such as stigmata, "born again" experiences, revelations, speaking in tongues, seeming cures or miracles, and claims of appearances of angels, prophets, and saints bearing revelations. Though some conversions can be lifelong, most are momentary trances created by suggestion, quick and shallow, having little permanent effect on the lifestyle of converts—seemingly full but soon void—"the stuff that dreams are made of".

These thoughts are not meant to be a definitive treatment of religious inflation, but aim merely to explore the application of the idea of inflation to sentimental symbols, to see a little more clearly what inflation in religion might consist of.

9

Fashion Inflation

Fashions are like human beings. They come in, nobody knows when, why, or how; and they go out, nobody knows when, why, or how.

"And by that sort of thing," added the tailor, Mr. Omer, in Dickens' *David Copperfield* (chapter 9), "we very often lose a little mint of money."

The present writer confesses to having a rack of old-fashioned garments that he could not bring himself to throw away because they were so "good" (who knows when they will be back in fashion?).

It is abhorrent to admit that, in our time no less than Dickens' styles come and go without anybody knowing why; but that is not far from the truth. Experts try to divine what is coming in a new dress style, song hit, best-seller, automobile body—wherever fashion holds sway—because great profits and risks are involved in fashion merchandise. They make elaborate market surveys to detect a trend. Producers of recordings of popular music use panels of experts (disk-jockeys, song writers, musicians) to listen to new tunes and try to pick out the next hit. Buyers of women's dress styles attend exclusive showings by designers, and stake their bets on which model to put into production. Editors court writers who have had a best-seller, hoping to hit the mark again. But, expert though they are, they are usually the first to admit that their choices are mostly inspired guesswork.

The mystery of fashion is that it is so hard to predict because it is not a logical development, not progress, not better than what it replaces. Take these examples, if you please: in men's clothing the bell-bottomed trouser's; in women's, the mini-skirt; in automobile bodies, large tail fins; in popular songs, "Mairzy-Doates." It would not be easy to prove that these are better than previous, nor that they are worse than subsequent fashions. There is little to tell us what the next hit in songs, dances, best-sellers, new looks, diets, therapies, or auto bodies will be because it is not a logical improvement or extension of what we already have or have had, but seems capricious and random, a rather abrupt—even silly—departure. So it is difficult to rationalize fashions on the basis of how useful they are. Technical knowledge gives little clue in predicting the fashion aspect. Consumers' reports do not identify fashionable items. This tells us that the reasons for adopting a fashion are quite different from why one purchases a better car battery.

Two things have much to do with what is happening in fads and fashions (though I do not suppose they are the whole story). First, fads and fashions come and go in unwitting response to emotional weather produced by emotional contagion (chap. 4)—that they are a kind of language of popular moods, could we but read it. (Some of these moods are described as "opening" and "closing" [Klapp 1978.] Fads and fashions come in and go out according to their success in dramatizing or signaling one's participation in popular moods, as is explicit in popular song lyrics.

Second, fads and fashions going out lose value by oversupply in a way similar to monetary inflation. For this reason we are interested in fashion, because it is a major subset, almost a paradigm of symbolic inflation. It is a process that resembles monetary inflation, except that "looks," not coins, lose value as their supply in the social marketplace increases. It is a process in which symbols float like a hot air balloon expanding, then descend as they run out of hot air, leaving merchandisers with stacks and racks of goods they cannot sell, because, though perfectly good, they are "out of fashion." Fashion is one of those symbols that lose value the more of them there are. It may not be apparent at first, but what happens to a dollar in inflation is very similar to what happens to a fashion. That is, when one tries to "spend" it, it does not "buy" so much as it used to.

What, then, is the logical relation of these two processes? I do not see monetary inflation as the authentic type which all others merely resemble, but general inflation (more becoming less), with both fashion and monetary inflation as subsets. To put it another way, both fashion and monetary inflation are synechdoches of general inflation.

Putting fashion alongside monetary inflation, for comparison may give us a better view of what is going on in both. How are fashion and monetary inflation similar? To my mind, the main points of resemblance between fashion and monetary inflation are: (1) an S-curve of adoption and discard, (2) people shopping for "looks" (display value that will enhance status), which parallels search in the economic market for monetary profits, (3) fashion and monetary symbols have a "purchasing power" which in the case of fashion is display value, a signaling function, (4) oversupply destroys both money and the display value of fashion, (5) a Gresham's effect occurs in fashion, in which poorer tokens displace better ones.

First, the course of a fashion strikingly resembles galloping (runaway, hyper) monetary inflation—a bubble-like boom followed by collapse of value.

During the boom phase, contagious imitation plays a large part. Everyone seems eager to get in, as in the stock market of 1929 and other booms and crazes so well described by Allen (1946). Going up such a slope is like a ride in a ski-lift, but coming down is like a fall off a cliff.

The second main resemblance I see between fashion and monetary inflation is that shopping for "looks" with display value that will enhance status parallels search in the economic market for monetary profits. People shop in the fashion market for "looks" by which to make themselves more interesting and enhance their status. The city is aptly described as a bazaar of people, in which we shop not only for economic goods and wages but experiences, entertainments, styles, status symbols, even ideas and faiths. Display of fashion looks is achieved by "seeing and being seen" at fashionable spots such as theatrical opening nights, posh restaurants, spas, ski resorts, Ascot races, the Henley regatta, or in Paris:

Sitting on the Boulevard St. Michele in a sidewalk cafe, one could watch the passing parade. Everybody seemed to have turned out: Sorbonne students, office workers, tourists, fashion models, and "characters" of all kinds—artists, bohemians, intelectuals, folk singers, impersonators of the opposite sex. Every "look" of fashion was there. All seemed to have turned out just to make the passing show more interesting. It was in some ways like the New York Easter Parade. There was a feeling of being "on show"; people seemed to be watching each other out of the corners of their eyes as they do when they are before a television camera. Many seemed to be theatrically made up just for the occasion: in wigs, monocles, eye patches, beards, goatees, bleached and dyed hair, odd coiffures and transformations, white mascara, green fingernails, every cut and color of clothing. Indeed, it seemed as though a score of theaters had suddenly discharged their casts in full makeup upon the street.

Media are showcases of fashion; and the largest cities, such as New York, Paris, and London, the centers from which styles diffuse. People scan the media, especially "people" magazines, for looks. New looks offer an adventure in identity not unlike wearing a costume in a play. Some idea of the variety of looks offered may be given by the following list from women's magazines: Classical, Rennaissance, Egyptian, Ballerina, Victorian, Space Age, Ethnic, Nostalgic, Gypsy, Peasant, Dallas-Dynasty, Mandarin, Coolie, Sailor, Crusader, Alpine, Bedouin, Russian, Musketeer, Edwardian, Lumberjack, Ruffles-and-Lace, Classic Tailored, California Casual, Floozie, Geisha, Little Girl, and so on. A department store posts a sign for its customers: "Let us help you find your look." Achieving a look may go beyond dress, cosmetics, hairstyles and grooming (Wax 1957), hair-transformation, even name-changing, face-lifting, steroids, silicon, and surgical operations. Men often achieve looks through vehicles and sports equipment. Guns and moustaches or beards play a large part in male identity, aiming perhaps at the macho look projected by actors such as John Wayne, Clint Eastwood, Charles Bronson, Chuck Norris, Sylvester Stallone. Youth may try to achieve a look by a grotesque haircut, or manner of manipulating a cigarette or beverage, or perhaps by a torn garment and other bizarre extremes aiming to shock. In this perspective, we think of fashion looks as props or costumes for a part an actor is to play. Such things as garments, hairdos, beverages, automobiles, food tastes, leisure activities are used to produce "looks," the purpose of which is to dramatize oneself and convey an impression to others that will earn social credit: perhaps a claim to belong to a certain social set.

A third parallel between fashion and monetary inflation is found in the concept of "purchasing power" extended to all sorts of tokens— not restricted to money. Fashion and money both have purchasing power. With money, it is the amount of commodities that can be bought, measured by price levels, as in the Fisher formula—the higher, the more inflation. In the case of fashion, purchasing power is display value, e.g., a "look" or sound (in the case of a popular song, or an accent) which "buys" prestige and glamour—a social rating. The style displayed is a basis on which to rate people and to improve—or at least preserve—one's social rating in the eyes of others. If everyone's rating were known and fixed, as in a military rank system, there would be little need for fashion. But in a society with an open social market, all can gain, and even the wealthiest bolster their standing, by making a good impression: looking one's best, driving a new car, living at a fashionable address, trimming one's lawn, skimming best-sellers, seeing the latest show, and so on. For most people, fashion is a major way, by appearance alone, to give oneself a promotion, so to speak. One who takes up a startling or "high" fashion can have an adventure in identity like wearing a costume in a play.

In a mass society, the style displayed may be the only basis by which to rate a person (no matter that his automobile is rented, yacht is borrowed, posh address temporary, "old school tie" not his own, even that his letterhead or certificate is fake). It serves, just as a seemingly large roll of bills does, to impress, for the moment, people who probably will not have opportunity or time to check further on the validity of the token. The fashion-user astutely seeks tokens that will give the maximum credit in impression and rating in return for the cost in effort and money. Such display is most useful in a mobile, anonymous, urban setting where impression counts, whereas it would not work in a small town where everyone knew everyone else too well to be impressed. The very anonymity and heterogeniety of people in the urban setting make fashion displays almost necessary to tell where people fit. Especially, the high expectations of urban life (stimulated by advertising) favor fashion, where so many are, so to speak, on the make.

Thus exchange of fashion tokens works in the social market to establish rating that are like prices. A social rating, like a market price, is a measure of the worth of what is offered in terms of what others will pay for it (to be sure, not in economic terms but less tangible values such as esteem, admiration, social acceptance, invidious distinction, mention in society columns, and so on—but no less than real money and economic goods). Also, ratings accumulate to make social worth, just as money invested accumulates to make net financial worth. In such ways, fashion is not just a race of Smith with Jones, but a market in which Smith and Jones are offering tokens to innumerable others for ratings that will make them richer in social worth.

The fourth, and perhaps for us most important, similarity of fashion to monetary inflation, is that tokens lose value as they become more plentiful. As we have argued throughout this book for other symbols, oversupply destroys both money and the display value of fashion, because both are subject to the law of supply and demand. The supply of tokens acts like the supply of money. For example, an increase in the amount of fashion tokens in relation to the prestige they can buy is like an increase in the supply of money versus the economic goods it can buy. This implies that market laws of supply and demand apply to fashion. The question obviously comes up: what happens if the supply of fashion tokens suddenly increases? Were money the tokens, economics has a ready answer: it is called inflation. In the case of fashion, it is called being merely "out of fashion."

As it runs its course, fashion loses value the way money does in a runaway or galloping inflation when the supply of money is recklessly increased. Too many dollars chasing too few goods raises prices generally, which means loss of purchasing power of money.

The parallel in fashion, of too many dollars chasing too few goods, is too many copies of a fashion chasing too little social credit or prestige. The increase in supply of the fashion, in which cheaper copies and even counterfeits flood the market, can bring about a loss of value of fashions, and especially of fads, as severe as that of the runaway inflation that ruined the German mark in 1922. In the case of fashion, the loss of value is illustrated by expensive, recently purchased, but now unwearable clothes hanging in the closet (the whole array of looks that are now "out," as can be seen in old magazines); or merchants' overstocks of perfectly good merchandise that now nobody wants at any price. Such loss of value occurs by the same law of supply and demand that devalues money when in too large supply. So if more and more women wear mink (because pelts are produced cheaply on farms), then that token fades as a sign of wealth. If too many drive Cadillacs, than one gets no special deference from a doorman who has just opened the doors of a dozen like it. A lady wearing a Givenchy original must feel cheated when she arrives at a party to see several other women wearing the same dress. Her original has been devalued to their copies. So it is with fashion as with money, that when too many have too much and try to cash in at once, the value collapses. Such copying defeats the purpose of high fashion, as it does of collecting art and antiques, since these activities are a search for *un*inflatable tokens, which cannot be turned out in cheaper versions. When a style becomes common it loses its ability to confer social credit, distinguish people by status-images, that is, loses its value for negotiating status. This corresponds to lost purchasing power of money. Carried to extreme, it means collapse of the fashion or currency and abandonment of that token. The death of fashion, as of money, occurs when it can no longer purchase anything.

The reason for loss of value of tokens is at least partly simple arithmetic. As with money, if twice as many tokens are presented for the same amount of purchasable goods, the value of tokens is cut in half. If the supply of goods runs out, the purchasing power of tokens plummets to zero. This would not happen were the supply of values so elastic that more was forthcoming, however many tokens circulated. But, alas, the supply of deference and elite status is limited. No matter how many people claim or deserve prestige, esteem, and so on, our ability to bestow them is limited. We cannot admire more than a certain proportion of people. Collectively, our capacity for heroes is limited. The reason for inelasticity of supply of elite values is twofold. On the sociological side, most hierarchies are constricted toward the top, and cannot give more elite status, only rotate persons among the same proportions of positions (as the joke says, you can't make the whole army generals). On the psychological side, there seems to be an equally rigid restriction: we are emotionally unable to give deference, esteem, and admiration beyond a certain number of people. If we have to give deference to more than that, we just spread it thinner, or give a perfunctory or mock performance. Suppose one is asked to admire a diamond. One does so earnestly. However, after ohing-and-ahing about that gem, along comes another person with a similar one, then another, and another. It does not take long to exhaust the emotional supply of admiration and esteem, even if stones get larger. In other words, there is a psychological limit to feelings people are able to generate in response to a token—and redundancy and imitation of fashions exceed this limit no less than with heroes' medals. This psychological limit combined with constriction of hierarchies means that elite values (other than sham) cannot be multiplied as fast as tokens claiming them. Tokens can always outstrip status values. And do!—which is the story of fashion.

Our fifth point of parallel between fashion and monetary inflation is usually called Gresham's law, according to which cheaper and inferior coins drive out "good" ones from circulation. The case with money is plain enough. If gold, silver, and paper currency in the same denominations are all circulating, there is little doubt after a time which would be easiest, and which hardest to find in trade, except as collector's items. Paper money would prevail, along with counterfeit well enough made not to be detected by most receivers.

A tendency to degrade in fashion and much of popular culture seems to come from copying something that was scarce, expensive, and good, rendering it into something plentiful, cheap, and bad.

Imitation for the sake of being in fashion soon becomes fakery of its symbols. We saw inflation by counterfeit credentials in chapter 7. Designer products are especially threatened by counterfeiting. When new dresses are worn by Diana, Princess of Wales or Sarah Ferguson, Duchess of York, copies are on the street within twenty-four hours after they were first worn. The counterfeiting of fashion includes a worldwide trade of fake products, invading trademarks and copyrights of designer merchandise like garments, handbags, shoes, and jeans. As can be imagined, this leads to mistrust of products and loss of reputation of trademarks (James R. Chiles, "Anything Can Be Counterfeited," *Smithsonian*, July 1986, pp. 35–43).

Something like Gresham's law seems to be operating when fake gems take the place of real. Fake gems are increasingly taking the place of real, even with the wealthiest women. Paste is worn, and the real ones stored in a vault. Knowledge that jewels are fake seems not to interfere much with their display value. The question remains: what will happen to display value when all jewels shown are known to be fake? Will a Gresham's effect degrade them all—or can a curious filip to status come from openly admitting one's jewels are fake—implying a huge hidden supply of real ones?

Cheapening by imitation also occurs in automobile body styles. A federal judge in California shut down a producer of imitation Ferraris because copycat cars were likely to damage the reputation of the manufacturer of the real ones—in our terms, the symbol would be degraded. Faking of auto body ornaments is widespread. Producers of Buicks for a time put holes—2, 3, or 4—on the side of engine covers to convey a sense of raciness (completely unfunctional). The 8-cylinder models had three, or even four, holes. Six-cylinder models got only two. When, one day, the manufacturers started putting three holes on the 6-cylinder model, they found sales of that model greatly improved, but got many angry letters from owners of 8-cylinder models, complaining that their cars had been cheapened by similarity to less expensive cars.

That even the rarest and most expensive items of fashion can be threatened by imitation and Gresham's law, seems to be illustrated by an extraordinary case of legal fine art counterfeiting in 1978 when Nelson Rockefeller tried to make masterpieces more available to private owners by producing and selling fine art reproductions so good that only experts could tell they were not authentic. For example, a Rodin copy (cost) could be had for $7,500. Soon after, the New York Metropolitan Museum of Art followed suit with a mail order and counter business of $12 million per year from its souvenir shop. Of course, new owners exulted in their acquisitions. But it aroused a storm of protest from art dealers. One critic asked, "How far do you go to provide the public with souvenirs? When do they become counterfeits?" (McBride 1980). It wasn't so much the cheaper prices of the copies as the fact that no longer could one be sure whether a Picasso or Van Gogh that one saw in a wealthy home was authentic. Copying had made precious originals a little too available.

From such examples we infer that a Gresham's effect seems to be built into fashion, even more than in money, due to copying and faking styles in ever cheaper versions—designer clothes, gems, art, automobile styles, and so on—a degradation of value by cheaper symbols entering circulation and taking the place of more valuable ones in a market, driving the better ones out of circulation, one might say, and leaving the market a little poorer for those who seek the best.

These aspects of fashion seem to justify the view that it is a form of galloping inflation, helped by Gresham's effect. Debasement of the quality of tokens turns the screw on other sorts of inflation already occurring from mere increase in supply.

Let us look further into the death of fashion, which occurs in two main ways, according to how it becomes oversupplied.

Perhaps the simplest way is sheer imitation, which multiplies inordinately the number of copies. Typically, a person sees a look he likes, on the street or displayed by opinion leaders or media models, then tries to copy or buy what he has seen. The style is copied widely. In this sense it circulates. If a physical object, it can be passed from hand to hand, also it may be manufactured and sold in huge quantities. If a label or surface feature, it can be put on. If a skill, it can be learnt by others. If a symbolic message, popular song, or vogue word, it can be diffused by media instantly to millions. Hairpieces, wigs, cosmetics, and plastic surgery can create uniform good looks. As noted in chapter 4, imitation is a sort of contagious communication, which makes people wish to be together and more alike. But all too soon the result of mass imitation is monotony and boredom, a wish for fresh looks while the old ones fade. So fashions drown in their own redundancy. But leaders strive against the monotony of fashion by personal *eclat*—soon copied. This helps us understand the paradox that fashion is that realm where everybody strives to be distinctive but winds up looking like everybody else.

But if sheer imitation helps explain the death of fashion by boredom, there is an opposite tendency that strongly helps its demise. The other way that fashions fade and why, even while they are "in," they never entirely prevail and flood the market, is explained by the ingenious theory of sociologist George Simmel, which asserts that there is a continual race for distinction as lower classes try to take the fashion up, causing upper classes to abandon that style and allow it to go to its doom.

> The fashions of the upper stratum of society are never identical with those of the lower; in fact, they are abandoned by the former as soon as the latter prepares to appropriate them. . . . Just as soon as the lower classes begin to copy their style, thereby crossing the line of demarcation the upper classes have drawn and destroying the uniformity of their coherence, the upper classes turn away from this style and adopt a new one, which in its turn differentiates them from the masses; and thus a game goes merrily on. . . . The very character of fashion demands that it should be exercised at one time only by a portion of the given group, the great majority being merely on the road to adopting it. As soon as an example has been universally adopted . . . we no longer speak of fashion. As fashion spreads, it gradually goes to its doom. (Simmel 1957, pp. 543–547)

What ruins fashion? In our terms of the "purchasing power" of a "look," it is too many others displaying the same look, which leads to loss of distinction (say a woman who has bought an exclusive dress design encountering at a social function others wearing that same "original"). Mass merchandising, reproducing the same in cheaper copies within a few weeks, floods the world with copies of copies, enabling many more people to enter the fashion race, until the fashion dies because it has lost distinction, until it is no longer chic but passe, not smart but "old hat." One cannot be both chic and mass. As a manager of a posh Swiss ski resort put it, "We don't want too large a clientele because then it's mass and not chic any more." The "look of success" described by a self-help book (Molloy 1978) showed an effort to find in business fashion a look that would distinguish winners from losers; but it does not tell what status is to be gained if *everyone* displays the same "look of success." We see, thus, that distinction is the function of fashion—however imitative it seems to be, it is really asserting the distinction of elite from mass values.

An illustration of how fashions die from both of these factors, imitation/redundancy and loss of class distinction, is found in the "Tut mania" of 1977–78. It showed the S-curve of adoption, then its death by loss of distinction by too many taking it up. The extraordinary enthusiasm to see the artifacts of this extinct monarch while on tour about North America grew until it reached a point described by newspapers as "mania"—standing in line for hours to get tickets; long bus rides; scalpers getting thirty dollars for a two-dollar ticket; King Tut motifs in clothing, jewelry, dinner plates, bed sheets, home decor—it was as though people were obsessed with the Tut-theme. Why did so many want so badly to see Tut? Archeological interest and love of beauty go only so far. People who had shown little interest in archaeology or the arts suddenly wanted to see Tut. Their wish was not all that hard to understand. *Not* having seen Tut, one had to admit one was "out of it," not up with what was going on, while others could capture the scene and hold forth for a time. Once having seen Tut, one could claim the spotlight, saying "Yes, I've seen the show," and give one's opinion before the silent if not spellbound audience—a satisfaction about the same as that of saying, "I just met Celebrity X, and this is what he told me"; or of appearing at a social function in the latest boutique style or cut of formal dress clothes drawing notice, compliments, and envy. In the case of Tut, it had little to do with love of art or archaeology.

Then, suddenly, it was over. People stopped talked about Tut because no distinction could be gained by telling about him. If one mentioned having seen the exhibit, everyone nodded knowingly, with just a hint of boredom. What distinction could there be in holding forth, when so many had—or claimed to have—seen it? Who was listening? The sudden artistic and archaeological interest evaporated. Discreetly one removed from the coffee table the Pharaonic bust, no longer a centerpiece for conversation. Sales of Tut souvenirs fell; ads announced:

> CLEARANCE SALE, UP TO 50%. Replicas of Tut, statues and Tut jewelry, from $7.50. Hundreds of Egyptian jewelry (electroplated), from $1.50. 14K Gold Tut Rings and Tut or Nefertiti charms, $28.00. T-shirts, slides, stamps, books, posters. . . .

The downturn in the S-curve and fall to extinction were rapid. Fad profits were over even if moderate sale of replicas continued at its normally subdued level. When too many people had seen the Tut exhibition, it ceased to be fashionable, no social credit was gained by talking about it or displaying its souvenirs. The case illustrates the sudden rise and death of a fashion that loses its "purchasing power" because its supply gluts the social market.

Thus fashion tells a story that could be reiterated for many symbols studied in this book: how in certain circumstances, such as oversupply, more becomes less, and too much proves to be not enough.

The broader perspective is to see a consumer society feverishly pursuing fashions and in so doing paradoxically losing those values by inflation. Practically everything in the realm of fashion fades and decays, its values melting like ice cream on a hot day. Doing so, fashion unintentionally portrays a world-view like that of Buddhism, where earthly values are transitory and unsatisfying. Doubtless this contributes to the malaise, the sense of cheapening, in modern life, which in chapter 1 I called the flatulence of affluence.

Even more pervasive does this sense of loss of value and meaning grow, when put in even broader terms as the inflation of information, in the next chapter.

10

Inflation Of Information

We turn now to the most general kind of inflation, trying to understand how information itself could lose value or degrade as it increases in amount. Two concepts especially help: John Stuart Mill's of the free market of ideas, and the contemporary concept of overload of information as a source of meaning lag. We explore these ideas not to prove them but to better see what they offer as metaphors for the most general kind of inflation, that of information itself.

Let us look first at Mill's idea.

The Free Market of Ideas

As with Adam Smith, the key of Mill's mechanism of progress is competition, without which testing and winnowing, ideas, instead of getting better, would mount up into a growing heap of prejudice, dogma, bigotry, and balderdash.

Since Mill wrote his famous essay, *On Liberty* (1859), the idea of a free market of ideas has provided an attractive metaphor for the flow of communication and formation of public opinion in an open (democratic) society. This metaphor is that the competition of ideas is like that of an economic market in which, according to Adam Smith, free competition of money, goods, and enterprises selects the better and eliminates the worse—improving products, hence progress.

To avoid such retrogression, Mill fashioned the most powerful argument for free speech that has ever been made, a sweeping claim of freedom for the individual in all spheres where society had no explicit right to intrude to protect itself: (1) "absolute freedom of opinion and sentiment on all subjects," including liberty of expressing and publishing same, (2) "liberty of tastes and pursuits . . . framing the plan of our life to suit our own character . . . doing as we like, subject to such consequences as may follow"; (3) "freedom to unite, for any purpose not involving harm to others." Mill did not call such an area of freedom a market, but recognized its parallel with Smith's free trade:

> It is now recognized, though not till after a long struggle, that both the cheapness and the good quality of commodities are most effectually provided for by leaving the producers and sellers perfectly free, under the sole check of equal freedom to the buyers for supplying themselves elsewhere. This is the so-called doctrine of Free Trade, which rests on grounds different from, though equally solid with, the principle of individual liberty asserted in this Essay (V).

What especially brought Mill into league with market theorists was his emphasis on utility as the "ultimate appeal on all ethical questions," including truth as a utility-value tested by free competition of ideas.

> I forego any advantage which could be derived to my argument from the idea of abstract right, as a thing independent of utility. I regard utility as the ultimate appeal on all ethical questions (I).

He accepted the presupposition of "absolute right," but rejected the motion of a social contract (IV), and built his argument on the utility of free competition, of which truth was a utility-value. Without free exchange and competition testing utility, we cannot tell what an idea is worth any more than we can tell the worth of a product. In such a market, an opinion so rare as to be regarded as eccentric (even were it Darwin's theory) has no market value of credibility or truth until demand puts it there. On the other hand, an accepted idea shows its public worth by the demand for it and the social utility value of the tokens—declarations, sacred books, best sellers, monographs, awards, academic regalia, legislation, and so on—that invest it with worth. But there must be free competition, not a monopoly, if information is to be properly tested and valued.

Above all, it was the way in which utility of ideas was to be tested that put Mill's doctrine into market theory. First, let us consider his famous principle that:

> If all mankind minus one were of one opinion, and only one person were of the contrary opinion, mankind would be no more justified in silencing that one person, than he, if he had the power, would be justified in silencing mankind (II).

Why all this concern for different—including many crackpot—ideas? It was the same concern one would feel about a small promising new enterprise in the market, say that of Thomas Edison.

> The peculiar evil of silencing the expression of an opinion is, that it is robbing the human race. . . . If the opinion is right, they are deprived of the opportunity of exchanging error for truth; if wrong, they lose, what is almost as great a benefit, the clearer perception and livelier impression of truth, produced by its collision with error. . . . We can never be sure that the opinion we are endeavoring to stifle is a false opinion; and if we were sure, stifling it would be an evil still (II).

Mill has such contempt for prevailing opinion because without competition from dissent, we have no way of telling which part of the current opinion is true and useful, since it all comes from the public, that miscellaneous collection of a few wise and many foolish individuals. Even good ideas, unless challenged continually, deteriorate (like market goods untested by competition):

> Not only the grounds of the opinion are forgotten in the absence of discussion, but too often the meaning of the opinion itself. . . . Instead of a vivid conception and a living belief, there remain only a few phrases retained by rote (II).

Such a "mischievous operation of the absence of free discussion" is what economists would call monopoly exerting its hand to stifle competition and set prices, in this case truth-values.

> There must be discussion, to show how experience is to be interpreted. Wrong opinions and practices gradually yield to fact and argument. . . . The whole strength and value . . . of human judgment, depending on the one property, that it can be set right when it is wrong, reliance can be placed on it only when the means of setting it right are kept constantly at hand. . . . Hearing what can be said . . . by persons of every variety of opinion, and studying all modes in which . . . looked at by every character of mind. No wise man ever acquired his wisdom in any mode but this. . . . The steady habit of correcting and completing his own opinion by collating it with those of others, so far from causing doubt and hesitation . . . is the only stable foundation for a just reliance on it . . . knowing that he has sought for objections and difficulties, instead of avoiding them, and has shut out no light . . . he has a right to think his judgment better than that of any person, or any multitude, who have not gone through a similar process (II).

So an invisible hand brings progress and truth from the clash of biased and selfish opinions. It hinges, of course, on the ability to recognize truth when one has tested it through rational arguments under open, temperate conditions. Without these, there is little hope:

> The dictum that truth always triumphs over persecution is one of those pleasant falsehoods which men repeat after one another. . . . History teems with instances of truth put down by persecution. . . . Christianity might have been extirpated. . . . It spread, and became predominant, because the persecutions were only occasional, lasting but a short time, and separated by long intervals of almost undisturbed propagandism. It is a piece of idle sentimentality that truth, merely as truth, has any inherent power denied to error of prevailing against the dungeon and the stake. . . . The real advantage which truth has, consists in that . . . it may be extinguished one, twice, or many times, but in the course of ages there will generally be found persons to rediscover it, until one of its reappearances falls on a time when from favorable circumstances it escapes persecution (II).

At the opposite pole from persecution are optimum conditions of competition for improving knowledge: constant debate, temperateness, Socratic dialectics, searching out the strongest opponent of an opinion—even a devil's advocate—to test it. Will this lead to disorder and confusion? On the contrary, knowledge will accumulate and society will progress:

> As mankind improve, the number of doctrines which are no longer disputed or doubted will be constantly on the increase: and the well-being of mankind may almost be measured by the number and gravity of the truth which have reached the point of being uncontested (II).

But all truths must be continually protected by dialectics in education from the "incurable defect" of being accepted through authority, not through reason.

Like Smith, Mill had to base his argument for freedom on the assumption that if society wants progress, it must grant freedom. Otherwise it must enjoy the dubious comfort of conformity to poor ideas and products. In this way progress in wealth is paralleled by progress in knowledge. The pricing system in one case is competitive sale of goods, and in the other, open debate, the outcome in either case being a moving equilibrium of progress toward a better society. The great power of Mill's idea, as of Smith's, was that it placed freedom on a utilitarian instead of a metaphysical basis, the latter being shaky in an age of positivism. In the free market, truth-value and price are parallel notions of utility.

According to Mill's argument, an open society must constantly face the challenges of new ideas or it will lapse into conformity. To avoid suppressing valuable ideas, it must tolerate deviant, even dangerous opinions and lifestyles, so long as they do not result in social injury. Censorship is abhorrent, for it implies the assumption of infallibility. The liberal must even tolerate ideas which threaten the free institutions on which he relies. Suppose he faces in debate an opponent who talks openly of establishing concentration camps. His dilemma is that if he denies his opponent the privilege of urging such proposals, he himself suppresses the free market of ideas. If he grants his opponent a hearing, freedom may be imperiled. A true follower of Mill must at this point rely on the probability of the free market of ideas working in the long run, over the certainty of damaging it by his own act of suppression. He must believe that an uncertain evil done by another is better than committing a certain one himself.

How then, in the light of Mill's doctrine of liberty, does inflation of symbols occur and information become degraded? The answer is that information is degraded when it accumulates and proliferates without being tested by free discussion: full, free, and fair debate. Information degrades when growing uniformity and stagnation result from the mischievous absence of free discussion—leading to uniformity, dogmatism, stagnation, monopoly, and loss of variety and creativity. This sterile and stagnant sector I have designated in other works (Klapp 1978, 1986) as "bad redundancy." The whole thrust of Mill's argument was to avoid such proliferation by the working of the free market of ideas.

And if there is a market of ideas, does it not follow that the symbols exchanged as tokens of those ideas can be inflated in the sense that, as they increase in numbers, they could denote less truth, meaning or other value—win less assent, be less credible—have less "purchasing power," as we have applied this concept to credentials, valentines, medals, fashions, and so on? If inflation is extended so far, then all such forms of inflation are synechdoches of the most general class of inflation, of information itself.

How, then, can information itself be inflated? I presume it does so, as does money, with growth in the token supply to a point where it is overextended and unable to deliver the values denoted, by redundancy, or sheer overload, or noiselike character of information. In such ways information can degrade and lose meaning as its supply increases.

So it seems to me that Mill provides an answer as to how, in the midst of rapid accumulation of knowledge, general cultural inflation could occur. If ideas pile up, uncriticized by free, fair, and full debate, then the intellectual enterprise, far from leading to progress, will proliferate into a great heap of bigotry and balderdash. That would be an inflation because information was increasing in amount but losing value. And authorities, experts, professors, and other purveyors of knowledge would be in a position like trying to spend devalued or counterfeit money.

Mill has stated the case of inflation by redundancy proliferating when criticism and freedom are lacking. Let us now turn to the other sector of inflation of information, by noise and sheer overload, as conceived in terms of information theory.

Information Overload and Meaning Lag

Another perspective useful for understanding inflation of information is commonly known as information overload. Familiar is the sense of being burdened more than helped by information. Modern society is generating a vast output of symbols to which it is often impossible to give sufficient attention and meaning. Perfectly good information becomes a glut, in amount and rate of production beyond any person's time and ability to digest, even with the help of information-processing systems. Paperwork inflation is a large part of this overload. Bureaucratic channels become more and more clogged with paperwork in multiple copies. Loaded files become harder to retrieve information from. Computer print-outs become longer. As bureaucracies become more complex, more and more reports have to be written and read to find out what is going on. Soon additional personnel have to be hired just to write, read, and file reports.

News agencies and journalism are also responsible for much inflation of information. When one has to generate a quota of words, day after day—story or no story, photo-opportunity or no photo-opportunity—inflation is inevitable. No newspaper has yet had the nerve to say, "Nothing today, folks."

Adding to news inflation is the inherent fleetingness, transience, or decay of media messages. As is well known, most messages from television, films, radio, newspapers, and magazines are consumed quickly and then perish. Their short life span emphasizes "timeliness, superficiality, or sensationalism in what is fundamentally a one-time chance to attract large audiences." Fleetingness lessens the ability of the audience to comprehend messages. However, video cassette recorders somewhat offset transiency by allowing a second look or hearing, and make it possible to save some otherwise unrepeated television programs and so reduce the rate of decay (Levy and Frank 1984). On the whole, though, it is evident that the faster messages decay, the more disconnected they are, and the less durable significance such information has.

Another source of inflation of information is closer to home for scholars. It is scholarship itself—especially those areas known as "publish or perish" and research grant reports, which require interim reports and articles and books, whether or not one has anything to say. This pressure to publish generates an enormous supply of articles and books in the academic marketplace competing for publication, authority, recognition, and prestige—as well as more tangible benefits in terms of promotion, tenure, and perhaps royalties. However, if during the time the scholar is writing, the number of competing authors doubles while the number of readers in that field remains constant, then a loss of value is to be expected in articles and books as tokens of academic prestige. All this tends to depress the academic market, a loss of morale in the world of scholarship because voices have multiplied but not ears.

In a world seemingly deluged with blab, chatter, trivia, advertising, junk mail, bad news, and other irrelevant or unwelcome messages, it is hardly surprising that a low value should be attached to information, indicated by such things as paperbacks thrown away on trains, students complaining of study loads and contemptuous of books, falling value of university degrees, tons of ephemeral literature unread the day after printed, degree-mill diplomas, and discounting expressions (blurb, sales talk, commercial, bafflegab, jargon, rhetoric, hokum, hype, garbage) applied to information rather as one might speak of inflated or counterfeit money.

In such a flood, people are seen to be inundated by information which is useless, meaningless, filled with hype, or sterile and redundant. As information becomes thus inflated, we pay less attention to it, feel bored by it, discount it as hype, and so on. It is more evident, then, why the modern attitude toward information is hardly one of unalloyed eagerness. To be sure, the modern appetite is voracious to the point of gluttony as people strive to consume media output and stay abreast. But the appetite, however huge, is tinged with contrary elements. First is satiety, a certain queasiness from overeating instead of the comfort of one who has dined well. The public palate is also jaded or blase, desensitized to what would have shocked the previous generation.

Third, there is a distinct thread of resentment of such things as television commercials, sex and violence content, and incessant ringing of telephones. More people than one might realize have become non-answerers of the telephone. They let it ring, cut off the ring, or record calls on an answering device. This is far from the enthusiasm of the community that listened in on the rural party line. There is also a defensive attitude, of fending off unwanted information. For the bulk of information, though some is momentarily useful, there is indifference or disdain, a throwaway attitude toward paperwork, magazines, and even books.

Finally, people are continually on the verge of boredom because so much information is irrelevant, meaningless, or trivial—or urgent but they can do nothing about it. We see boredom as having a defensive function as a barrier against noise.

What such negative elements in the appetite for information suggest is that along with the growth of information there has been a decline in its marginal value or meaning. The point might be made with the economist's idea of marginal utility. Yet another useful economic analogy which we are emphasizing here is that the decline of value of information was rather like an inflation of currency: the more there was of it, the less it seemed to "buy" in meaning.

In another study (Klapp 1986) I have tried to explain how a society could become boring in spite—indeed because—of huge loads of information. The information society is not only not immune but is susceptible to its own kinds of boredom, resulting from degradation of information in two ways, redundancy and noise, which outstrip the "slow horse" of meaning. It is a major paradox that the growing leisure and affluence and mounting information and stimulation that we call progress leads to boredom—a deficit in the quality of life. No small item of this deficit is attrition of meaning along with the vast accumulation of information.

What the information society of the late twentieth century seemed to be demonstrating was that information is not necessarily an answer. It, too, is a problem, like everything else (Klapp 1986, p. 9). Information in large amounts degrades in two main ways. One is by becoming sterile and banal, helping to make life flat and insipid.

The other main way in which information degrades is by becoming noiselike. This is a high-input society. It seems that not a minute may be wasted in consuming commodities and communicating with as many people as possible. But in a Babel of signals, we must listen to a great deal of chatter to hear one bit of information we really want. We discover that information can become noiselike when it is irrelevant or interferes with desired signals, so tending to defeat meaning and making it harder to extract from information, just as it is hard to extract metal from low-grade ore. All too often, media and computers speed up the impact of information upon us without adding to its meaning for us. By taking in too much noise, a person becomes cluttered, not integrated. The result for our information society is that we suffer a lag in which the slow horse of meaning is unable to keep up with the fast horse of mere information.

Both of these types of degradation we shall now call inflation, conforming to the minimal definition: the more of something (in this case tokens in a marketlike situation), the less value. The loss of value is now called loss of meaning because of overload of information in which there is too much redundancy and noise.

It was only in the last few decades that social scientists discovered that it was possible to have an overload of information (an idea that could not have been envisaged by Mill, who hitched progress to abundance of information)—as with money, too much of a good thing. One of the first to notice information overload was the turn-of-the-century sociologist Georg Simmel (1950, p. 415), who wrote of the attitude of reserve by which city people shield themselves from "indiscriminate suggestibility." He wrote of the overload of sensations in the urban world, causing city dwellers to become jaded and develop a kind of psychic callus, the blase attitude, "an incapacity . . . to react to new situations with the appropriate energy" (pp. 410, 414). James G. Miller (1960) reported pioneering experiments in information overload of individuals and groups. Karl Deutsch (1961) noted that "communication overload" was a "disease of cities," in which freedom of choice is jammed by the very efficiency of communication and transport; so many things call for attention that people lack time to attend to anything or anyone. Richard Meier

(1962, p. 132) theorized broadly about information overload in cities, calculating that dwellers in modern cities, like San Francisco, bore 100 times the load of dwellers in less modern ones such as Addis Ababa, Djakarta or Tehran, and predicted a saturation in communications flow and crisis of overload within the next half century. Lucien Pye (1963, p. 126) noted in developing countries an unselective hunger or eagerness for media, whereas the West was "nearly saturated," requiring people, "as a means of self-defense" to "develop the capacity to ignore much and to become selective." A psychiatrist (Meerlo 1967) commented that the media "have become ensnarled in a gigantic traffic jam," whose overloading had caused a breakdown in some patients' communication systems. By 1970, Alvin Toffler characterized the crisis from information overload as "future shock."

And now we have an information society, in which a large amount and high rate of information seem like noise when they reach overload: a rate too high for the receiver to process efficiently without distraction, stress, increasing errors, loss of meaning, and other costs making information poorer. If the human channel capacity for a given task—say supermarket checker—is 8 bits per second, but the checker is trying to handle 10 bits, then perhaps it is reasonable to say that 2 bits are acting like noise, interfering with information, increasing errors, and omissions. In such cases, one might say, information gets in its own way. What it comes down to is a growing burden of coding from ever larger masses of information, much of which is unsorted and unconnected, like the unfitted pieces of a jigsaw puzzle. The higher the meaning, the more judgmental the task, the more pieces there are to fit into a more intricate pattern. So our society, for all its hardware, and however large its organizations, suffers information overload because the bottleneck of coding has not been widened. It is still just as hard to make complex judgments of pattern and meaning as ever—and more need to be made!

The trouble with large amounts of information is not only in its possible loss of quality per se but, however good, its amount exceeding channel capacity, and especially human capacity to use information and form meaning. Overload occurs when facts (with their due quota of errors) mount up and outstrip meaning, which is a slow horse unable to keep up in the race (Klapp 1986, p. 109). This results in a growing lag of meaning formation behind information accumulation in the modern society (Klapp 1986, p. 111), Since a crisis of meaning has occurred in the midst of a flood of information, there seems little reason to be confident that increased quantities of public information—whether from science, computers, news agencies, publishing, education, or official pronouncements—will restore a meaning that seems to be slipping away.

One way to conceive the overload of information and slowness of making sense is by the following metaphor. Suppose one is seated at a table fitting pieces of a gigantic jigsaw puzzle. From a funnel overhead, pieces are pouring onto the table faster than one can fit them. Most of the pieces do not match, indeed, they do not all belong to the same puzzle. In this metaphor, the pieces of the puzzle represent facts rapidly accumulating; the pattern is the meaning, slowly emerging, perhaps never found. The irregularity and confusion in the heap of pieces, impeding finding a fit, might be called the noise of the puzzle.

According to this notion (meaning lag resulting from noiselike information), the amount of inflation depends on how noisy information is. This theory of inflation by information overload gives noice a central place, for it is the noise that in inflationary—by becoming noiselike large amounts of information lose meaning and value—more becomes less.

Let us look at various ways in which information becomes noiselike. The most obvious way is by sheer loudness, when it drowns out other stimuli that might be signals. Today competition to be heard so adds to the stridency and amplification of entertainment, advertising, and political messages, that each is many times louder than they would need to be in tghe absence of the others. But loudness is not merely a matter of decibels; it can occur in other sensory modalities, as in a twenty-foot-high billboard above smaller ones, or a certain style or color said to be "loud" (meaning, perhaps, that it steals attention from quieter styles and colors).

Amount and rate of information are also parameters of noise when they reach overload, a rate too high for the receiver to process efficiently without distraction, stress, increasing errors, and other costs that make information poorer.

A third way in which information becomes noiselike is lack of apparent relation to other information with which the receiver is concerned: irrelevance or disconnectedness makes it harder to find a pattern (what Alfred North Whitehead called the "fatal disconnectedness" of subjects in education). When information is too disconnected, finding its meaning becomes like working on the gigantic, endless jigsaw puzzle whose pieces do not fit.

Yet another noisy characteristic of information is excessive difficulty in decoding. Ciphers are, one might say, a deliberately contrived noise (scambling) to hide a signal, which deciphering overcomes. Past a point, decoding difficulty makes any communication noiselike, if the code acts more like a cipher than a signal, and the work of deciphering ipso facto carries no desired information and preoccupies the receiver at cost of other things that might have been learned during the same time. Ambiguity adds much to semantic noise and the work of decoding, to say nothing of giving negative information if the wrong meaning is chosen. Besides, today so many more signals are exogenous—not immediately understood, but strange in origin, referring to things with which one has had little direct experience, coming from people one does not know, requiring continual definition, calculation, and testing.

A clue to a fifth way in which information becomes noiselike comes from brain research suggesting that our culture overloads the left hemisphere with calculativee, verbal, digital information while inadvertently neglecting pattern recognition and intuition by the right. If there is such a difference in hemispheric function, then much information is bound to seem noiselike when unsuited to the hemisphere trying to process it. The remedy seems to be either achieving brain wave coherence or making less noise on one side interfering with signals of the other.

Finally, a sixth way in which information becomes noiselike in modern society is lack of feedback while the volume of communication increases. Today media bombard, they do not answer us; messages seem random and chaotic from the receiver's point of view. Such abundance of information without feedback does not help solve problems but adds to the difficulty of finding the fact or meaning one wants. Beer (1972, p. 31) observes that corporate managers are "engulfed in a sea of useless facts," very little of which is feedback to anything they have done or decided. Such a dearth of feedback helps turn information into noise. It is also often true of personal interaction that few messages are direct feedback to anything one has said or done. While many people are talking, it is surprising that so few are listening. Voices have multiplied but not ears.

In such ways—loudness, overload, disconnectedness, burden of decoding, interference between brain hemispheres, and dearth of feedback—information becomes noiselike and noise degrades communication, adding to meaning lag in modern society.

I hope these ideas of sterile redundancy and noise overload may provide helpful models in terms of information for understanding how more becomes less. It would seem reasonable to suppose that either of these models, the market of information or channel overload, could be adapted to throw light on how information loses value as its amount of tokens increases. We have suggested that the social problem called information overload can be usefully conceived as an inflation of information. Here the tokens are whatever form information may take as signal or marker, the market being the entire domain of public communication and social interaction. There seems no reason, in principle, why what has been said of credentials, medals, smiles, fashions, and so on, may not be extended to the entire range of communication, insofar as symbols are used as tokens. Wherever symbols are used as tokens communication becomes marketlike and inflation of those tokens is possible. One may then speak meaningfully of negotiation, shopping, supply, demand, and price as a general understanding from market feedback of a "going value" of tokens or what they buy or are worth in exchange. The broadest possible formulation of the idea of inflation is that any disproportionate increase in the supply of tokens can devalue them in terms of what they are worth in human response, through a marketlike mechanism in which laws of supply and demand set the "price" (social worth, going value) of those tokens. The social price is established by a ratio between the amount of tokens offered and the amount of values denoted by those tokens that happen to be available in the social market and can be delivered in exchange when appropriate tokens are offered or displayed. But then they are felt to be inflated when they lose "purchasing power," i.e., pricing feedback tells that they do not buy so much in terms of attention, interest, response, significance, recognition, or prestige; and communication is discounted by names like hype, ballyhoo, rhetoric, noise, chatter, clutter, selling pitch, computer garbage, gobbledegook, and so on. In market terms, it is a loss of marginal value of information from oversupply. The average value (per bit or message) declines as supply increases relative to demand (willingness to give attention, size of audience). The harder senders compete to "sell" their messages, and the more they supply, the less attention and significance people are able to give to any. At some point, the marginal value of signals approaches zero, or even less if messages are disliked. Discounting was the term we used for receivers' perception of inflation—that communication is worth less than face value.

The more there is of such inflated communication, the more it seems to call for filters to cut out noise and unwanted information. So a top executive's staff gathers for him the best information and keeps him from being swamped in a sea of useless facts. And it is not surprising that professors have been known to rely on research assistants and graduate students to abstract literature and compile bibliographies.

In television viewing, a moderately effective filter is a muting or "blab-off" remote control, which enables viewers to play a sort of game with producers of commercials to see how much they can cut off and still enjoy the show. A drawback, however, is that the viewer may get so habituated to noise that he neglects to push the muting button.

Sheer boredom acts as a sort of filter when it helps a person to tune out information he is not interested in and seek better luck elsewhere.

Less successful in filtering are postal services delivering "junk mail" (second and third class) in the same box with first class. Mechanically addressed to names from a mailing list that is sold to anybody—or addressed to nobody in particular, but a mere category such as "resident" or "occupant"—junk mail pours upon people whether they want it or not. It is estimated that in a year an average resident of the United States receives some fifty-five and in England some sixty pounds of mail from parties he does not choose to hear from. Boon though this cheap mail service may be to mail-order businesses and people spreading propaganda, it is generally regarded as a nuisance to receivers, who have to go through it for fear it may contain something important. Both the United States and English postal services are looking into the feasibility of reducing the amount or kinds of junk mail—perhaps delivering only first class and returning to source or destroying all other (this would assure, at least, that the addressee gets mail valued by the sender at more than the first class postage). And at least it would reduce the total load of mail handled by the much criticized postal services.

Libraries offer a potential threat of information overload by their ever greater stacks of books, tapes, and electronic services. But this is not inevitable; librarians have an important filtering function according to Lester Asheim (1982), who gives a picture of how librarians can use their expertise to help researchers find what they want and reduce overload of information that is not needed, being active partners of research rather than passive custodians of information. Asheim distinguishes two kinds of filter function performed by the librarian, both of which serve to

> bring to the user a manageable store of information from which to select. Original selection by the librarian in the building of the collection attempts to provide the largest possible store, so that all needed items are available. . . . But once a library patron comes with a request for information . . . a new filter function faces the librarian: the manipulation of the flow of information from the total store to focus on that part of it that meets the user's need insofar as the librarian understands the expression of that need. As the negotiation proceeds, new questions may be raised. . . . The librarian's goal should be to use our special knowledge of sources, content, retrieval techniques, and bibliographic control inventively and imaginatively in each case to help the individual find his or her way— not ours—through the complex and many-faceted store of information. (pp. 220– 21)

To screen out the redundant, the banal, the meaningless, and the noisy elements of modern communication, many gatekeepers and filters may be needed. "Someone must scan, process, and select from the great domain of total information the *needed* information to suit the individual seeker." Asheim suggests that the librarian can be such a monitor (p. 224).

Effectiveness of filtering will help determine how well our society deals with inflation by overload of information and how much of a problem it will be. It seems to me that the most benefit to society will come not so much from the sheer amount of information—inflated as it is—as from how well it is filtered to get the most of the best signal and least of the worst noise. If the noise is in junk mail, I would like to see some way of filtering it and directing it to those who want it. If the noise is in television commercials, I would like to see it become more controllable by muting (bearing in mind that this is one's own selection, not censorship by somebody else). If the noise is overflowing library shelves with poor access and servicing, I would like to see more skilled librarians with an active role in cooperation with researchers, as Asheim suggests. Filtering can work for or against us. Let us do what we can to improve it.

11

Factors Favoring Social Inflation

In this book we have looked at various cases of how symbols shrink in value as their supply increases, a process that in the case of money economists have called inflation. We distinguished five sorts of social magnification that make things seem bigger or more important than they really are: overstatement, crusading, contagious communication, emotional hitchhiking, and oversupply of tokens in a market-like setting. Some go up like balloons which take people where they want to go, others like bubbles that arouse enthusiasm but carry nobody very far.

At the heart of social inflation is the fact that, when any token markedly increases in supply—while values represented by the token do not so increase—people become disappointed because their tokens do not "purchase" as much as they formerly did. In chapter 6 we sought a generic concept of inflation that could apply to symbols other than money. We did so by defining three conditions under which any sort of symbol could inflate: (1) symbols are used as tokens in social exchange; (2) social exchanges comprise a market in which laws of supply and demand operate, however obscurely; and (3) some sort of pricing, however informal, occurs both of values sought in exchange and tokens of those values. Inflation, then, could occur wherever the supply of tokens increased in proportion to the supply of values (too many dollars chasing too few goods), as demand drove up price, ipso facto, devaluing tokens.

Our aim at this point is not to prove but to explore symbolic inflation as a concept, to see better how it applies in particular cases, to fill out its denotation as a concept. In all cases we have been concerned to study examples where the supply of tokens grew inordinately, giving rise to a sense of cheapening, of "more becoming less." At this point, I do not claim to know how large the scope of all these kinds of symbolic inflation may be. That awaits better indicators and quantitative studies. Even so, in studying cases, incomplete though they may be, we may get some notion of what causes cultural inflation that will offer at some remote date hopes of mitigating it, assuming that that in fact is desired (and recalling that much of it is fun).

Indeed, it is not quite clear that society is against all five forms of symbolic inflation. Some are (at times) downright enjoyable, as in overstatement, when one allows oneself the pleasure of boasting for one's tribe or herd, bamboozling others, or running off at the mouth. Enjoyment is also found in the earlier stages of crusades (that type of moralistic overstatement making one's opponent a villain and oneself a hero), while enthusiasm is high, war weariness has not set in, and the price in blood and tears has not grown too great. Only when reality calls the bluff does the pain of overstatement set in. (But is there any assurance that prevailing ideologies—so comfortable themselves—will be challenged by the pain of reality?) Business is loaded with overstatement. Religion thrives on its fables. Our media are full of hype aiming to impress people that something is better or worse than it really is. We live in a bubblebath of overstatement—it is a shock only when the hot water runs out and cold pours in.

Crusading shows the difficulty of evaluating symbolic inflation, for it often has about equal numbers of partisans on opposite sides, equally sure that they are right, and ready to fight. Nor can it be denied that in spite of intransigence, many crusaders achieved their goals, in the short run at least (to mention a few successful ones: Margaret Sanger, Ralph Nader, Gandhi, Oliver Cromwell, William Lloyd Garrison, Emmaline Pankhurst, John Brown). But as a social policy, crusading has undeniable faults: (1) it is easily magnified into hysterical fears, holy wars, magical fulfillments, grails, white knights, and the like; (2) it is inexcusably arrogant, fostering authoritarians and bigots who are ready to impose their views on others; and (3) perhaps its worst fault is encouraging a search for scapegoats and villains—a process of vilification that can go to extremes such as McCarthyism, and has little effect on social problems beyond emotional satisfaction (Klapp 1959). Even so, with all these disadvantages, Americans do seem to prefer crusading to steady, pragmatic action—gradualism, ameliorism. They like dramatic conflict with a knockout punch to the villain, the very least of which that can be said is that it is exciting (whereas pragmatism and compromise are often boring).

Inflation is greatly helped by contagious communication, herdlike processes that get many people doing the same things (laughing, cheering, yelling, weeping, jostling, fighting, fleeing, stampeding, praying, speaking in tongues, repeating catchwords) for no particular reason except that others, a few models or the majority, are doing such things. Contagious communication is highly enjoyable when one has the satisfaction of consensus with one's herd or tribe, "letting go" (catharsis) emotionally, adulation of popular heroes and celebrities, and obedience to leaders whose main claim to authority is an undefined charisma.

Contagious communication is inflationary because it multiplies in the minds of many a thought or action that was perhaps not even worthy of being in *one* mind; making something seem important even when it is trivial or stupid, or ephemeral and soon to fade. Thus contagion contributes to bubbles, such as the stock market boom of 1929, war fever, the Tut mania, dance fads from the Charleston on, hysterias such as McCarthyism and other red scares, ghetto riots in Los Angeles and other cities, and other contagions well known to sociologists such as the Phantom Anaesthetist of Mattoon, the June Bug, and the atomic shelter panic of 1962-63. Such bubbles seem good and true at the time but are only the mood of a particular crowd or multitude.

People also get much enjoyment from emotional hitchhiking, living through the more or less happy lives of others, without permission, but without objection. Such hitchhiking extends our own small scope by vicarious experience of innumerable other people's—real or fictitious—lives. The growth of media has much helped this. Each sits in his chair, watching one or more screens, and attains a Mitty-like existence in which dreaming takes the place of doing. Here is where those energetic celebrities earn their keep: to provide symbols that will give meaningful and interesting, if second-hand, identities to innumerable Mittys. We must admit, though, that emotional hitchhiking is a cheaper way of expanding one's identity than getting out and doing something with or to other people. Modern man, dwelling in media, has become a sort of clearinghouse of identities trooping through his brain, soliciting attention and imitation, and sometimes loyalty, pride, and commitment. Unlike in traditional societies, identity is not taken for granted; modern man must maintain multiple identities and identifications to be anybody or amount to anything at all.

How is emotional hitchhiking inflationary? It is so because it multiplies in the minds of many people experience that they cannot get in reality themselves. It inflates because it is a kind of covert self-abandonment, a trip in which one leaves an old self behind and vicariously participates in others' lives, roles or deeds. It inflates in two main ways: it *multiplies* the number of people who can ride on the same vehicle; and, if one happens to identify with a hero, it *enlarges* the scale of the devotee, perhaps to the stature of a superman (which applies to those larger-than-life heroes I call group superselves, who can provide a vehicle for an entire tribe, nation, or people).

But modern man, plugged into innumerable media, can become over-inflated by too many, too large, inappropriate, or disappointing identities, which fail to give him a satisfactory lift or fit. Then he becomes a seeker, rather than possessor, of identity, searching through avenues such as television serials, television evangelism, sports and their heroes, cults, heroes and their fans—the cult of celebrities that is such a prominent institution in modern life. When this happens, it seems plain that emotional hitchhiking is not just an amusement but is an important compensation for a mass society which is failing to offer to millions of television viewers enough real life identity—and has not inherited a credible myth of the sort that Carl Jung and Joseph Campbell wrote about, but turns to fictitious identities in media to fill the gap with anything that is there. So Rambo, James Bond, and J. R. Ewing replace Ulysses, King Arthur, and Robin Hood on center stage.

Finally, among the five types of symbolic inflation we have identified, are cases which best fit a market concept of supply and demand affecting the value ("price") of symbols when they are over-supplied. We saw, for example, that steel axes among the aborigines had become of great importance as a status symbol, but lost value when there were too many of them, when making steel axes available to everyone—even women and children (from the generosity of missionaries)—destroyed not only the prestige value of stone axes but the status of native chiefs, whose own stone axes became worth less, either as symbols of male authority or as practical instruments.

Other tokens—credentials, diplomas, academic degrees, grades, academic regalia, greeting cards, smiles, kisses, religious tokens, medals, trophies, applause, and ovations—were seen as examples where tokens can become less valuable as their supply increases. In the case of standing ovations, we saw that such a vogue in audiences of the performing arts spoiled its meaning as a supreme accolade; and, by rewarding too many mediocre performances, destroyed ability to recognize, discriminate, and reward truly superior achievements.

From such examples, we might say that a generic cause of inflation is oversupply of tokens which cannot deliver the value they denote, because they have outstripped the available supply of that value. Values such as prestige, honor, love, affection, status, are conceived as limited in supply, so that too great a number of those symbols circulating can outstrip the supply of value and lose "purchasing power." The basic trouble is increase in symbols without proportionate increase in values they are expected to purchase.

This emphasizes the need for scarcity of symbols if they are to keep their market value. If money were not comparatively scarce, it could buy nothing—and so for tokens. Medals and trophies are of special interest here because of the high value they place upon scarcity. Performance beyond the call of duty is inherently rare; one simply cannot give awards of honor and distinction for achievements that are commonplace. We noted four ways in which medals can be "cheapened" by oversupply.

As we conjectured in the preceding chapter, information itself can be thought of as subject to inflation, if meaning lags behind sheer information (meaning formation being considered as a slow horse in the race with accumulating information). Here the inflation is thought of as an overload of useless information (such as banal redundancy and noise [Klapp 1986]), leading to loss of meaning in the society taken as a market where information is exchanged. Loss of meaning from oversupply of symbols is considered as the most general kind of inflation possible. I hope that future theorizing will say more about this.

Fashion offered not merely examples but, one might say, a paradigm of galloping inflation because of the swiftness and inevitability of its fading—its march to doom—as a result of increase in numbers and cheapness of its tokens. I suggest that the fading of fashion is perhaps the best example of loss of display function from oversupply in a social market in a manner resembling galloping monetary inflation.

The root cause of symbolic inflation is inability to restrain the supply of tokens versus a supply of real values that does not so expand, a shortcoming masked, to some extent, by consolations of placebo institutions.

Having admitted so much enjoyment in symbolic inflation, we can hardly condemn it as a policy to be avoided. Yet, should there be any wish to control social inflation—to lessen its role in modern life, or, for that matter, to increase it, since many are doing just that—it may be of value to take note of some of the factors that favor it.

Without claiming to know all the causes of symbolic inflation, I might point out nine things that seem to contribute to it, as illustrated by one or more cases. Briefly, these factors have to do with: (1) supply, (2) fashion-orientation, (3) scarcity, (4) egalitarianism, (5) suggestibility, (6) group egotism, (7) massness, (8) anonymity, (9) exposure to information overload.

1. It is almost tautological, stemming as it does from our definition of inflation as loss of value of tokens as their supply increases, to say that anything which increases the *supply* of symbols is likely to inflate those symbols (be they money, fads, fashions, credentials, etc.) unless balanced by increase in the values denoted ("purchased") by the symbols.

2. Anything which increases *fashion-orientation* favors inflation. We all know that poor fellow who is working day and night to keep up with Jones, who in turn is keeping up with Smith, who in turn is keeping up with Smythe, and so on. The race for status symbols is never won for long. I call this fashion-orientation. It occurs in a market of people who think it is necessary to keep up with the latest. The new is always better than the old. Styles go to a quick death, from redundancy leading to boredom and loss of display functions of distinction. We suggested in chapter 9 that fashion is almost a paradigm for marketlike inflation of symbols. On the other hand, in traditional societies, where people are not oriented to fashions, and display of new symbols cannot gain Jones status, culture changes slowly and fashion as a type of social inflation is least to be expected.

3. A *loss of scarcity* or increase in abundance of tokens tends to inflate them. We saw in cases like medals, ovations, and credentials

that scarcity is essential for preserving the value of highest symbols if they are to honor the distinction of best from mediocre. On the other hand, symbols given out too plentifully are regarded as "cheapened" by their abundance. Affluence, reducing scarcity and encouraging people to spend more on status symbols, favors symbolic inflation. This, or course, fosters consumerism as a lifestyle focused on the perpetual pursuit of commodities as the goal of life, and quality of life being judged by the amount of things consumed. Where there is such eagerness for commodities (which can be keener than hunger as a motivation), the mass market is easily flooded with tokens making a marketlike inflation likely. Then, as commodities pile up and turn to clutter, the irony of affluence becomes perceptible and consumerism is seen as hollowness of the American dream.

4. Anything which increases *egalitarianism* favors symbolic inflation, because it encourages people to expect equal access to status symbols, at least a "level playing field"; and entitles all to the same amounts and kinds of symbols if properly earned. In an egalitarian society everybody feels equal (whatever the fact), and feels free to imitate anybody he pleases. All this makes Jonesism ever more competitive and encourages inflation because it invites everyone to make claims for status and prestige by easily obtained and multiplied symbols. This constitutes a pressure to vastly increase the supply of status symbols. In chapter 7 we considered cases—credentials, academic degrees, grades, and medals—where increasing supply of symbols, often by counterfeiting them, threatened to devalue them in a way similar to monetary inflation.

5. Anything which increases *suggestibility* increases the likelihood of inflation in forms like bubbles, fads, hysterias, crowd emotions, and crusades, able by contagious communication to draw people in, and cause them to give in to crowd pressures (as in riots or standing ovations), and to uncritically accept messages of rumor and media. It is easy to evoke the herd mentality (by rhetoric and other demagogic tactics), and harder to put it to rest, even when institutions such as courts, schools, and science demand rationality as a sine qua non. Obedience is surprisingly high among supposedly independent-minded people, as shown by classic studies, and by fanatical followers of cult leaders.

6. Collective pride encourages inflation by overstatement. It is easy to point to overstatement as an individual fault (such as vanity);

but much more of it comes from *group egotism*, which permits brag-ging for one's own group, team, leader, culture or ideology in terms that would be obnoxious if applied to oneself. Group egotism encour-ages overstatement by pride, boasting, swaggering, wagering, threatening, bullying, bluffing, chauvinism, superpatriotism, boost-erism, and hero worship. It especially favors the moral rhetoric and self-righteousness of crusading. When group pride is operating, a member feels free to do as much of this sort of thing as he likes— even to the fatuity of "my country right or wrong." It sanctifies bigotry, fanaticism, zealotry, sectarianism, authoritarianism, and ethnocentrism. Epic poets and saga-tellers have a special mandate to inflate the glory of their nation, tribe, or people. Deflating this glory is the job of critical historians and debunking biographers of great men.

7. Anything which increases *massness* in social life favors sym-bolic inflation. As understood by sociologists, massness is the fact that many people today are crowded but alone and lonely—a "lonely crowd," a "society of strangers." Where such is the situation, people are mobile, relationships are numerous but tenuous, roots are shallow, social networks are diffuse and temporary rather than dense, durable, and cohesive (as one would find them in a tribal society or a sect like the Amish).

Why does massness favor symbolic inflation? One obvious reason is that since people have numerous relationships and weak social ties it is necessary to appeal to the mass by symbols that will be persua-sive to strangers, such as bargaining, sales talks, propagandas, or threats. If the rhetoric of loyalty, friendship, and sentiment is used, it must be rather empty and thin describing how people really feel; symbols proliferate and outstrip realities. Another reason that mass-ness inflates is that it generates anxiety from loneliness and being alone. So it contributes to suggestibility as a vulnerability to contagi-ous communication, propaganda, hysterias, scapegoating, and bub-bles of one kind or another as promised by cults and leaders. Some of the inflation from massness comes also from the factor of availa-bility. We expect that rootless people, not tied by local loyalties, and having little to lose in terms of memberships and privileges, will be easily drawn into new alignments, not excluding bizarre cults and ex-tremist movements which can grow rapidly. Massness contributes to social inflation also because it generates dissatisfactions, such as loneliness, frustration, boredom and meaninglessness, for which people try to compensate by identifying with celebrities, and placebo institutions (Klapp 1986) like soap operas, carnivals, lotteries, and violent sports, which paint life in brighter, less humdrum colors. In such ways, by proliferating symbols, mass society cheapens them because people are able to obtain little of what the symbols portray and promise.

8. Anything which increases *anonymity* in social relationships favors inflation because it reduces accountability, releases people from responsibility for symbols and actions they present to others. This is obvious in crowd behavior, but it extends to the entire social market where one can pass oneself off to strangers by symbols which no one can verify, where people do not know a person well enough to tell whether he is entitled to his claims and pretensions. As in the case of masquerades and carnivals, anonymity favors social inflation because it removes the normal limits on identity claims; anybody can be anybody, so to speak. Anonymity provides an opportunity for self-abandonment that is rather like that of a masquerade: freedom from conventional identity to be somebody else for the moment. Thus countless nobodies can be somebodies.

9. Where there is a vast and open media system, with worldwide and instantaneous diffusion of stimuli, images, and models, anything which heavily increases *exposure* to information from media can lead to the kind of overload we call meaning lag—treated in chapter 10 as the broadest kind of inflation: loss of meaning in information itself.

These nine factors seem to be conducive to symbolic inflation, or to play some part in it. They are offered not as final conclusions but as conjectures exploring how the idea of inflation might apply to social symbols other than money.

While we may not know exactly what to do about it, we should at least be critically aware of symbolic inflation and the risks it carries of loss of values from culture, especially on four scores.

The first is crusading as a type of moral overstatement. Though a sword of reform, crusading carries moral arrogance and high social costs. Its militancy threatens to rip the social fabric while "doing good."

The second is herd-thinking (contagious communication). Herd-thinking can be enjoyable (the main reason for some sports contests). It also contributes to evangelistic conversions, the experience of being "saved." But it stampedes individual judgment and also contributes to chauvinism and witch-hunting, with appalling results, as in Germany during the 1930s. Dare we say that Americans are immune?

We should also be critically aware of inflation of sentimental symbols (smiles, kisses, flags, religious icons) which, overworked and recognized as cliches, are perceived as shallow and hypocritical, lose meaning, and give rise to boredom and alienation.

Fourth, perhaps the most subtle form of symbolic inflation is not visible early but creeps into the award of tokens of approval (credentials, medals, degrees, honors, academic grades, ovations), until given too easily, they reward mediocrity and lose the ability to distinguish excellence. The remedy for such inflation is plainly holding up and sticking to higher standards. A generous spirit of egalitarianism is often a justification of mediocritization; so also is a desire for abundance which loses sight of the fact that scarcity is a basis of valuation. An important dimension of mediocritization is the idolatry of celebrities who do not hold up higher values.

I offer these thoughts with the hope that they may throw light on the flatulence of affluence—that puzzling experience in the consumer society of more becoming less. If many things beside money are inflating, it makes little sense to keep one's eye solely on money. From looking at various types of inflation, I hope we can get a better view of the ambivalence of affluence in modern life.

Above all, let me not end with overstatement.

References

Abelman, Robert, and Kimberly Neuendorf,. 1985. "How Religious is Religious Television Programming?" *Journal of Communication* 35: 98–110.

Alinsky, Saul David. 1946. *Revelle for Radicals*. Chicago: University of Chicago Press.

Allen, Frederick Lewis. 1946, 1931. *Only Yesterday, the Fabulous Twenties*. New York: Bantam Books.

Amory, Cleveland. 1957. *The Proper Bostonians*. New York: E. P. Dutton & Co.

———. 1960. *Who Killed Society?* New York: Harper.

Asheim, Lester 1982. "Ortega Rivisited." *The Library Quarterly* 52 (July): 215–26.

Barnett, James H.. 1949. "The Easter Festival, a study in Cultural Change." *American Sociological, Revue* 14: 463–69.

———. 1954. *The American Christmas: a Study in National Culture*. New York: Macmillan.

Beaufort, John. 1976. "What Comes After the Standing Ovation?" *Christian Science Monitor*, 10 February.

Beer, Stafford. 1972. *The Brain of the Firm*. New York: McGraw-Hill.

Berkley, George E. 1976. "On Being Called Doctor." *Journal of Higher Education* 41 (October): 556–61.

Berne, Eric. 1964. *Games People Play*. New York: Grove Press.

Bethel, May. 1969. *How to Live on our Polluted Planet*. New York: Pyramid Publishers.

Birdwhistell, Ray L.. 1970. *Kinesics and Context, Essays on Body Motion Communication*. New York: Ballantine Books.

Black, Norman. 1980. " 'Electric Church' Growing," *San Diego Union*, 1 February.

Blau, Peter M.. 1955. *The Dynamics of Bureaucracy*. Chicago: University of Chicago Press.

———. 1964, 1969. *Exchange and Power in Social Life*. New York: John Wiley & Sons.

Blumenthal, Albert. 1932. *Small Town Stuff*. Chicago: University of Chicago Press.

Blumer, Herbert. 1939. "Collective Behavior," in *An Outline of the Principles of Sociology*, ed. R. E. Park, pp. 221–80. New York: Barnes and Noble. New edition, A.M.Lee, ed., 1946, pp. 167–224.

———. 1969. *Symbolic Interactionism, Perspective and Method*. Englewood Cliffs, N. J.: Prentice-Hall, Inc.

Bode, Carl. 1959. *The Anatomy of American Popular Culture, 1840–1861*. Berkeley: University of California Press.

Boulding, Kenneth E.. 1970. *A Primer on Social Dynamics*. New York: The Free Press.

Burger, Ralf. 1988. *Computer Viruses, a High-Tech Disease*. Grand Rapids: Apacus, a Data Becker Book.

Carnegie, Dale. 1937. *How to Win Friends and Influence People.* New York: Simon & Schuster.

Collins, Randall. 1979. *The Credential Society, an Historical Sociology of Education and Stratification.* New York: Academic Press.

Csikszentmihalyi, Mihaly. 1975. *Beyond Boredom and Anxiety.* San Francisco: Jossey-Bass Publishers.

Daly, Herman E., ed.. 1980. *Economics, Ecology, Ethics: Essays Toward a Steady-State Economy.* San Francisco: W. H. Freeman & Co.

Darnton, Robert. 1989. "What Was Revolutionary About the French Revolution?" *New York Review of Books,* (January 19): 3–4

Deutsch, Karl W.. 1961. "On Social Communication and the Metropolis." *Daedalus,* 90: 99–110.

Dorfles, Gillo. 1969. *Kitsch: The World of Bad Taste.* New York: Universe Books.

Douglas, Mary, and Isherwood, Baron. 1979. *The World of Goods.* New York: Basic Books.

Draper, Theodore, 1987. "Iran-Contra Autopsy." *New York Review of Books* (December 17): 68–9

Eckert, Thor Jr. 1983. "To Boo or Not to Boo — It's a Matter of Tradition." *Christian Science Monitor,* (March 23).

Ehrlich, Paul R., and Ann H.. 1974. *The End of Affluence,* New York: Ballantine Books.

Ekman, Paul, and Friesen, Wallace V. 1975. *Unmasking the Face: a Guide to Recognizing Emotions from Facial Cues.* Englewood Cliffs, N. J.: Prentice-Hall, Inc.

Evans-Pritchard, E. E.. 1937. *Witchcraft, Ordeals and Magic Among the Azande.* Oxford: At the Clarendon Press.

Filler, Louis. 1939. *Crusaders for American Liberalism.* Yellow Springs, Ohio: Antioch Press.

Firth, Raymond. 1956. "Rumor in a Primitive Society." *Journal of Abnormal and Social Psychology.* 53: 122–32.

Follett, Wilson. 1966. *Modern American Usage, A Guide.* New York: Hill and Wang.

Fowler, H. W.. 1974. *A Dictionary of Modern English Usage.* Oxford: at the Clarendon Press, second edition revised.

Galbraith, John Kenneth. 1958. *The Affluent Society.* Boston: Houghton Mifflin.

Gamson, William A.. 1968. *Power and Discontent.* Homewood, Ill.: Dorsey Press.

Georgescu-Roegen, Nicholas. 1971. *The Entropy Law and the Economic Process.* Cambridge, Mass.: Harvard University Press.

Goldman, Ivan. 1979. "Just Don't Get Any Students Angry." *Washington Post* (April 29).

Goode, William J.. 1978. *The Celebration of Heroes, Prestige as a Social Control System.* Berkeley: University of California Press.

Gorz, André. 1967. *Strategy for Labor, a Radical Proposal.* Boston: Beacon Press.

Hardin, Garrett James. 1972. *Exploring New Ethics for Survival, the Voyage of the Spaceship Beagle.* New York: Viking Press.

Heath, Anthony. 1976. *Rational Choice and Social Exchange, a Critique of Exchange Theory.* Cambridge: Cambridge University Press.

Hecht, Ben. 1964. Quoted in Roy Newquist, *Counterpoint,* Skokie, Ill.: Rand McNally, p.348.

Henderson, Hazel. 1978. *Creating Alternative Futures, the End of Economics.* New York: G. P. Putnam's Sons.

Hochschild, Arlie Russell. 1983. *The Managed Heart: Commercialization of Human Feeling.* Berkeley: University of California Press.

Hofstadter, Richard. 1955. *The Age of Reform.* New York: Random House. pp. 16–7.

Homans, George C., 1958. "Social Behavior as Exchange." *American Journal of Sociology* 63 (May): 597–606.

Hirsch, Fred. 1976. *Social Limits to Growth.* Cambridge, Mass: Harvard University Press.

Horsfeld, Peter G.. 1985. "Evangelism by Mail: Letters from the Broadcasters." *Journal of Communication* 35 (winter): 89–97.

Kahn, E., Jr. 1947. *The Voice.* New York: Harper and Row. pp. 45–54, 68, 83–4.

Kapferer, Bruce, ed. 1977 *Transaction and Meaning: Directions in the Anthropology of Exchange and Symbolic Behavior.* Philadelphia: Institute for Study of Human Issues.

Keating, Edward M. 1966. "The New Left: What Does it Mean?" *Saturday Review* (September 24): pp. 25–7, 64.

Kerckhoff, Alan C., and Back, Kurt W. 1968. *The June Bug: a Study of Hysterical Contagion.* New York: Appleton-Century-Crofts.

Kilborn, Peter T., 1989. "Federal Reserve Sees a Way to Guage Long-run Inflation." *New York Times,* (June 13): pp.D1,D7.

Klapp, Orrin E.. 1972. *Heroes, Villains and Fools, Reflections of the American Character.* San Diego: Aegis Publishing Co.

———. 1978. *Opening and Closing, Strategies of Information Adaptation in Society.* New York: Cambridge University Press.

———. 1986. *Overload and Boredom: Essays on the Quality of Life in the Information Society.* Westbrook, Connecticut: Greenwood Press.

———. 1959. "Vilification as a Social Process." *Pacific Sociological Review* 2: 71–6.

Kohr, Leopold. 1977. *The Overdeveloped Nations: the Diseconomics of Scale.* New York: Schoken Books.

Krier, Beth Ann. 1980. "Spreading the Gospel of Tax Avoidance, Mail-chartered Churches Claim IRS Exemptions." *Los Angeles Times* (March 13).

Lapham, Lewis H. 1987. *Money and Class in America.* New York: Weidenfield and Nicolson.

Lerner, Daniel. 1958. *The Passing of Traditional Society.* New York: The Free Press.

Levy, Mark R., and Edward L. Fink. 1984. "Home Video Recorders and the Transience of Television Broadcasts." *Journal of Communication* 34 (Spring): 56–71.

Linder, Staffan Burenstam. 1970. *The Harried Leisure Class.* New York: Columbia University Press.

Lorenz, Konrad. 1974. *Civilized Man's Eight Deadly Sins.* New York: Harcourt, Brace Jovanovich.

MacDonald, Dwight. 1957. "A Theory of Mass Culture," in *Mass Culture: The Popular Arts in America,* ed. Bernard Rosenberg and David Manning White. Glencoe, Ill.: The Free Press.

Malinowsky, Bronislaw. 1922. *Argonauts of the Western Pacific.* New York: Dutton.

Marcuse, Herbert. 1964. *One-Dimensional Man.* London: Routledge & Kegan Paul, Ltd.

Maslow, Abraham H.. 1968. *Toward a Psychology of Being.* New York: Van Nostrand and Reinhold C.

McBride, Stewart. 1980. "Albert Elsen: He Knows When Picasso Isn't Picasso." *Christian Science Monitor,* (February 6) pp. B6–7.

Mead, George H. 1934. *Mind, Self and Society*. Chicago: University of Chicago Press.

Meadows, Donella H., Dennis L. Meadows, Jorgen Randers and William W. Behrens. 1972. *The Limits to Growth, a Report for the Club of Rome's Project on the Predicament of Mankind*. New York: Universe Books.

Medalia, N., and O. N. Larsen. 1958. "Diffusion and Belief in a Collective Delusion: the Seattle Windshield-pitting Epidemic." *American Sociological Review*, 23:221–32.

Meerloo, Joost. 1967. In *Human Communication Theory*, ed. Frank E. X. Dance. New York: Holt, Rinehart & Winston. p. 133.

Meier, Richard L. 1962. *A Communications Theory of Urban Growth*. Cambridge, Mass.: Joint Center for Urban Studies of M.I.T. and Harvard University, M.I.T. Press.

Mencken, H. L.. 1982. *The American Scene*. New York: Alfred A. Knopf.

Menninger, Karl. 1973. *Whatever Happened to Sin?* New York: Hawthorn.

Miles, Rufus E., Jr.. 1976. *Awakening From the American Dream: The Social and Political Limits to Growth*. New York: Universe Books.

Miller, James Grier. 1960. "Information Input Overload and Psychopathology." *American Journal of Psychiatry* 116 (Feb.): 695–704.

Millis, Walter. 1935. *Road to War: America 1914–17*. Boston: Houghton Mifflin.

Mills, C. Wright.. 1951. *Whitecollar, the American Middle Classes*. New York: Oxford University Press.

Mishan, E. J.. 1980. "The Growth of Affluence and the Decline of Welfare." In Herman E. Daly, ed., *Economics, Ecology, Ethics: Essays toward a Steady-state Economy*. San Francisco: W. H. Freeman and Co.

Molloy, John T.. 1975, 1978. *Dress for Success*. New York: Warner Books.

———. 1977. *The Women's Dress for Success Book*. New York: Warner Books.

Morris, Desmond, Peter Collett, Peter Marsh, and Marie O'Shaughnessy,. 1979. *Gestures, Their Origins and Distribution*. New York: Stein and Day.

Newman, Charles. 1985. *The Post-modern Aura, the Act of Fiction in an Age of Inflation*. Evanston, Ill.: Northwestern University Press.

Odegard, Peter H.. 1928. *Pressure Politics: the Story of the Anti-Saloon League*. New York: Columbia University Press.

Packard, Vance. 1959. *The Status-Seekers*. New York: D. McKay Co.

Plowden, Allison. 1979. *Tudor Women*. London: Weidenfeld and Nicolson.

Pye, Lucian W., ed. 1963. *Communications and Political Development*. Princeton.: Princeton University Press.

Rexroth, Kenneth. 1966. Quoted in *Time* (February 25): p. 108.

Rifkin, Jeremy. 1980. *Entropy, a New World View*. New York: Viking.

Roosevelt, Theodore. 1954. "The Man with the Muck-Rake." In John Eric Nordskog, ed., *Contemporary Reform Movements*. New York: Scribner. pp. 386–87.

Rosenberg, Bernard and David Manning White, eds. 1957. *Mass Culture, the Popular Arts in America*. Glencoe, Ill.: The Free Press.

Rosnow, Ralph L. and G. A. Fine. 1976. *Rumor and Gossip: the Social Psychology of Hearsay*. New York: Elsevier.

Sahlins, Marshall. 1972. *Stone Age Economics*. Chicago: Aldine-Atherton, Inc.

Samuelson, Paul A.. 1970. *Economics*. New York: McGraw-Hill. 8th edition.

Schonberg, Harold C. 1981. *Facing the Music*. New York: Summit Books.

Schumacher, E. F.. 1973. *Small is Beautiful*. New York: Harper & Row.

Scitovsky, Tebor. 1976. *The Joyless Economy.* New York: Oxford University Press.

Seabrook, Jeremy. 1978. *What Went Wrong: Why Hasn't More Made People Happier?* New York: Pantheon Books.

Schrank, Jeffry. 1977. *Snap, Crackle and Popular Taste: the Illusion of Free Choice in America.* New York: Dell.

Shames, Laurence. 1989. *The Hunger for More: Searching for Values in an Age of Greed.* New York: Times Books.

Shannon, Claude E. and Warren Weaver. 1949. *The Mathematical Theory of Communication.* Urbana: University of Illinois Press.

Sharp, Lauriston. 1952. "Steel Axes for Stone Age Australians." In Edward H. Spicer, ed., *Human Problems in Technological Change, a Case Book.* New York: Russell Sage Foundation. Pp. 69–92.

Shibutani, Tamotsu. 1962. "Reference Groups and Social Control." In Arnold Rose, ed., *Human Behavior and Social Process.* Boston: Houghton Mifflin Co.

Simmel, Georg. 1957. "Fashion." *American Journal of Sociology* 62: 541– 58.

Simmel, Georg. 1950. *The Sociology of Georg Simmel,.* ed. and trans. by Kurt H. Wolff. Glencoe, Ill.: The Free Press.

Skidmore, William. 1975. *Theoretical Thinking in Sociology.* Cambridge: Cambridge University Press.

Sorokin, Pitirim. 1950. *Altruistic Love, a Study of American "Good Neighbors" and Christian Saints.* Boston: Beacon Press.

Strauss, Anselm L. 1978. *Negotiations: Varieties, Contexts, Processes, and Social Order.* San Francisco: Jossey-Bass Publishers.

Toffler, Alvin. 1970. *Future Shock.* New York: Random House.

Tönnies, Ferdinand. 1887. *Gemeinschaft und Gesellschaft.* In *Fundamental Concepts of Sociology.* Ed. and trans. by Charles P. Loomis. New York: American Book Co., 1940.

Tumin, Melvin M. and Arnold S. Feldman. 1955. "The Miracle at Sabena Grande." *Public Opinion Quarterly* 19: 124–139.

Turegano, Preston. 1984. "U.S. suspects that 164 doctors bought degrees." *The Tribune,* San Diego, May 7.

Veblen, Thorstein. 1899. *Theory of the Leisure Class.* New York: Macmillan.

Voyer, Roger D. and Mark G. Murphy. 1984. "A View of Canadian Economic Development and the Environment." in *Global 2000.* Toronto and New York: Pergamon.

Wachtel, Paul L.. 1983, 1988. *The Poverty of Affluence: a Psychological Portrait of the American Way of Life.* New York: the Free Press.

Waller, Willard. 1937. "The Rating and Dating Complex." *American Sociological Review* (October). pp. 727–35.

Watterson, Thomas. 1982. "With Jobs tight, falsifying resumes appears on the rise." *Christian Science Monitor,* (January 21).

Wax, Murray. 1957. "Cosmetics and Grooming." *American Journal of Sociology* 62: 588–93.

Wiegner, Kathleen. 1978. *Forbes* (August 7): pp. 47–53.

Zorbaugh, Harvey. 1929. *The Gold Coast and the Slum.* Chicago: University of Chicago Press.

Index